CHINESE FOOTBINDING

The History of a Curious Erotic Custom

CHINESE FOOTBINDING（全一册）

著　者：HOWARD S. LEVY

發行所：南天書局有限公司

登記證字號：行政院新聞局局版臺業字第一四三六號號

出版者：南天書局有限公司

台北市羅斯福路三段二八三巷14弄14號

電　話(Tel)：(〇二)三六二〇一九〇

電　傳(Fax)：(〇二)三六二三八三四

郵政劃撥帳戶：〇一〇八〇五三一八號

印刷者：國順印刷有限公司

板橋市中正路二一六巷2弄13號

中華民國七十九年十月影印

SMC PUBLISHING INC.
PO Box 13-342, Taipei, Taiwan
Republic of China 10764

ISBN 957-638-028-6

CHINESE FOOTBINDING

The History of a Curious Erotic Custom

by HOWARD S. LEVY

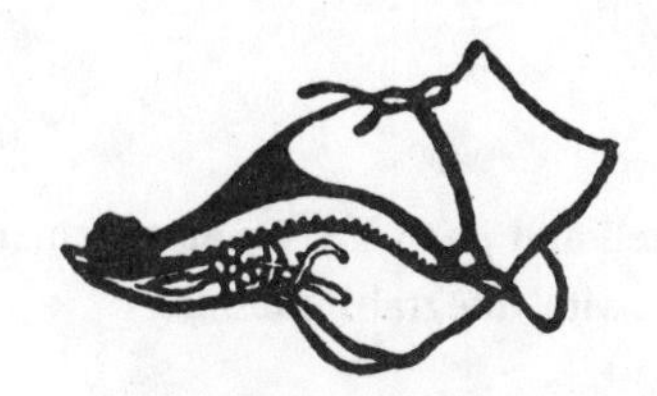

Foreword by
ARTHUR WALEY

Introduction by
WOLFRAM EBERHARD

SMC PUBLISHING INC.

Library of Congress Catalog Card Number: 65-28030

ISBN 957-638-028-6

Reprinted and published by arrangement
with Integral Publishing

For

NAGAO RYŪZO

SOCIOLOGIST

Observer of Chinese
customs for more
than forty years

The characters mean Golden Lotus, euphemism for the bound foot, and were done by Liu Ch'iu-yeh for this book. The calligraphy is patterned after that of a famous Sung calligrapher-emperor named Hui-tsung and in a style called "slender gold."

Foreword

I have for long been interested in footbinding not so much as an isolated Chinese institution but rather as the most striking example of the strange things that women do or have done to them, in almost all cultures, in order to make themselves more attractive to men. One non-Chinese example of such propensities, which has intrigued me for fifty years, is the habit of women in old Japan of shaving off their eyebrows and painting false eyebrows higher up on the forehead, and again of blackening their teeth. One thinks of the women in Africa who elongate their necks and adorn them with innumerable necklaces; and others who wear large round disks suspended from their lower lips. One of the values of Mr. Levy's well-documented book on footbinding in China is that it will give material to anyone writing a general anthropological study of such self-mutilations or self-modifications in all parts of the world.

On the psychological side this book would have fascinated Havelock Ellis, who in discussing sexual abnormalities stresses the attractiveness to some men of lameness or an uncertain gait in women. There is no doubt that this and other small perversions became institutionalized in the cult of the bound foot in China, and Mr. Levy's book plainly shows that the perhaps more familiar sexual fixation on boots and shoes played its part in the appeal of the footbound woman's minute shoes. In short, Mr. Levy's book has among its many merits that of supplying material for future general works on both anthropology and sexual psychology.

ARTHUR WALEY

Acknowledgments

The research on footbinding required that more than 1,500 pages of material be examined, most of it in Chinese. My wife, Henriette Liu Levy, gave me invaluable assistance, aiding me in reading and in clearing up problem areas with a minimum of wasted time. Preservation of the footbinding record is due to the prodigious accomplishment of one man, Yao Ling-hsi, who accumulated much of the available primary evidence in the nineteen-thirties, when the custom was still flourishing. My contribution to the study of footbinding has been to draw largely upon Chinese sources and translate, collate, and rearrange materials according to theme. Mr. Maurice Schneps, Editor of *Orient/West*, read the manuscript in draft and indicated ways in which it might be improved. Mr. Walton H. Rawls suggested revisions in content and arrangement which proved invaluable. Bibliographical assistance was rendered and important references were brought to my attention by Dr. Edwin G. Beal of the Library of Congress and Mr. Kanenobu Watanabe of the Toyo Bunko Research Institute.

HOWARD S. LEVY

Table of Contents

List of Illustrations

(Except where indicated in the text, the illustrations are derived from those found in the volumes of *Ts'ai-fei lu,* edited by Yao Ling-hsi.)

Introduction

We are flooded by books on China which try to explain what happened in the last decade and what might happen in the future. The great majority of these books discuss the astonishing fact that China, so proud of its long history and unique culture, should be the only country which has of its own will embraced an ideology of the West which is totally antagonistic towards all values of the East; whereas, for centuries China resisted the attempts of missionaries to convert the country to another Western world-concept.

Many authors tend to contrast the stability and so-called stagnation of pre-Communist China with the rapid transformation of the present time and give the impression that China was a backward country until 1948. More recently, others have attempted to correct this picture by showing, for example, that the nineteenth century was a period of thorough change, and that much of what is now credited to the Communist regime had already begun some eighty years ago and was widely spread before World War II. More and more, all these discussions—if they are serious—circle around the problem: is Communist China heir to the old imperial, Confucian China, with only a few new techniques and trimmings, or is it a new society—of the East European variety of Western society? Since this is intrinsically a socio-psychological problem, sociologists as well as psychologists have started to go beyond the well-known generalizations about "national character" and have tried to develop methods to get reliable insight into the psychology of the Chinese. This attempt is made extremely difficult since China, together with all other Communist countries, does not allow foreigners to do social science research along modern lines. The aims of their work in this field, as they freely admit, are political and practical, and the work is done with methods which in the West are regarded as antiquated. Fortunately, there are still some other ways open. There are today three Chinas: the Mainland, Taiwan, and the Overseas Chinese (including Hong Kong); in two of them, modern social scientists can work and find congenial, modern-trained Chinese colleagues with whom they can collaborate in the study of modernized Chinese. Furthermore, there are more than two thousand years of a tremendous literature in Chinese at our disposal, covering innumerable topics. The examination and analysis of this literature has just begun.

What has footbinding to do with all this? Footbinding is one element, among many others, belonging to the central problem of the position and role of women in Chinese society, a sociological and psychological problem par excellence. Rarely does one see today a Chinese woman who still has bound feet. The custom is dead. Most Westerners who saw bound feet did not try to find answers to their questions, but simply detested and deplored the custom. They justified their objections by saying that footbinding was "unnatural." But, what is "natural"? A part of being human is that people do not even let basic "instincts," like hunger and sex, operate "naturally"; these impulses have been harnessed by social institutions, and various societies have found different ways to do this. Then it happened in the nineteenth century that Western society set up the cult of "nature" and began fighting against what certain people considered "unnatural." Yet, even today, few Western men dare or wish to let beard and whiskers grow as they grow naturally, and few women are proud of hair on their legs and in their armpits. All men and women shape their hair in different coiffures, and many remove their body hair. Most Western women "bind" their breasts and many their waists, and these "unnatural" forms are called an improvement over nature. No part of the body has not been the object of special attention at one or another time and in one or another society; many have been of sexual importance. For example, most Westerners have preferred and still prefer women with small feet; many people adore the feet of ballet dancers, which do not appear too different from the bound feet of the Chinese; millions of men enjoy seeing women in shoes with heels so high that the foot appears to be deformed, that walking becomes precarious, and that the whole movement of the body is changed. What men in the West feel when they see all the "unnatural" female apparel is surely not too different from what a Chinese felt when seeing a bound foot. We should keep this in mind before passing judgment upon the traditional Chinese's love of small feet.

Each custom and even each fashion somehow express social or psychic values of the whole society, or of that part of society which cherishes the custom; behind each custom there is a whole system of ideas. The study of customs and fashions often opens up insights into aspects which are inaccessible otherwise, either because the topic is taboo or because the psychology behind the custom is unconscious to the person performing it.

Footbinding lasted for more than a thousand years. Is this a proof that Chinese society was stagnant? A look into the origin and development of the custom shows that it has undergone many changes. In the beginning, as far as we know, it was a fashion developed by court dancers who performed on carved lotus flowers or carpets with lotus flower designs much in the way that ballerinas dance in the West. Court circles and the upper class at large imitated the fashion, and it soon became a status symbol. In the course of the following centuries, the middle and even the lower classes imitated the upper-class fashion—a process well known still today in all societies, even in the so-called "classless societies." This process has always been one of the main agents of change: the social leaders wanting to stay aloof from the masses tend to give up a status-symbol custom for a new status symbol as soon as it is used by everybody. Therefore, as the custom of footbinding spread, its meaning changed. It became a convenient way to express and enforce the new concepts of female chastity which China developed in the twelfth century. A chaste wife had to stay in the house and was not to be seen in the fields or streets. Bound feet made walking painful and difficult. At the same time, bound feet indicated economic status. A man who had a wife with bound feet proved to the world that he was rich enough to feed a wife with his earnings and did not need her help in the fields or in the shop.

The Manchu conquerors of China in the seventeenth century were the first to turn against the now all-pervasive custom. They again took pride in the large, natural feet of their women, thus setting them apart from the conquered Chinese. With the end of the eighteenth and the beginning of the nineteenth centuries, long before Western ideas of the equality of sexes came to China, Chinese leaders began to fight for women's rights, and soon this also included a fight against bound feet. The famous novel *Ching-hua yüan,* written 1810 to 1820, contained a whole program for the emancipation of women and decried footbinding as degrading. Later, foreign missionaries and their wives took up the fight, not so much for equality of women as against "unnatural" customs. The Chinese learned from them new techniques of influencing public opinion and of organization which finally led to the first step toward abolishing footbinding, an imperial decree of 1902.

But footbinding was more than just a custom. Howard S. Levy shows in this book that footbinding belongs together with many other elements centering around the sexual psychology of the Chinese. Until the researches done by R. H. van Gulick, almost nothing was known about sexual psychology in China. However, van Gulick's work does not cover the last three hundred years of Chinese history. Here, Levy's work, of which this book is only a small part, will help. He worked for many years in Taiwan and Japan and is eminent in both Chinese and Japanese studies. Naturally he cannot give us "hard facts" in the form of tests and statistics, but he has succeeded in bringing together essays and documents concerned with footbinding which, at the same time, allow us insights into a part of Chinese social life which an outsider hardly ever can observe and about which few writers dare to write directly. Even if we know social and political structure, painting, and philosophy, our knowledge of Chinese society, old and new, is incomplete unless we know something of the way Chinese men and women lived together and what they felt in the most intimate field of human relations. By his thorough familiarity with a type of Chinese literature well known to many Chinese, but, significantly, rarely if ever read by Americans, Howard Levy has been able to present texts which give us this very insight. He has studied the erotic literature of traditional China together with the sentimental novels of the time. But he has also delved into modern magazines, journals, and the literature which is sold on the newsstands. These are, like some of our American magazines and best-sellers, not of the highest literary quality, but they are full of lively and realistic detail about private life in present-day China.

WOLFRAM EBERHARD
University of California
Berkeley, California

Part One

HISTORY

CHAPTER ONE

Introductory Remarks

Footbinding, a vivid symbol of the subjection of woman, survived countless dynastic changes and flourished for centuries. It was an integral part of a man's society which taught women to obey a strict and comprehensive moral code hallowed by time and tradition. A lady of virtue passively accepted her role as an intellectual inferior and remained ignorant of the outside world. Her reading was restricted to the orthodox canon, and she learned only household tasks and approved hobbies. She was inaccessible to view and safe from the dangers of flirtation, since she spent most of the day modestly concealed within the women's apartments. It was considered laudable for her to submit to the dreaded pain of footbinding in early childhood with stoical endurance, fighting back the tears in order to please her mother by achieving the criterion of beauty sanctioned through the ages.

The success or failure of footbinding depended on skillful application of a bandage around each foot. The bandage, about two inches wide and ten feet long, was wrapped in the following way. One end was placed on the inside of the instep, and from there it was carried over the small toes so as to force the toes in and towards the sole. The large toe was left unbound. The bandage was then wrapped around the heel so forcefully that heel and toes were drawn closer together. The process was then

Steps In Binding

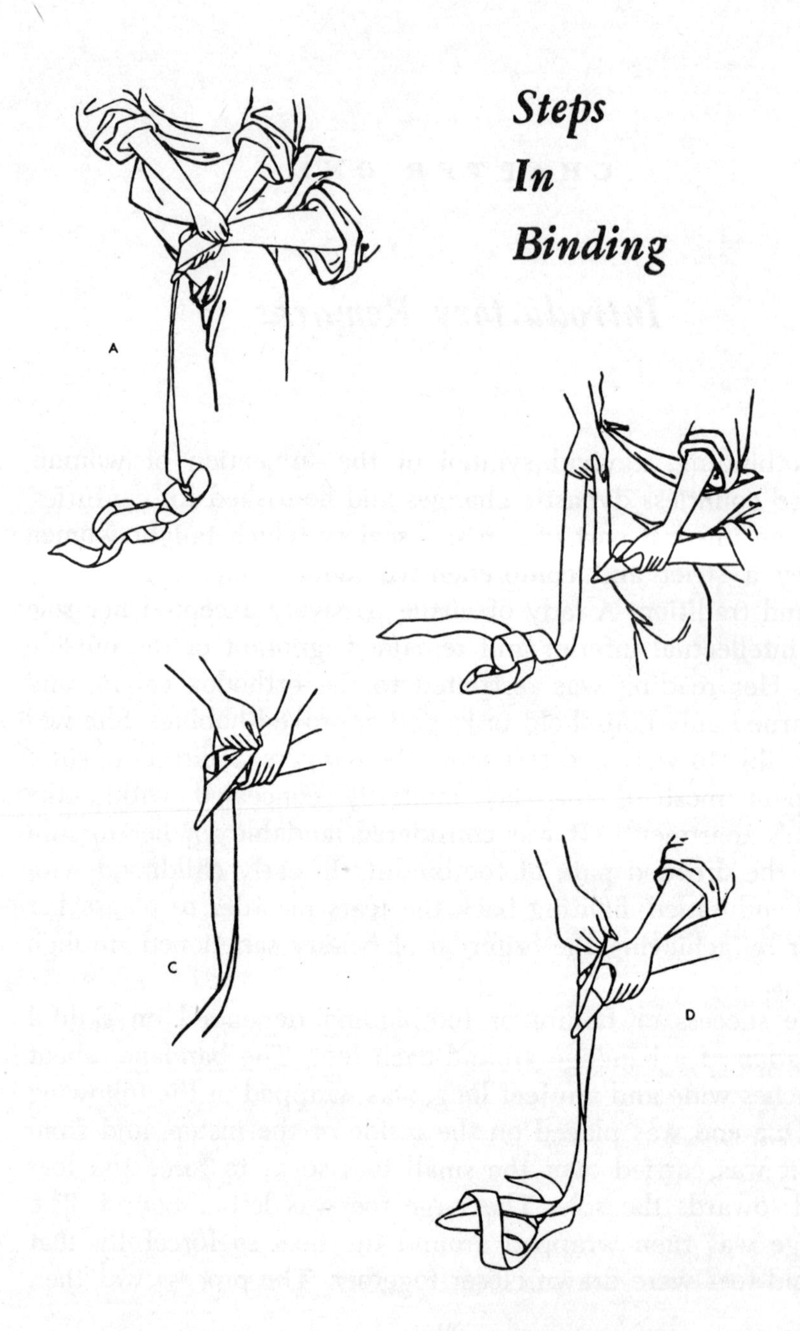

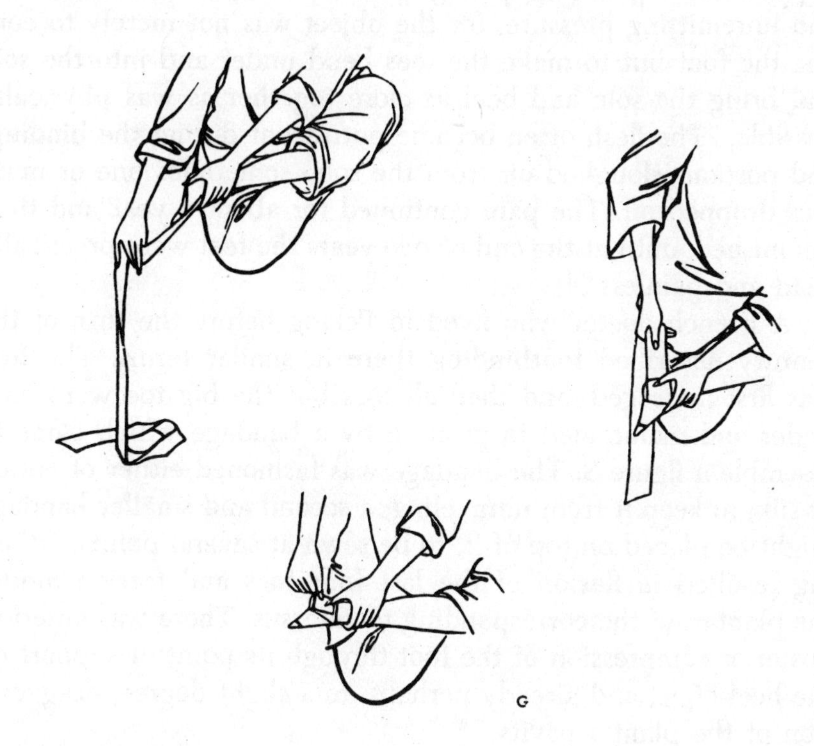

A. Bind the four toes once around.

B. Then pull the binding toward the outside; turn it toward the plantar, tightly binding the four toes.

C. From the inside of the foot, pull the binding toward the front point and turn it tightly around the big toe.

D. Wrap the heel from the outer side of the foot, and pull the binding toward the front point. Wrap the front, except for the big toe.

E. Wrap over the instep, go around the ankle, and return to the instep.

F. Turn toward the heel, and wrap the binding from the inner side of the foot to the front point.

G. Wrap from the inner side and over the instep to the outer side. Wrap around the heel and pull the binding back towards the part the binding cloth on the instep.

repeated from the beginning until the entire bandage had been applied. The foot of the young child was subjected to a coercive and unremitting pressure, for the object was not merely to confine the foot but to make the toes bend under and into the sole and bring the sole and heel as close together as was physically possible. "The flesh often became putrescent during the binding, and portions sloughed off from the sole; sometimes one or more toes dropped off. The pain continued for about a year and then diminished, until at the end of two years the feet were practically dead and painless."[1]

A French doctor who lived in Peking before the turn of the century described footbinding there in similar terms. The foot was first massaged, and then all toes but the big toe were bent under and maintained in position by a bandage which came to resemble a figure 8. The bandage was fashioned either of cotton or silk; to keep it from unraveling, a second and smaller bandage might be placed on top of it, to be sewn at several points. "Binding resulted in flexion of the last four toes and torsion, under the plantar, of the corresponding metatarsus. There was anterior-posterior compression of the foot through its point of support on the heel-bone, and already perhaps, to a slight degree, exaggeration of the plantar cavity."[2]

The young girl was subjected to this process by her mother, who bound the foot initially and prevented loosening of the bandages. Evidence that the child suffered intensely during the early stages is overwhelming:

> Born into an old-fashioned family at P'ing-hsi, I was inflicted with the pain of footbinding when I was seven years old. I was an active child who liked to jump about, but from then on my free and optimistic nature vanished. Elder sister endured the process from six to eight years of age. It was in the first lunar month of my seventh year that my ears were pierced and fitted with gold earrings. I was told that a girl had to suffer twice, through ear piercing and footbinding. Binding started in the second lunar month; mother consulted references in order to select an auspi-

cious day for it. I wept and hid in a neighbor's home, but mother found me, scolded me, and dragged me home. She shut the bedroom door, boiled water, and from a box withdrew binding, shoes, knife, needle, and thread. I begged for a one-day postponement, but mother refused: "Today is a lucky day," she said. "If bound today, your feet will never hurt; if bound tomorrow, they will." She washed and placed alum on my feet and cut the toenails. She then bent my toes toward the plantar with a binding cloth ten feet long and two inches wide, doing the right foot first and then the left. She finished binding and ordered me to walk, but when I did the pain proved unbearable.

That night, mother wouldn't let me remove the shoes. My feet felt on fire and I couldn't sleep; mother struck me for crying. On the following days, I tried to hide but was forced to walk on my feet. Mother hit me on my hands and feet for resisting. Beatings and curses were my lot for covertly loosening the wrappings. The feet were washed and rebound after three or four days, with alum added. After several months, all toes but the big one were pressed against the inner surface. Whenever I ate fish or freshly killed meat, my feet would swell, and the pus would drip. Mother criticized me for placing pressure on the heel in walking, saying that my feet would never assume a pretty shape. Mother would remove the bindings and wipe the blood and pus which dripped from my feet. She told me that only with removal of the flesh could my feet become slender. If I mistakenly punctured a sore, the blood gushed like a stream. My somewhat-fleshy big toes were bound with small pieces of cloth and forced upwards, to assume a new moon shape.

Every two weeks, I changed to new shoes. Each new pair was one- to two-tenths of an inch smaller than the previous one. The shoes were unyielding, and it took pressure to get into them. Though I wanted to sit passively by the *k'ang*, Mother forced me to move around. After changing more than ten pairs of shoes, my feet were reduced to a little over four inches. I had been binding for a month when my younger sister started; when no one was around, we would weep together. In summer, my feet smelled offensively because of pus and blood; in winter, my feet felt cold because of lack of circulation and hurt if they got too near the

> *k'ang* and were struck by warm air currents. Four of the toes were curled in like so many dead caterpillars; no outsider would ever have believed that they belonged to a human being. It took two years to achieve the three-inch model. My toenails pressed against the flesh like thin paper. The heavily-creased plantar couldn't be scratched when it itched or soothed when it ached. My shanks were thin, my feet became humped, ugly, and odoriferous; how I envied the natural-footed! [3]

Foreign visitors in China about the turn of the century were appalled by the crippling effect of footbinding and the untold suffering which it caused. They denounced the practice as barbaric and, in the larger cities, were especially effective in organizing public sentiment against it. After the Manchus were overthrown, these foreign efforts were overwhelmingly supported by leaders of the new Republic, who made a determined effort to eradicate the practice once and for all. Footbinding was denounced as a reactionary and anti-democratic vestige of an autocratic age, and articulate opposition to it became widespread. The rationale behind footbinding in earlier times was gradually forgotten. Prior to the Revolution, however, there were many reasons for its perpetuation in China.

The preference for small feet by the Chinese went back to remote antiquity and was poetically expressed before the age of Confucius. The ancient admiration of women who took small and measured steps was part of an over-all code of feminine behavior which stressed the cultivation of gracefulness and poise.[4] Large feet belonging to either sex were associated with lower class background. Even in the twentieth century, a concerned mother might confine the feet of a young son in tight linen socks to inhibit growth. A Chinese friend from Peking once remarked to me that residents there always wore socks and shoes and had small feet; by way of contrast he derided the Taiwanese, who usually wore wooden clogs or went about barefoot, for having large, wide feet.

Palace dancers probably originated footbinding in about the

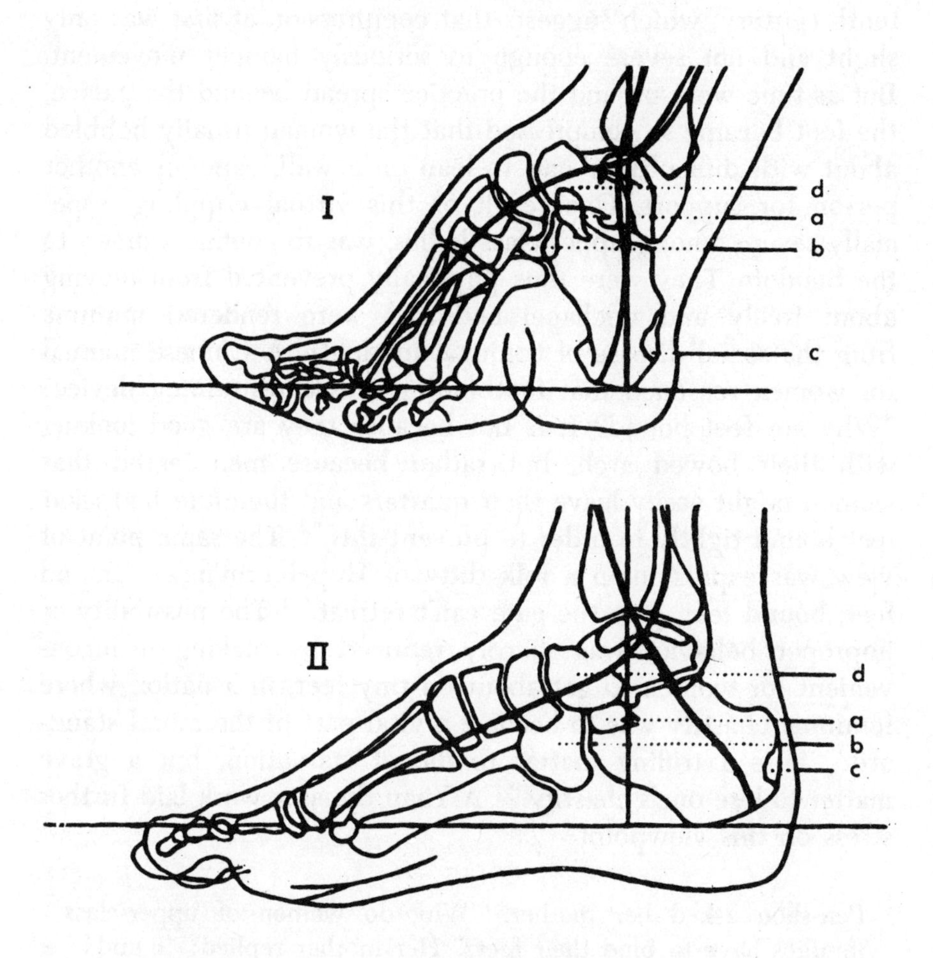

X-RAY COMPARISON OF BOUND AND NORMAL FOOT (PROVIDED BY A CHINESE AND AN ANNAMESE WOMAN OF THE SAME HEIGHT)

a. Small protuberance of the heel bone.

b. Cuboid.

c. Insertion of the Achilles tendon.

d. Top of the anklebone.

(from Vincent, *La Medicine en Chine au XX Siecle*)

tenth century, which suggests that compression at first was only slight and not severe enough to seriously hamper movement. But as time went on and the practice spread beyond the palace, the foot became so compressed that the woman usually hobbled about with difficulty or had to lean on a wall, cane, or another person for support. One result of this virtual crippling, especially severe among upper-class ladies, was to confine women to the boudoir. They were thus physically prevented from moving about freely and unchaperoned and were rendered immune from the social disease of conjugal infidelity. A Chinese manual for women reasoned that footbinding was a restraining device: "Why are feet bound? It is not because they are good looking with their bowed arch, but rather because men feared that women might easily leave their quarters and therefore had their feet bound tightly in order to prevent this." [5] The same point of view was expressed in a folk ditty of Hopei Province: "Bound feet, bound feet, past the gate can't retreat." [6] The possibility of improper behavior was sharply reduced by making it inconvenient for women to get about on tiny feet, in a nation where feminine chastity was to become a vital part of the moral standard: "It is a trifling matter to die of starvation, but a grave matter to lose one's chastity." [7] A Yüan dynasty work laid further stress on this viewpoint:

> Pen-shou asked her mother: "Why do women of upper-class families have to bind their feet?" Her mother replied: "I understand that the sages looked upon women with gravity and did not permit them to flit about. For this reason, they bound their feet. Their sphere of operation therefore did not extend beyond the women's quarters. If they wanted to go out, they had to do so in sedan chairs which were concealed by screens. There was, then, no need for them to use their feet." [8]

Traditional apologists asserted that footbinding, by making the woman's foot much smaller than the man's, more clearly defined visual points of difference between the sexes. They criticized the natural-footed female because her feet lacked diminutiveness and were therefore unfeminine and referred to her by such derisive names as Duck-foot and Lotus Boat. To rebel against footbinding was as unthinkable as to oppose traditional Chinese mores, with their insistence on maintaining a sharp cleavage between men and women. In order to ensure separation of the sexes, girls seven or older were forbidden to sit together with boys. Young ladies were even instructed to avoid speaking with brothers-in-law, as this might be interpreted as a presumption of intimacy. Conservative thinkers of the past alleged that applying rouge, putting on make up, piercing the ears, and binding the feet were all necessary practices which enabled women to conform to the social dictum that they had to differ from men in every visible physical aspect.

Another reason why this custom survived the vicissitudes of a millennium of history was its profound appeal to the Chinese male. Later chapters present the attitudes of critics and proponents, and from the pros and cons one fact becomes undeniably clear: the sexual appeal of footbinding to the Chinese male was never questioned. Those in favor of abolition condemned the tiny foot as lewd and lascivious, because it led man astray and prevented him from fulfilling his social responsibilities. There were apologists, on the other hand, who explained the persistence of the custom in terms of feminine psychology. Women from time immemorial and throughout the world showed a willingness to maim themselves to achieve male-defined standards of beauty and win love and admiration, and footbinding was therefore no different in its essential nature from the wearing of unnaturally high heels, plucking the eyebrows, or undergoing face-lifting operations.

We find this deformity of the feet ridiculous, but it pleases the Chinese. What would we say in Europe if a society of celestials made a campaign against the corset? Deformity for deformity, which is the more ridiculous: that which consequently produces a certain difficulty in walking, or that which, compressing the stomach, dislocating the kidneys, crushing the liver and constricting the heart, often prevents women from having fine children? [9]

From antiquity to the recent past, the Chinese regarded the beauty of the tiny foot as a mark of gentility and refinement. During the latter part of the Ming dynasty (early 17th century), China suffered from Tartar invasions. To save the day, a scholar named Ch'ü Ssu-chiu[10] made the following proposal:

The reason these barbarians are able to leave their own territory easily and swiftly and come to invade us from a great distance is that there are no beautiful women in their northern regions. If we want to control these northern barbarians, we should bring it about so that they have many beauties and cause their men to be ensnared and deluded by feminine charm. We should teach them footbinding and persuade them to imitate us in dress. They will prize women with a willow waist and a lotus gait and a weak and alluring attitude. Barbarians who have been deluded by such women will then lose their cruel and harsh natures.

The mystery of the foot enhanced its appeal. It was washed in strictest privacy and bound in the intimacy and inaccessibility of the boudoir. Male curiosity was aroused; stealing a covert glance at one's beloved with bindings unraveled thrilled the beholder and stirred his passions. The impact must have been greater than that felt by a Westerner who accidentally sees his enamored in the nude, for the feminine figure in China was usually entirely concealed. The flesh revealed by summer dress or bathing suit leaves little to the Western imagination, but the Chinese male let his thoughts dwell on the tiny foot barely revealed beneath the full-cut trousers and then transferred his fancy upwards to the forbidden Jade Gate.

The tiny and fragile appearance of the foot aroused in the male a combination of lust and pity. He longed to touch it, and being allowed to do so meant that the woman was his. Golden

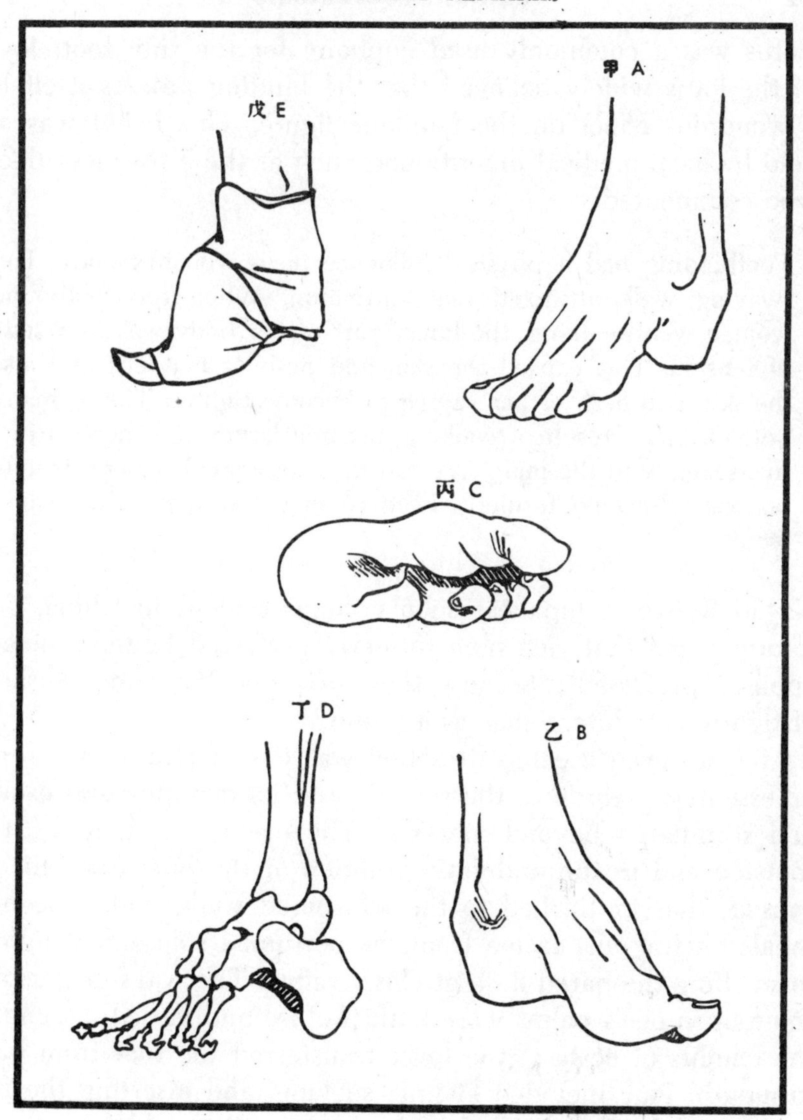

STAGES OF THE FOOTBINDING PROCESS

A. Early results, all toes but the big one bent under the metatarsal. B. and C. Process complete, with toes entirely bent under the metatarsal. D. Resultant change in bone configuration. (Based on a specimen kept by the Natural Foot Society in Taipei, Taiwan, in 1905.) E. The foot which has changed in form tightly bound by a strip of cloth. (from *Shina kanzoku no joshi ni okonawaruru tensoku no fu*)

Lotus was a commonly used euphony for the tiny foot; lovers of the lotus widely believed that the binding process itself had a wondrous effect on the feminine figure. This belief was also held by local medical practitioners such as the Taiwanese doctor who commented:

> Footbinding had a physical influence on a woman's body. Her swaying walk attracted male attention. When the footbound woman went walking, the lower part of her body was in a state of tension. This caused the skin and flesh of her legs and also the skin and flesh of her vagina to become tighter. The woman's buttocks, as a result of walking, became larger and more attractive sexually to the male. We can thus see that there are definite reasons why men formerly liked to marry women with bound feet.[11]

Nagao Ryūzo, a Japanese scholar long resident in China, once informed me that rich men formerly preferred bound-foot concubines, professedly because they gave one the same sensation of tightness in intercourse as a virgin.[12]

But an even greater attraction was the foot itself. It formed an essential prelude to the sex act, and its manipulation excited and stimulated beyond measure. The eye rejoiced in the tiny footstep and in the undulating motion of the buttocks which it caused; the ear thrilled to the whispered walk, while the nose inhaled a fragrant aroma from the perfumed sole and delighted in smelling the bared flesh at closer range. The ways of grasping the foot in one's palms were both profuse and varied; ascending the heights of ecstasy, the lover transferred the foot from palm to mouth. Play included kissing, sucking, and inserting the foot in the mouth until it filled both cheeks, either nibbling at it or chewing it vigorously, and adoringly placing it against one's cheeks, chest, knees, or virile member. The devotee willingly washed his beloved's feet, trimmed the toenails without hesitation, and even ate watermelon seeds and almonds placed between the toes.[13]

This introductory chapter has touched upon some of the general aspects of footbinding. Subsequent chapters and appendices record history and development, the revolutionary fervor to abolish the practice, critical comments by abolitionists and counter arguments by apologists, sexual implications, relevant social customs and superstitions, details on binding and the areas where it flourished, and interviews with and biographies of the tiny-footed. The subject is as vast and sprawling as China itself and impossible to neatly delineate, for variations on the binding theme were limitless. For example, it was of course considered a feminine monopoly, but there were proven instances of male footbinding. It is generally taken for granted that only the Chinese practiced it, but some Chinese writers assert that towards the close of the nineteenth century, Korean women also compressed their feet.

Pain and binding of the feet were synonymous terms. One apologist explained that women suffered willingly in order to please men and that all of womankind would be eager to purchase a modern medicine which could painlessly reduce the foot. That women generally want their feet to be small is undeniable, but footbinding was a far from easy formula. As a natural-footed female critic once stated:

> I don't know when this custom began;
> It must have been started by a despicable man!

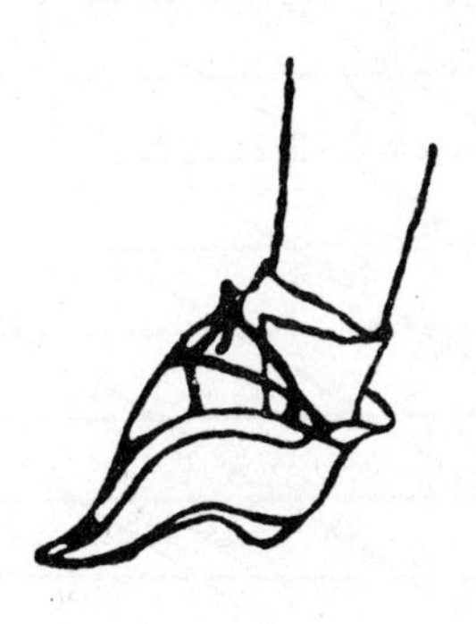

CHAPTER TWO

Origin and Presence

Questions concerning the beginning of footbinding in China have invited learned speculation from the Sung dynasty onwards, with widely varying opinions. The nineteenth-century sinologist Du Halde, for example, believed that the last empress of the Shang dynasty started it in about the twelfth century B.C.:

> Her own feet being very small, she bound them tight with fillets, affecting to make that pass for a beauty which was really a deformity. However, the women all followed her example; and this ridiculous custom is so thoroughly established that to have feet of the natural size is enough to render them contemptible.[1]

Chinese folklore attributed the origin of footbinding to a fox who tried in this way to conceal its paws while assuming the human guise of the Shang empress mentioned by Du Halde. And, as the story goes, the imperially-favored fox then set a palace fashion. A similar version alleged that the empress, who had a clubfoot, persuaded her timid spouse to make the compression of feet obligatory for young girls. This enabled the empress to set forth her deformity as a model of beauty and elegance.[2] Scholars attributed the start of footbinding to various later dynasties. They relied largely on veiled classical poetic or prose references, but failed to resolve the persisting problem as to whether the references were to bound or merely small feet.[3] Small feet had been esteemed in China since antiquity, but prior to the tenth century there was no verifiable proof that feet were bound. Even as late as the T'ang dynasty, as it was stated in one history of the period, women of the upper class wore dress and shoes in imitation of their husbands.[4] This statement is partially borne out by figurines of the period, which show that both men and women wore a court shoe which resembled a boat with a high prow.[5]

The available evidence for the T'ang weighs heavily against footbinding. Women depicted in eighth and ninth century paintings are robust and vigorous physical types without the slightest hint of needing support or of walking with a hobbled gait. Primary references make it clear that T'ang ladies were encouraged to engage in many athletic events requiring strenuous physical exertion, such as horseback riding, polo, and ball kicking, which were much better suited for a natural-footed participant. Polo and ball kicking were also popular among palace ladies, which would not have been so if tiny feet had already become an imperial harem vogue. The story was told of an old lady at Ma-wei who displayed a tiny shoe of Yang Kuei-fei's (d.756) after her death, but this version was a late Sung fabrication. The earlier account said instead that the consort's stocking was shown to curiosity seekers at Ma-wei for a fixed price.[6] This again, as Lin Yutang points out, is evidence that Consort Yang had natural feet, and there is nothing in the historical details of her life which might lead us to believe otherwise.[7] Futhermore, a late-eighth-century manual written by a palace lady gave detailed instructions to women of the time on how to sit, walk, and behave properly, and in so doing gave no indication that any of its intended readers might be hampered in movement by compressed feet.[8]

Chang Pang-chi,[9] a commentator who lived in the early twelfth century, made an unequivocal reference to footbinding. He stated that the practice was a recent one and that former allegations about its much earlier origins were contrary to fact. He cited a reference, no longer extant, to the effect that foot-binding had begun during the Southern T'ang dynastic rule of sovereign-poet Li Yü (r.961-75), a ruler who controlled one region of a divided China prior to reunification by the Sung. According to the reference, Li Yü had a favored palace concubine named Lovely Maiden who was a slender-waisted beauty and a gifted dancer. He had a six-foot-high lotus constructed for her out of gold; it was decorated lavishly with pearls and had a carmine lotus carpel in the center. Lovely Maiden was ordered to bind her feet with white silk cloth to make the tips look like the points of a moon sickle. She then danced in the center of the lotus, whirling about like a rising cloud.[10]

The construction of a lotus out of gold represented an old if little-known palace tradition, begun in about 500 A.D. by an emperor of Northern Ch'i. The emperor had his Favored Consort P'an walk on top of the golden structure and said in admiration that she was giving rise to lotuses with every step.[11] The "golden lotus" which became a euphonious term for bound feet was therefore originally a special apparatus on which palace dancers walked and later danced. The making of a lotus out of gold may have been in imitation of Indian tradition, for the fifth-century pilgrim Fa Hsien stated in his travel account that an Indian king made one in honor of an assemblage of priests.[12] The Buddhist pilgrim Hsüan Tsang (596-664) recorded an Indian tale about a deer lady which probably supplied the ideological basis behind the construction of a golden lotus in the Chinese palace. A Rishi was once bathing in a pure stream, said Hsüan Tsang, when a roe-deer who had come there to drink conceived and brought forth a female child. She was beautiful beyond human measure, but she had the feet of a deer. The Rishi adopted her as his child. One day she walked to the hut of another Rishi; wherever her feet trod, she left the impressions of lotus flowers upon the ground. Soothsayers predicted that she would bear a thousand sons; this she did, with each child seated on one leaf of a thousand-leafed lotus flower.[13] It seems likely that this Indian tale was known in the Northern Ch'i court and that the monarch constructed the lotus so that his consort might visually represent the heroine. The popularity of the story may have stemmed from its emphasis on fecundity, and its enactment may have been restricted at first to the imperial harem, as were, for example, special dances in the T'ang period.[14] The story should have been known to Li Yü, reigning in south China more than four centuries afterwards. He therefore may have had his consort bind her feet to represent more faithfully the traditional theme, in which the feet of the beautiful child remained those of an animal and would have been disguised. The consort's feet may have been bound in a special way to portray the moon over the lotus in dramatic artistic form. Chinese folklore may have adopted the dim outlines of the Indian story to explain the origin of footbinding, replacing the deer with a beautiful fox in human guise. In both instances the feet alone failed to assume human shape.

Twelfth-century writer Chang Pang-chi revealed that, while footbinding had begun in the Five Dynasties period, it was infrequent until the end of the eleventh century. However, by his day (ca.1130) it had become so widely imitated that people were ashamed not to practice it. The custom probably started in the imperial harem in a way similar to that described above, at the end of the T'ang or in the interim period preceding the Sung, at a time when there were myriad trained dancers in the empire.[15] The palace may have, in effect, started a vogue for a special and artistic dancing effect achieved through footbinding which slowly set the fashion for the rest of the Chinese world. The early connection with dancing was unmistakable; we know, for instance, that while Li Yü's favored danseuse bound her feet in the new moon style, his empress was natural-footed.[16] The pre-Sung binding must have been only slightly constricting in contrast with the much more rigorous later application, which crippled women so that walking could be accomplished only with difficulty. After the Sung, increasingly tighter binding led to stagnation of the art of dancing and its virtual disappearance.[17] The early association of tiny bowed shoes with dancing is further corroborated by a statement in the Sung dynastic history. When a pair of tiny bowed shoes was brought into the palace in 1064, a court official in attendance asked of what use such dancing shoes were to his prince.[18] It was from the early twelfth century onward that such shoes acquired a more general use. "Perhaps the style of shoe in the tenth century required excessively small feet, and the dancer's solution of the problem was rapidly and widely adopted by other women."[19] Adoption at first, however, was neither wide nor rapid; there was a gradual evolution from the palace dancer to the upper classes and finally down to the masses, in a north to south geographical direction.

While footbinding may have begun as an innovation of the palace dancer, its diffusion in the Southern Sung was facilitated because it came to be regarded philosophically as a device for the suppression of women:

> Why must the foot be bound?
> To prevent barbarous running around![20]

During the Sung dynasty, there was a change in masculine viewpoints, with a gradual shift away from the liberal attitudes towards chastity and remarriage which had characterized the T'ang. Women of the T'ang remarried fairly frequently, either after divorce from or death of the first husband. There were often two and sometimes three recorded marriages of women in the imperial clan.[21] T'ang courtesans wrote direct and frank revelations of their feelings in verse, showing that their intellectual development was unhindered.[22] While remarriage in the Sung was still commonplace, several noted thinkers took a dim view of feminine liberty and intellectual freedom, laying the groundwork for the belief that a woman of virtue should be a conventional lady of little talent. The eleventh-century historian Ssu-ma Kuang felt it advisable to let women read proper classi-

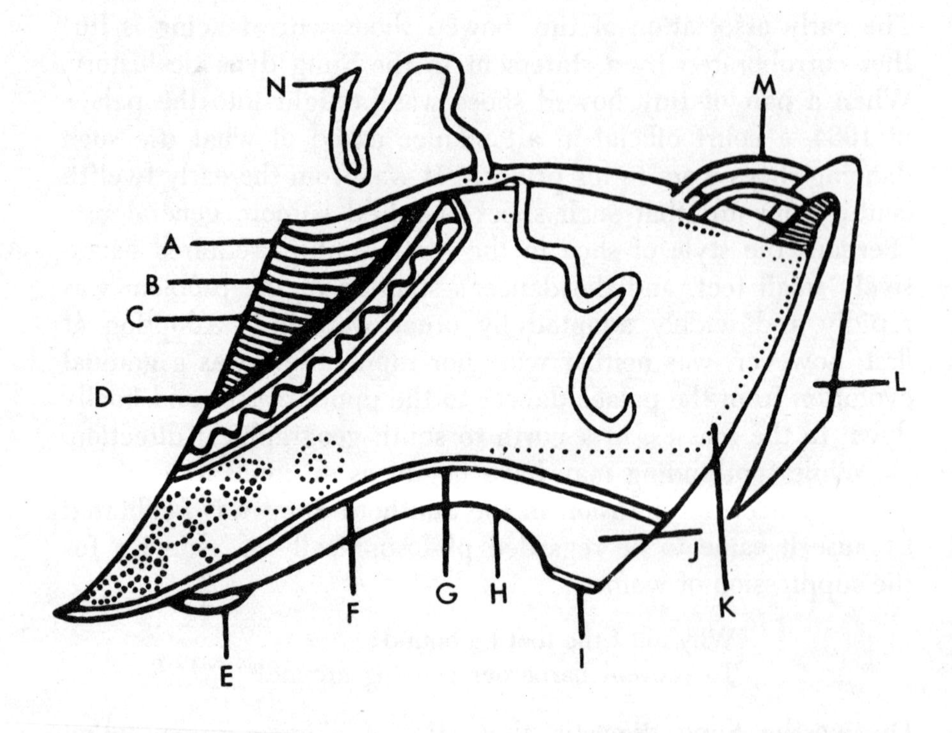

DETAILED DRAWING OF A TINY SHOE, NORTHERN STYLE, POPULAR IN THE EARLY 1920'S

A. Temple Gate; also called Moon Gate.

B. Ladder rungs.

C. Bound foot surface; also called aperture surface.

D. Aperture point.

E. Front sole support.

F. Border strip.

G. Middle joint.

H. Center of the sole.

I. Rear sole support.

J. Perfume storage.

K. Inner high heel.

L. Heel lift.

M. Heel lift reinforcement.

N. Shoe fastener.

(from *TFL* 1.225-26)

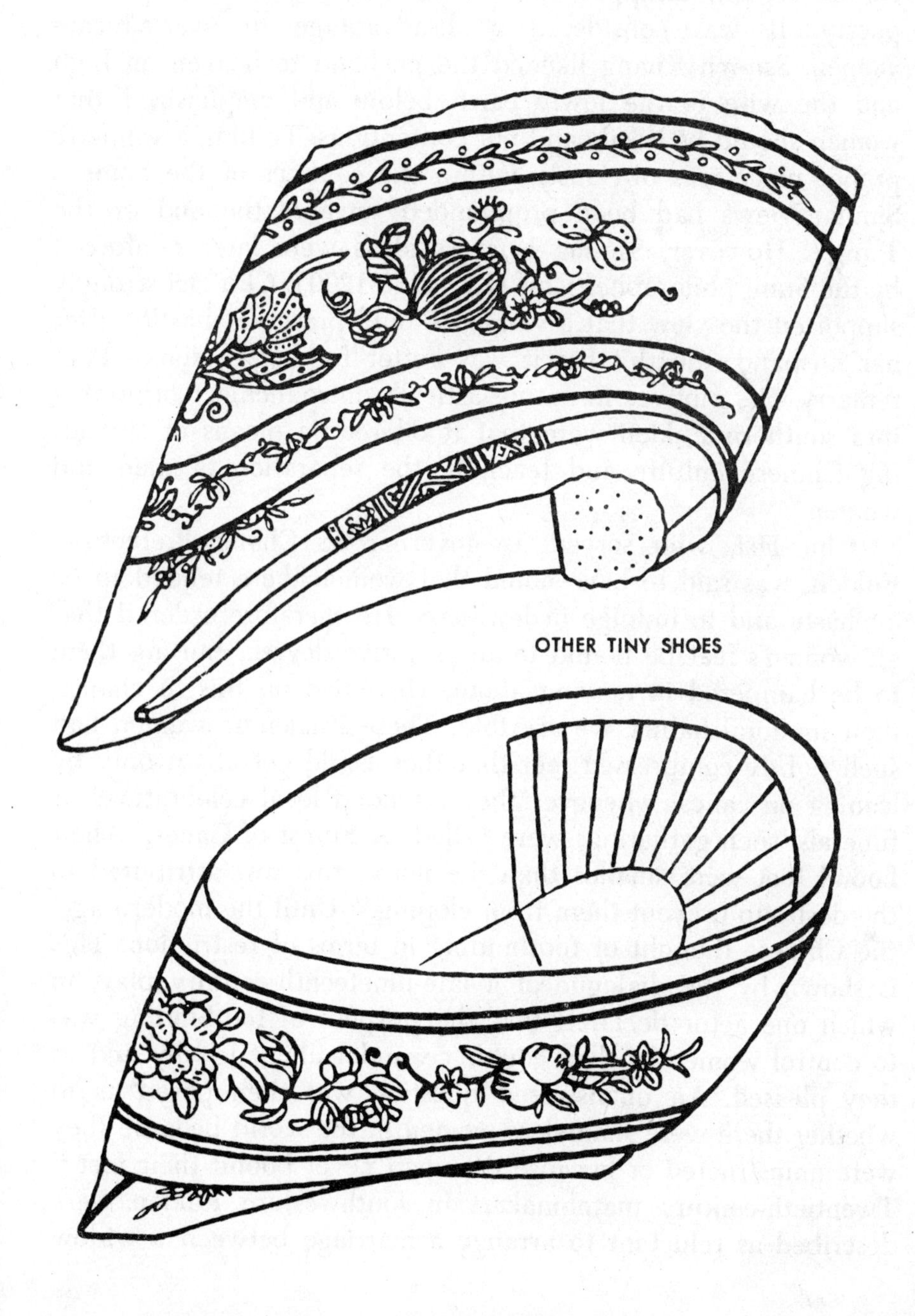

OTHER TINY SHOES

cal works, but disapproved of their learning to sing or write poetry. It was considered a disadvantage to over-educate women. Ssu-ma Kuang likened the husband to heaven on high and the wife to the lowly earth below and emphasized that woman should be docile and not contentious. To him, a woman's proper place was obviously within the confines of the home.[23] Similar views had been propounded towards the end of the T'ang.[24] However, Ssu-ma Kuang's ideas were later reinforced by the Sung philosopher Chu Hsi (1130-1200). Chu Hsi strongly supported the view that a woman should preserve chastity after her husband's death, that it was better for her to starve than remarry. His motives in enthusiastically introducing footbinding into southern Fukien were that it offered "a means of spreading Chinese culture and teaching the separation of men and women."[25]

Chu Hsi, who served as governor in Chang Prefecture, Fukien, was said to have noted that women there tended to be unchaste and to indulge in lewdness. He therefore ordered that all women's feet be bound to an excessive degree, causing them to be hampered in moving about. He relied on this to change their immoral habits, we are told. These Fukienese women had such tightly compressed feet that they could get about only by leaning on canes; whenever they attended local celebrations or funerals, such gatherings were called "A Forest of Canes." Their bound feet were smaller than the norm; this was attributed to the desire to prevent them from eloping.[26] Until the modern age, the Chinese thought of footbinding in terms of restriction. This is shown by the dialogue of a late-nineteenth-century play, in which one actor declared that the purpose of footbinding was to control women so they couldn't wander about lewdly and as they pleased. An unanswered question was then posed as to whether there were shameless women in the world because they were uninstructed or because they had never bound their feet.[27] Twentieth-century matchmakers in southwestern Fukien were described as reluctant to arrange a marriage between a widow and a young bachelor, believing that it would bring the man bad luck.[28]

As we have seen, the custom of footbinding probably originated toward the end of the T'ang dynasty or in the decades which immediately followed. It was limited at first to a palace innovation practiced by trained dancers, whose feet must have been only moderately compressed. By the twelfth century it had become accepted throughout the imperial palace.[29] From then

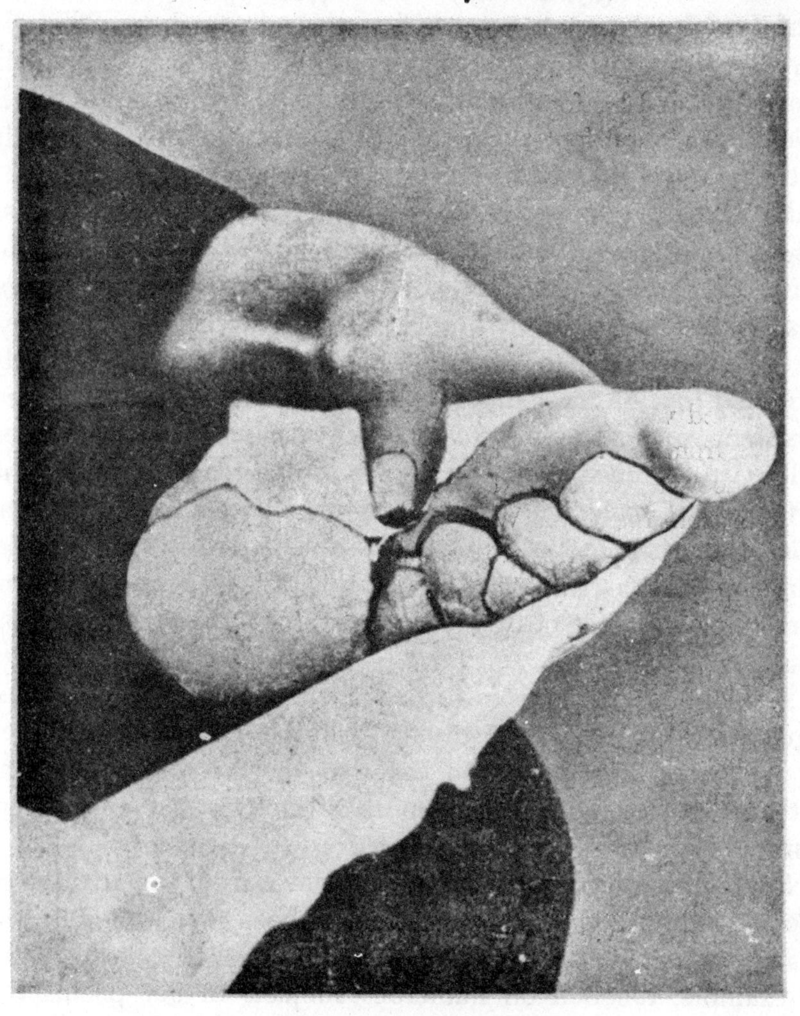

on, its impact as a hallmark of gentility and correct fashion was felt increasingly by the upper class. It also helped to ensure that a woman remain in her proper place—at home. It was so inconvenient for the bound-footed to get about that her chances for indulging sexually as did the Chinese male were greatly lessened. Footbinding proved to be a significant and lasting development in a nation whose outlook on feminine morality became increasingly stringent.[30] This philosophical outlook was reinforced in the centuries which followed the Sung. That the tiny foot came to be considered a mark of gentility was equally significant. From the Yüan dynasty onward, families which claimed aristocratic lineage came to feel compelled to bind the feet of their girls, with utmost severity and diligence, as a visible sign of upper-class distinction. An ideal of conspicuous leisure required diminutive feet and hands as well as a slender waist, for these features indicated that the person affected was incapable of useful effort and had to be supported in idleness by her owner. Veblen used this argument to explain why the deformed foot of the Chinese woman enjoyed such a wide and persistent vogue. The fact that the foot was bound to the smallest and a virtually incapacitating degree as one reached the heights of the social scale, and that upper-class Korean and Manchu ladies under Chinese influence also strove to achieve feet smaller than the norm, is further evidence that it was a distinguishing mark which set the aristocratic lady apart from the plebeian class.

A Yüan dynasty treatise further justified footbinding because it guaranteed feminine chastity.[31] A Chinese manual for instructing women similarly pointed out that the purpose in binding feet was not to make them more attractive, but to prevent women from easily being able to leave their quarters.[32]

Footbinding was not yet commonplace during the Sung, even among the upper class who would have been first to imitate the palace style. The famed poetess Li Ch'ing-chao (born 1080), for example, touched on numerous subjects in her poems but never mentioned binding. In one line she wrote of having once walked barefoot through the snow, proof that she was never personally exposed to the practice.[33] During the Sung, binding was unknown in Kwangsi and Annam. It probably was rare in the southern areas of Kwangtung, Kiangsu, and Chekiang, for there were poems about women in these localities going about in bare feet.[34] Su Tung-p'o (1036-1101), who also referred poetically to natural feet, wrote one of the earliest verses in praise of footbinding:

> Anointed with fragrance, she takes lotus steps;
> Though often sad, she steps with swift lightness.
> She dances like the wind, leaving no physical trace.
> Another stealthily but happily tries on the palace style,
> But feels such distress when she tries to walk!
> Look at them in the palms of your hands,
> So wondrously small that they defy description.[35]

There was a verifiable late-thirteenth-century reference to a prominent official towards the close of the Sung who had lived in a region of Shensi where women neither pierced their ears nor bound their feet. The writer thought it relevant to note that certain women did not observe such customs, indicating that by the start of Mongol rule natural-footedness in Shensi must have seemed rather unusual.[36]

During the Yüan dynasty, footbinding was gradually transmitted from the north to the center and south of China. The Chinese may have emphasized it in order to draw a clearer cultural distinction between themselves and their large-footed conquerors. Perhaps the Mongols encouraged it in order to weaken the Chinese by impairing the health of their women.[37] In songs, poems, and plays of the period, there were frequent references to three-inch golden lotuses. The following poem by Sa'dulla (born 1308) implies that by the fourteenth century the foot was probably much more compressed than it had been in the Sung:

Caught by the gentle wind,
Her silk skirt ripples and waves.
Lotus blossoms in shoes most tight,
As if she could stand on autumnal waters!
Her shoe tips do not peek beyond the skirt,
Fearful lest the tiny embroideries be seen.[38]

Footbinding, as we have seen, widened its popular base under Mongol rule. We should therefore expect to find frequent notice of it by foreigners then coming to China for the first time. And yet, there was apparently no mention of it in the records of visitors prior to or during the Yüan dynasty, with the exception of one. The reason may be that feet were not then bound to so small a degree that a foreigner would notice the difference in contrast with a natural foot, or that women of the upper classes who had diminutive feet were carefully secluded and kept out of the view of foreigners. Marco Polo (1254-1324), writing when footbinding was practiced by the courtesan as well as the genteel lady, surprisingly made no reference to it in his chronicle. This may be a reflection on his faulty powers of observation. A contemporary of Marco Polo named Friar Odoric of Pordenone (died January, 1[illegible]), in northern China about 1324, was the first foreigner to write about the custom, stating in his travelogue: "And with the women the great beauty is to have little feet; and for this reason, mothers are accustomed, as soon as girls are born to them, to swathe their feet tightly so that they can never grow in the least."[39] This Western record was slightly earlier in actual date of publication than the Chinese reference which stated that footbinding had originated in Li Yü's imperial harem towards the end of the Five Dynasties period.[40]

Footbinding was more popular during the Ming dynasty than in any before it, receiving official and popular sanction. Palace ladies wore a special tiny bowed shoe, different from all others.[41] The first Ming emperor had an unusually large-footed empress. He once jokingly asked her how she had ever become so eminent with such large feet; she replied that large feet had been essential in order to firmly pacify the nation. Her remark was a reminder to the monarch that, because she was natural-footed, she had been able to accompany him on military expeditions prior to unification. On Lantern Festival Day, occurring during the first lunar month, the emperor went strolling about the streets disguised as a commoner. It was then the custom for people to write or draw riddles on lanterns during the festival as amusement for the passers-by. The emperor saw a drawing on one lantern of a big-footed woman sitting and holding a watermelon in her lap. He guessed that she was supposed to be from Anhwei and that the empress was being made the target of ridicule. The next day, he ordered the clan responsible for the drawing executed, down to the remotest relative; over three hundred lost their lives.[42] This incident shows that footbinding so flourished in early Ming that the natural-footed woman was considered ridiculous. During Ming rule, Mongols still living in the Chekiang area were officially discriminated against by being prevented from engaging in studies if men or from binding their feet if women. Binding was as highly regarded for the proper woman as learning was for the cultivated man, and conservative families transmitted the saying, "If you care for a son, you don't go easy on his studies; if you care for a daughter, you don't go easy on her footbinding."[43]

Toward the close of the Ming dynasty, rebel Chang Hsien-chung occupied Hsiang-yang in Hupeh and cut off the hands of men and the legs of women whom he captured. He made two large and separate mounds from the severed hands and feet. The mound of hands was called the Peak of the Jade Arms; the mound of feet was called the Peak of the Golden Lotuses. He did this, according to one account, to fulfill a vow to Heaven that he would offer up to it two trays of candles if he were cured of malarial attacks. No one understood what he meant, but upon being cured he ordered the mounds constructed and severed the slender legs of one of his concubines in order to place them on top of the pile.[44] This gruesome incident further proves that footbinding flourished as never before toward the close of the Ming dynasty. Another account, written about a palace lady who alone escaped massacre of the occupants of a royal harem at Hsiang-yang by the forces of Chang Hsien-chung, alleged that the rebels played a gambling game with the feet after they were severed.[45] The last Ming emperor was a lover of the lotus who esteemed his Precious Consort T'ien because her feet were both tiny in appearance and perfectly compressed in form.[46] He once reputedly became extremely displeased because the Pre-

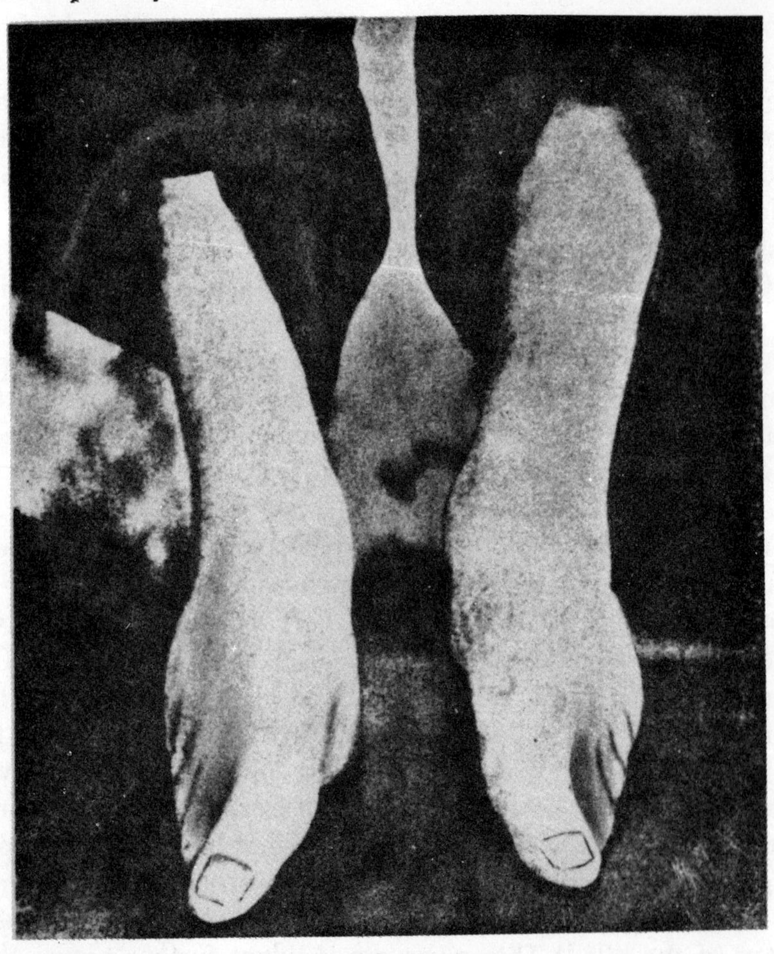

cious Consort accepted a gift of elegant tiny shoes from an official admirer, reproved the woman, and became ill-disposed towards the man.[47]

Ming poets, novelists, and diarists frequently referred to bound feet and praised their dainty beauty. *Chin P'ing Mei,* for instance, the late-sixteenth-century erotic novel made accessible to the West through Clinton Egerton's four-volume translation,[48] revealed how the tiny foot was regarded by affluent society of the author's day. It was advertised by matchmakers as a praiseworthy attribute; the shoe in which it was encased flirtatiously suggested concealment, mystery, and boudoir pleasures. Well-to-do ladies took pride in their small and well-proportioned "golden lotuses," designed shoes for them of crimson silk, and wore especially attractive models when preparing for bed. The sleeping shoes, scarlet in hue, were intended to heighten male desire through a striking color contrast with the white skin of the beloved. Making the shoes was a painstaking process, and a lady might become infuriated if her shoes were dirtied or stolen. In a fit of rage, she might cut a rival's shoes to shreds. The shoes played a role in drinking games, but wine was not drunk directly from them, as Egerton erroneously translates, but from cups placed in them.[49]

Bound-foot ladies rode in sedan chairs when they visited friends or attended such formal occasions as funerals. The implication in *Chin P'ing Mei,* however, is that the tiny feet which peeped from beneath a woman's skirts did not prevent her from moving about quickly and painlessly.

Hsi-men Ch'ing, the central character of the novel, was a profligate who cared more for the thing-in-itself than its outer trappings, of which the lotus was but one. He was in no way an avid lotus lover and might have looked askance at the aficionados who even willingly drank the foot-washing water when the passion seized them. (There are numerous verified references in *Ts'ai-fei lu* to this sort of bizarre behavior.) Hsi-men Ch'ing might tie a woman's legs to trellis or bedpost with her own bindings, but his sexual manipulations of the lotus go unmentioned. He might admire the feet aesthetically and raise them above his shoulders during intercourse, but in *Chin P'ing Mei* the usual insistence of the lotus lover on smelling, rubbing, and caressing the bared flesh was conspicuous by its absence.

The Manchus were opposed to footbinding from the start. But during their centuries of rule, attempts at eradication were sporadic and unsuccessful; the custom continued to grow in popularity. A detailed Western description of how footbinding flourished in the decades before organized opposition to it got under way is recorded in *The Chinese Repository*, an early-nineteenth-century journal of sinological scholarship and missionary observation.[50] One writer stated that in 1835 it prevailed more or less throughout the entire empire, but only among the Chinese. It was socially sanctioned; a majority of women in the large towns and cities, as well as in "the most fashionable parts of the country," had their feet compressed. The writer estimated that five to eight out of every ten females had bound feet, depending on locality. He reports that the process began in infancy, with a tendency towards applying the bindings more tightly and rigorously as one went up the social scale. Ladies of rank and fashion might be rendered quite unable to walk. "The effects of this process are extremely painful. Children will often tear away the bandages in order to gain relief from the torture; but their temporary removal, it is said, greatly increases the pain by causing a violent revulsion of the blood to the feet." Women in Canton and vicinity who could avoid it seldom appeared outside the confines of their homes, except in sedan chairs. However, since such seclusion was impossible for members of the poorer classes, in order to walk any considerable distance they had to rely on a stick or the shoulder of a matron or servant. "In walking, the body is bent forwards at a considerable inclination, in order to place the centre of gravity over the feet; and the great muscular exertion required for preserving the balance is evinced by the rapid motion of the arms, and the hobbling shortness of the steps."[51] The remainder of the article consisted of a paper written by a surgeon to Guy's Hospital named Bransby Blake Cooper read before the Society on March 5, 1829. Doctor Cooper medically analyzed a bound foot amputated from a woman's corpse which had been found floating in the river at Canton; it had been sent to England for scientific evaluation.[52]

While footbinding started solely as a Chinese custom, some Manchu ladies imitated it in defiance of official decree; upper-class Korean women also practiced a less severe form of foot compression. Professor Francis L. K. Hsu, writing in 1953 about a former Jewish colony in Honan, said that these Jews had lived like Chinese, using Chinese forms of their Hebrew names: ". . . and their elderly women, like their Chinese sisters, had bound feet."[53] Non-Chinese peoples living in China such as the Mongols, Tibetans, Hakka, and Miao were natural-footed, as were most Mohammedans in Kansu Province. But Mohammedans who moved elsewhere often bound their feet in imitation of the Chinese. The Hakka, originally from Shansi and Honan, gradually moved southward from the late ninth century onward; the fact that their women never had other than natural feet is evidence that footbinding was little practiced, if at all, in these northern areas during the late T'ang and Sung periods.

The difference in the extent to which footbinding was adhered to in China depended largely on social class. Women of the poorer classes, such as those who worked in the fields, were often barefooted; in areas such as Kwangtung and Kweichow, meticulous footbinding was associated with families of wealth and eminence. A tiny-footed concubine in Kwangtung was politely referred to as "aunt," but if natural-footed she was derisively called "bare foot" and was not allowed to wear socks and slippers until after one of her sons married. The best "lotus" specimens in this area tended to be round and so short that they could be placed on a small dish.[54] There were both tiny and natural-footed Cantonese prostitutes; the large-footed came from poor village families. The domestic who attended to boudoir needs was usually tiny-footed and attractive looking, in contrast to the homely servant who performed manual tasks.[55]

Footbinding was uncommon in that part of Kiangsu Province north of the Yangtze River, villages in Kwangsi and Szechwan Province, northern Anhwei, Kiangsi, Fukien, Hunan, and parts of Hupei and Chekiang. But in northern provinces like Suiyuan, Chahar, Shensi, Shansi, Honan, and Hopei, footbinding still flourished as late as the first two decades of the twentieth century. The women in Shansi and Shensi provinces and vicinity reputedly had the smallest feet in China:

> I have wandered about everywhere. The places which have the smallest feet, still capable of being walked upon, are undoubtedly Lanchow in Shensi Province and Ta-t'ung in Shansi Province. The feet of Lanchow women are three inches at the most or less than three inches.[56]

Another who traveled through Honan and Shensi in the Manchu era noted that even women of the lowest classes there, such as beggars and water carriers, had tiny and regular feet which pointed upwards like water chestnuts.[57] These remarks were equally valid for the period before the revolutionary insistence on change achieved effect. Ta-t'ung women were known for their tiny feet as early as the Ming, and a lotus style emerged which consisted of being slender, small, pointed, bowed, fragrant, soft, and regular. Perfume was used in the washing; however, this failed to blunt the criticism of a southern apologist about the odoriferousness of northern women:

> Northern women have three offensive odors. They like to eat onions, so their breath is offensive. They don't wash their private parts, so these are offensive. And they don't wash their feet, so their feet are offensive.

To reinforce his last remark, the critic mentioned the experience of his friend, a Mr. Yang, who was once sitting beside a northern prostitute. The prostitute suddenly placed her lotus hooks on Yang's knees, and he inhaled such a strong odor that he hurriedly put them down. She did this again, almost causing him to go into a faint.[58] The odoriferousness of the seldom-washed bound foot must have been repugnant to all but the confirmed lotus lover, for it was made a part of the Chinese language in the form of a popular saying about a Mrs. Wang's binding cloth being both long and smelly.[59]

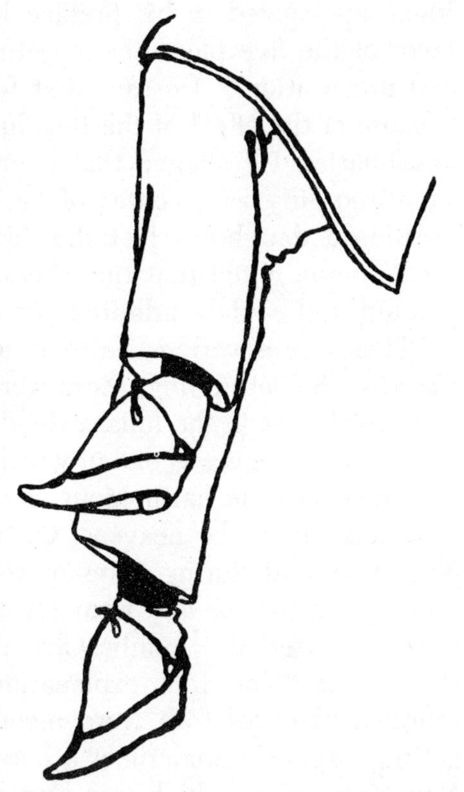

The women in several counties in southern Suiyuan were alleged to be fanatically devoted footbinding enthusiasts. They opposed prohibitionists and surreptitiously continued the practice in defiance of governmental decree even in the early nineteen-thirties. They dressed rather shabbily but went in for elegant shoe adornment. Women almost always made their own shoes and worked on them diligently; very few were sold commercially. Red and green were the preferred colors; white was used only on shoes to be worn at funerals or to indicate mourning. It was concluded that while these Suiyuan women did not dare publicly to advocate footbinding, those in average and wealthy families were still striving to keep the custom alive.[60]

Inoue Kobai, a Japanese observer who compiled a three-volume study of Chinese customs, described the presence of footbinding in Shanghai and vicinity during 1919 and 1920. Mr.

Inoue apologized in his preface for having been prejudiced in favor of the five pleasures of eating, drinking, gambling, opera, and prostitution.[61] He said that footbinding had declined more because of the effect of the Revolution than the efforts of foreign missionaries. He alleged that poor parents in Yangchow, famed from antiquity as a center of beauty, still hoped that by compressing a daughter's feet they could sell her later for greater profit. Inoue noted that tiny shoes of Yangchow were extremely pointed and widely admired for their superlative beauty.[62]

There were various customs and superstitious beliefs associated with footbinding; these were coordinated with auspicious or festival days in the lunar calendar. According to Taoist belief, an auspicious day was one in which male and female elements in the universe were harmonious, creating the possibility for felicitous activity in the heavens. On national holidays such as the New Year and during plays or temple festivals, women would go about in groups and wear lovely bowed shoes. One superstition associated the number five propitiously with the start of footbinding. The folk explanation was that the word "five" sounded identical to a word meaning "to stop" (the foot from getting larger).[63] Sometimes a five-year-old nominally started on New Year's Eve, which was also called the Fifth Night-Watch, but did not really tightly bind the feet until spring. Propitious days for starting footbinding were recorded in various books which were consulted by the girl's family. An old lady who had enjoyed good fortune might be asked to give the first turn of the binding, or a shepherd or woodcutter might do this instead, signifying that the girl could later move about with agility. The young girl might bite the tip of a writing brush or grasp a water chestnut, both symbolizing a hope that the foot might become thin and pointed. She might burn incense and kneel in worship, either on her birthday or on an auspicious festival day. An old lady of good omen might pray before the Kitchen God, after which necessary objects such as bindings and shoes would be placed in a kitchen basin. These would include a knife, signifying that the bones of the foot were to be diminutively reduced.

Village girls sometimes began binding about the middle of the seventh lunar month, when the Hemp and Corn Festival was held, in the hope that the foot might achieve the slenderness of a stalk of hemp. The most frequent starting day was the twenty-fourth day of the eighth lunar month, in celebration of the birth of a goddess appropriately called The Little-Footed Miss.[64] On this day, the protection of the Kitchen God or the goddess Kuanyin was also sought. Dumplings made from cooked grain and red beans were eaten by the girl so that her foot might become as soft and as small as a dumpling.

Before starting the binding, some mothers made an elegant pair of tiny shoes. These were taken to an altar before Kuanyin and placed directly above the incense burner so that it looked as if they had come down from Heaven. Incense was burned daily, and prayers were offered up that the foot about to be bound might assume as beautiful a shape as the newly-made shoe. On the first day, mother and daughter might pray to Kuanyin that the child's foot be painlessly and beautifully bound. The holding of this festival in the eighth lunar month coincided with the advent of cooler weather in late September or early October, consequently reducing perspiration and odor and allowing the necessary initial attention to be devoted to binding after the harvest. Sometimes footbinding began on Kuanyin's birthday, the nineteenth day of the second lunar month. In some regions it started exactly four months later, on the day that the goddess attained enlightenment. There was also a custom of praying to Kuanyin for nineteen days prior to her birthday; these practices varied by area and were not universally observed.[65]

Footbinding was a prerequisite to a proper marriage, and the golden lotus received its due share of attention. The shoes to be worn by the tiny-footed bride were handmade and embroidered with good luck wedding sayings such as "Harmonious for a Hundred Years," "Wealth and Eminence Until Our Hair Turns

White." In the north, such bridal shoes were called "Good Fortune"; in the south, they were called "Stepping into the [Bridegroom's] Hall." Such shoes were considered good luck omens; after the wedding they might be removed and secretly stored away. They were worn again for the celebration when a baby boy became one month old. The shoes were supposed to alleviate foot pain. Sick women often requested them from a bride, because the wearing of three pairs was considered a cure for consumption. The bride's dowry might include four pairs of brocade shoes, for this word had the same sound as one meaning that everything would be perfectly achieved.[66]

On the last night before her wedding, the southern Fukienese maiden placed two cooked eggs in a basin of heated water. She then removed the bindings and washed her feet in the water. After washing, she took out the "Feet Washing Eggs" and brought them to the home of the groom. There she boiled them in sugar and presented them to him. When her husband got into bed first on the wedding night, the bride secretly put her bound feet into his shoes. According to one observer, she did this to intimidate him.[67]

The Chinese for more than a millennium have enjoyed a custom of having relatives and friends play pranks on bride and groom on their wedding night. Still practiced today in modified form, this is appropriately called "Disturbing the Bedroom."[68] One popular Shansi game on the wedding night consisted of turning over four to eight wine glasses and placing them in a straight line, about three inches apart. The name of the game was "Turning Over The Glass," which the bride had to do with the tip of her toe. Another game was called "Crossing the Bridge." There were two lines of parallel glasses, with a chopstick placed across each pair. The paired glasses were about three to four inches apart, and the bride had to walk between the pairs without breaking the "bridge." If she knocked down the bridge because her feet were too large, everyone laughed at her. Peking guests on this night might play with the bride's shoes and even grab at her tiny feet. She had to allow this, displeased as she was, for only then would they finally desist. It was a village custom to stand quietly outside the bedroom window on the wedding night, hearing and remembering every sound made by the nuptial pair. These were then mimicked on the following day as a form of rustic amusement.[69]

Tiny-foot beauty contests were popularly held during Buddhist temple festivals in both north and south. There, women

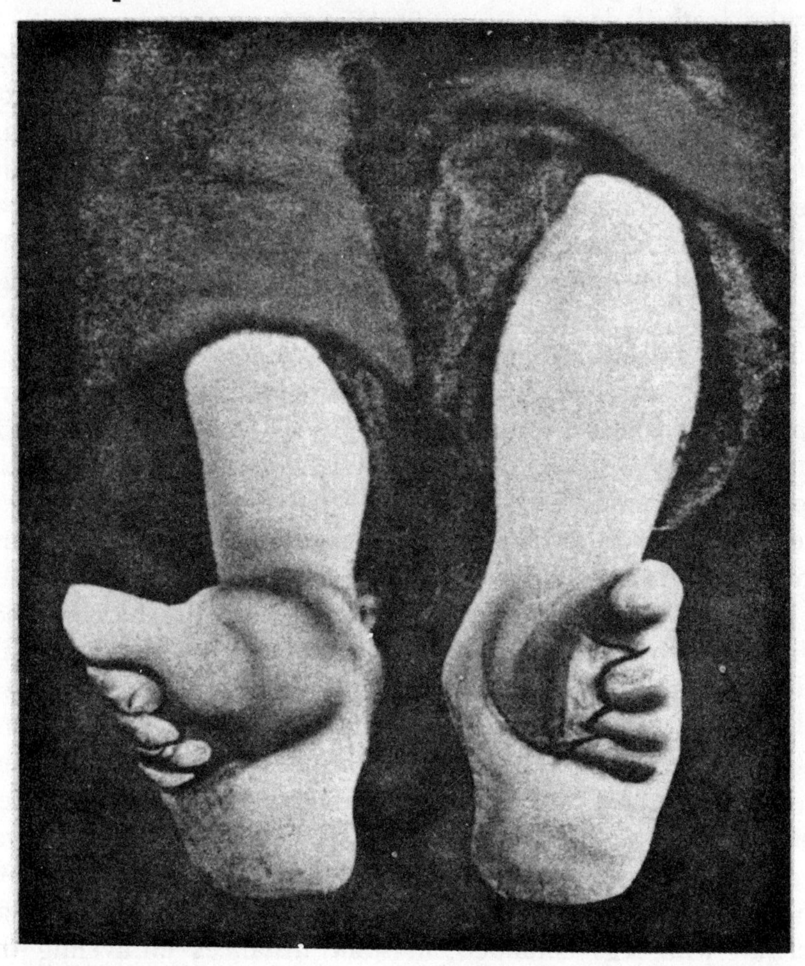

usually confined to the home enjoyed moments of freedom. The large-footed wife concealed herself from view, feeling a social embarrassment which the unhappy husband shared. Those with feet small but substandard in shapeliness might decline on the pretext of illness, only to be found out by relatives and laughed at for having lacked the necessary competitive qualifications. The contests were not held specifically for that purpose alone, but were rather part of the over-all celebrations observed during regular festival days.

The most famous of the many contests was the Assemblage of Foot Viewing held yearly at Ta-t'ung in Shansi on the sixth day of the sixth lunar month. A custom of sunning armor *(liang-chia)* on this day was observed during the Manchu dynasty, and the theory was advanced that this practice gradually came to an end and was replaced by one of tiny-footed women assembling at the temples in large numbers. People who still partially remembered the name came to associate it with the foot festival and called this "sunning the feet" *(liang-chiao)* instead.[70]

A person who had twice seen the tiny-foot festival in Ta-t'ung supplied the following information. He witnessed it when north China was controlled by Feng Yü-hsiang and also after the Japanese occupied Ta-t'ung. He said that it was held on a back-street which was probably once especially reserved for that purpose. These meetings may have been originally organized to exhibit prospective candidates for the imperial harem, since Ming emperors would select concubines from among young ladies whose feet were tiny and perfectly proportioned. He believed that the principal purpose of the showing was not competitive, but was rather to give everyone a chance to comment on and appreciate the diminutive sizes and proportioned shapes. The first time he attended, an old lady over sixty years old was awarded first prize from among five or six hundred participants, having feet less than three inches long. The ladies sat on small benches with legs extended, in some instances unraveling the bindings for the benefit of the onlookers who came into the city from all directions. Ta-t'ung maintained its enthusiasm for bound feet at a time when the rest of the nation was abandoning the custom, and to such an extent that even Feng Yü-hsiang was ridiculed in doggerel verse for being an advocate of the natural-foot movement.

> Feng Yü-hsiang fidgets on his seat,
> Walls filled with drawings,
> Covered with big and little feet.
> Big feet for his old lady,
> But little feet for his mother![71]

Another observer described how Ta-t'ung ladies displayed their feet when plays were given there. They sat along three sides of the theater, heavily adorned and formally posed, their feet stretched out in a row like scales as they tried to gain each onlooker's praise. The shoes were meticulously embellished. Some had small bells attached to the heel to attract the audience's attention with each foot motion. Others placed thin silk butterflies with movable wings on top of the shoes, so that the wings trembled as if in flight. Admirers walked back and forth in groups; if the feet were especially small they inspected them closely but were not allowed to touch them with their hands. "It was just like going to a department store to see an exhibition!"[72] On the evening of the sixth lunar day and month, after the competition, some wealthy families liked to dye the feet red. They spread a dye which turned the feet the color of a red chestnut, feeling that this innovation added to their beauty and charm.

Let us briefly recapitulate views concerning the origin and presence of footbinding in China for the past millennium. It arose either at the end of the T'ang dynasty or in the decades which preceded the Sung, an innovation of palace dancers which slowly set the fashion for the rest of the empire. The binding of the foot gradually became more severe, and the fashionable foot became smaller. Thinkers of the Southern Sung dynasty, such as Chu Hsi, made it part of an ideology of feminine suppression and elevated the practice as a convenient device to ensure the separation of the sexes and prevent woman from leaving the confines of the home. The bound foot also became a symbol of aristocratic gentility and a proof of affluence on the part of the master, for it was a demonstrably incapacitating feminine appendage. The Yüan and Ming dynasties made a love fetish of the tiny foot, and the shoes became symbols of passionate love and an integral part of drinking games in which amusement with courtesans provided the main attraction. To lovers of the lotus, a woman's sexual attraction came to center in the mystery of her bound feet, which were almost never bared to view. The caressing of the diminutive foot in innumerable ways became part of the prelude to the sex act. The rationale came about that binding the foot resulted in a heavier thigh and that the genital region tightened and became much better developed. These scientifically invalid ideas were, nevertheless, widely believed.

The abolition of footbinding by imperial decree, attempted by the Manchus as early as the seventeenth century, was doomed to failure because it was attempted unilaterally in a male-dictated society which relegated woman to the role of an ignorant and fettered plaything. It was not until the present century, when anti-footbinding came to be regarded as part of a larger movement to emancipate the Chinese woman from her age-old inheritance of social inequality, that progressive headway was finally made. The fervent pleas of revolutionary leaders to free woman from her spiritual and physical bondage made an increasing psychological impact on China's masses. This liberal dissemination of thought, combined with positive action by local officials, gradually brought to an end this unique contribution by Chinese culture to the history of feminine suffering.

纏脚原委圖說

攷婦女纏脚之風古所未有起於南唐李
後主宮中行樂有宮嬪名窅娘纖纖善舞
後主使其以帛纏足層層緊扎狀似弓彎
故今名繡履為弓鞋一時遊戲相習成風
始則宮中行之繼則民間效之羣傳為纏
足之濫觴矣然而誨淫造孽貽累今朝猶
未醒悟也惜哉

A WORK DESCRIBED AS THE EARLIEST ANTI-FOOTBINDING PUBLICATION (ca. 1894)

Translation: "The custom of footbinding by women proves, upon investigation, to have been unknown in antiquity. Later Ruler Li of the Southern T'ang dynasty originated it as a means of amusing himself in the palace. Palace concubine Lovely Maiden was slender and skilled in dancing; he had her bind her feet tightly with layers of cloth until they resembled a curved bow. And that is why embroidered sandals are now called bowed shoes. What arose as amusing fancy was transmitted until it became a custom. Binding started in the palace and came to be imitated by the masses; this is the popular account of its origin. But the imparting of this lewdness has involved our nation in harmful ways to the present day. And still there is no awakening. How pitiful!" (from *TFL* 1. The illustration on the following page faced the above text.)

窅娘纏腳

CHAPTER THREE

Emancipation Movements

Footbinding was part of a set of mores which insisted on coercing women and treating them as intellectual inferiors, but widespread opposition did not make itself felt until the start of the twentieth century. It was then that revolutionary demands for the education of woman and her treatment as a social equal began to be increasingly heard. Throughout the centuries, enlightened and liberal thinkers criticized footbinding, but they failed to change or even slightly modify the traditional view. The earliest anti-footbinding spokesman on record was a Sung dynasty (960-1279) literatus named Ch'e Jo-shui, who was quoted as having said:

> I don't know when footbinding began. Children not yet four or five years old, innocent and without crime, are caused to suffer limitless pain. What is the use of binding and restraining [the feet in this way]?[1]

The Manchus who conquered China in the seventeenth century tried in vain to abolish footbinding by fiat, making this effort in an era when the tiny foot was universally admired by the Chinese male Another reason for failure during their reign was the unchanging view of woman as an unlettered and sheltered plaything. The Manchus at first strove to abolish footbinding because they looked down upon it as being culturally backward. They circulated a saying about a ". . . large-footed wife, but a tiny-footed servant." They taught this to their young daughters, telling them that a natural-footed girl would one day become the wife of a great official, but that a girl with tiny bound feet would never amount to anything more than the servant of a great official's wife.[2]

The constant failure of official Manchu attempts to prohibit footbinding seems to indicate that it could not be effectively combatted unless it were regarded as only one aspect of the struggle to liberate woman. The futile attempts at prohibition are listed in Chinese sources.[3] As early as 1642, heavy penalties were threatened for those who bound their feet. This proved fruitless, and in 1645 and 1664 bound-foot women were barred from the imperial harem. However, it is doubtful that even this part of the decree was fully effective. The objective of enforcement was the natural-footed child; footbinding of any daughter born after 1662 was strictly enjoined, with penalties to be meted out to the father. He was to be relieved from office if an official, and flogged forty times and exiled if a commoner. If the head of a household pleaded that he had merely been remiss and unaware that his daughter's feet had been bound, he was to be flogged forty times and forced to wear the cangue, a square wooden device confining the neck, for one month. Civil and military officials who proved recalcitrant in carrying out the edict were to be investigated and punished according to the individual circumstances. The edict tried to prevent evasion by setting forth punishments for those who sought to avoid compliance by falsely reporting that daughters had been born prior to 1662, the year when feet could no longer be bound. But this was still an age in China when the tiny foot as a sign of beauty, gentility, and desirability was philosophically unchallenged. Opposition to reform was discreet but influential. Soon after the edict was issued, a story was circulated about the foolish official who sent up a memorial to the emperor to the effect that he had been the first to let out his wife's big feet.

The failure to eradicate an ingrained custom through legislation was admitted three years later, when the decree was rescinded. The influence of footbinding and other aspects of Chinese culture was increasingly felt by the Manchus as the years went by; men came to prefer the tiny foot, and their wives invented a kind of imitation. They compressed the foot, as did the Koreans, to achieve a slender and narrow knife-like effect, but did not bend the toes under as the Chinese did. The style of footwear which Manchu ladies came to adopt was further evidence that they wished to emulate the tiny-footed, for at the bottom of their ordinary shoes they affixed a small white support, about two inches high, to give the onlooker an illusion of smallness. When the skirt concealed the regular shoe, this

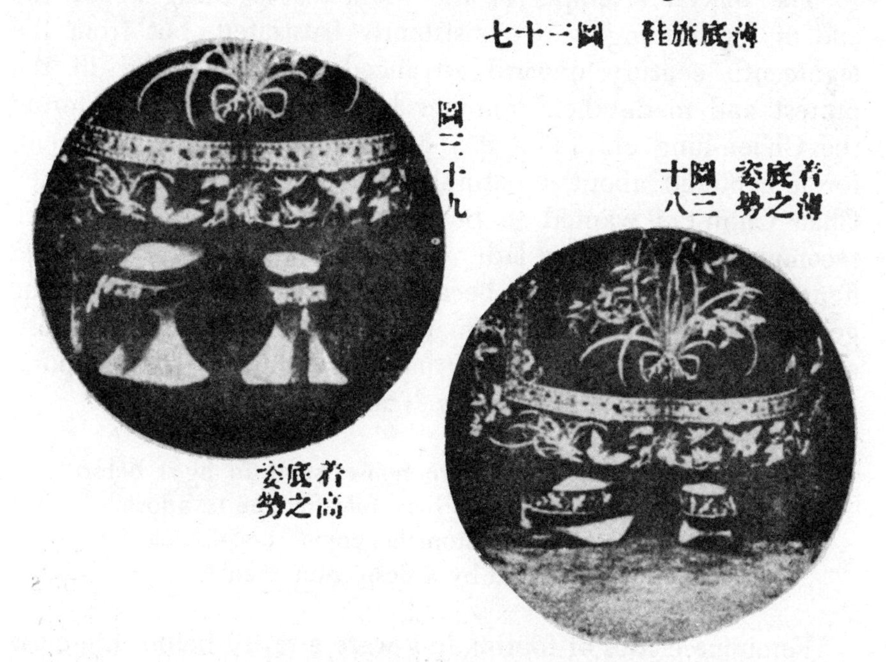

MANCHU IMITATIONS OF THE TINY-FOOTED
(from Vincent, *La Medicine en Chine au XX Siecle*, 114)

support was the only thing which protruded. The Manchu woman became the official target of several later edicts, in which she was strictly ordered not to emulate the footbound.[4]

Manchu efforts against footbinding proved ineffectual throughout their reign, since traditional views in its favor were never seriously challenged. As late as 1847 still another edict was issued, and it was as ineffectual as its predecessors. Part of the argumentation is of interest, for it shows that the appeal for change was directed toward the upper class:

> The women of Han have all had bound feet for a long time. This injures the natural harmony. Distinguished families should endeavor to encourage everyone [to have natural feet], in the hope that this old custom can then be eliminated.[5]

The official attempts of the Manchus to bring about the end of footbinding were consistently frustrated, but from the eighteenth century onward advanced thinkers joined in the protest and made their opinions known. One incident during the Ch'ien-lung era (1736-95) aroused considerable comment, for it centered about a natural-footed poetess. A man named Chao Chün-t'ai wanted to buy a concubine. The go-between recommended a young lady who was beautiful in face and figure, but Chao demurred because her feet were unbound. The go-between said that the woman was an accomplished poetess, and Chao therefore requested that she compose an extemporaneous poem about bowed shoes. This was her poem:

> Three-inch bowed shoes were non-existent in ages before,
> And Great Kuanyin had two bare feet for one to adore.
> I don't know when this custom began;
> It must have been started by a despicable man![6]

Feminine critics of footbinding were a rarity before the close of the Manchu dynasty, and in this instance, significantly, the dissent was made by a woman of intellectual training. When

Yüan Mei (1716-98), the liberal scholar whom we have already cited, heard of the incident, he sent Mr. Chao the following letter:

> Women revere elegance and gracefulness. It is elegant and graceful for a woman's neck to be of termite length and for her waist to be neat and trim. But this is certainly not to say that she should stand unsteadily. If a woman has a three-inch bowed foot but a short neck and thick waist, how can she ever give a light appearance when walking, as if she were skimming over the waves?[7]

Yüan Mei based his argument on the inappropriateness of exclusively admiring tiny feet while disregarding other essential attributes of beauty and tried to dissuade one individual. But he did not generally attack the practice as he had elsewhere.

There were advocates of natural feet for women among writers and political leaders of the Manchu period, whose arguments were part of a wider plea for a liberal attitude toward woman and her education. Anti-footbinding and the granting of women's rights were indivisible. Li Ju-chen (c.1763-c.1830) used fiction as a propagandistic device to achieve this goal. He was the first person of note to advocate foot emancipation forcefully and unequivocally, and his fictional technique of having men assume feminine roles probably assured him both an interested and sympathetic reading audience. His liberal sentiments were echoed by Kung Tzu-chen (1792-1841), a foremost scholar and political reformer. Kung was a forerunner of the modern reform movement and expressed the radical opinion that women should be encouraged to have unbound feet. He showed a poetic preference for the natural-footed, stressing that binding and feminine beauty were unrelated. In one poem he said in part:

> How lucky to get a Cantonese wife!
> A face like jade, large feet like an immortal's! [8]

Taiping Rebellion leader Hung Hsiu-ch'uan prohibited footbinding in areas under his control, as part of a more general reform which included the outlawing of prostitution and slave trading. During his stay in Kiangsu Province, Hung once ordered women there to unbind their feet and decreed decapitation as the penalty for disobedience. It was later reported that many women in areas under his jurisdiction let their feet out, including more than half of the bound-footed in Kwangsi and Kwangtung.[9]

A type of theoretical attack on footbinding, launched with increasing frequency in the two decades preceding the overthrow of the Manchus, is to be found in the writings of Cheng Kuan-ying. Cheng, who worked actively in favor of emancipation in the latter half of the nineteenth century, advanced a series of arguments intended to sway the general populace:

> The custom of footbinding is unknown throughout the vast universe, with the exception of China. Now there is nothing that parents will not do through love of their children, with the lone exception of this cruel and senseless custom in which they indulge. When a child is four or five, or seven or eight, parents speak harshly to it, and frighten it with their looks, and oppress it in every conceivable manner so that the bones of its feet may be broken and its flesh may putrefy. They are then happy in their parental hearts, feeling that when she later gets married, they will be very proud of her. But if the foot is round and six inches long [i.e., of natural size], relatives and neighbors all feel that this is shameful. This kind of trivial fashionableness is even more revered in the cities than in the countryside. Great families especially favor footbinding and follow one another in imitation. A person is unfortunate in being born a woman, but still more unfortunate if born a Chinese woman. [Men commonly regarded being born as a female retribution for the evil of a former life; a mother might remind her suffering daughter that she was subjected to the pain of footbinding because of evil done in a previous existence.[10]] Her own person is injuriously maltreated in this way, with injurious effects on health, while her flesh and bones are so tightly restrained that the blood flows unceasingly. It is as if she has incurred a most heavy penalty, contracted a

> most serious illness, or encountered a major calamity. As a young child, she suffers from having her feet virtually dismembered and her skin despoiled. If she is delicate, her health is damaged. . . . If she is lucky enough to remain alive, all day she requires the support of others. How can she get water from the well or pound the pestle? If there occur calamities such as flood, fire, or bandits, she has to sit and await death, unable to do more than hobble about. The injuring of her physical well-being is looked upon as beautiful, and doing such a profitless thing is regarded as profitable. This is the height of lewdness! [11]

The anti-footbinding thesis put forth by two ladies at the start of the Manchu dynasty stressed the immorality of mutilating the body and was not concerned with the more practical aspect of impairment for household tasks. In expressing their gratitude to the emperor for his having issued a decree of abolition, they cited the Confucian doctrine that since the body was a gift bestowed by one’s parents, it should not be tampered with or altered. It was also argued that it was wrong to upset in any way the inextricable relationship of the four limbs. The duty of the parent was to love the children equally: “Now parental love by its very nature does not discriminate between boys and girls. Can only girls be without persons [to feel compassion for them]?” [12]

Towards the end of the Manchu dynasty, opposition to footbinding became more widespread, within the larger movement for reform, modernization, and feminine equality. Two of the chief proponents were reform leaders K’ang Yu-wei and Liang Ch’i-ch’ao. K’ang Yu-wei advocated abolition in Kwangtung Province as early as 1882, but failed to evoke a mass response because the time was still premature. Later, his younger brother K’ang Kuang-jen propagandized likewise and achieved some results. K’ang Yu-wei started an Unbound Foot Association at Canton in 1894, later moved it to Shanghai, and made this one of the reforms for which he struggled.[13]

K’ang’s most eloquent writing on the subject was probably

the memorial which he submitted to the throne in 1898, decrying the survival of footbinding as an outmoded vestige of the past which helped to prevent China from taking its rightful place in the modern world. He requested that further binding be prohibited and that women all be ordered to let their feet out. The penalty he proposed was somewhat reminiscent of the early Manchu edict; remiss officials were to be deprived of their privileges and householders were to receive a monetary fine, doubled if the tiny-footed offender in the family were under twelve. One of his principal arguments was that China was losing face among the community of nations:

> . . all countries have international relations, so that if one commits the slightest error the others ridicule and look down on it. Ours is definitely not a time of seclusion. Now China is narrow and crowded, has opium addicts and streets lined with beggars. Foreigners laugh at us for these things and criticize us for being barbarians. There is nothing which makes us objects of ridicule so much as footbinding.

K'ang traced the evolution toward a more enlightened culture in China, showing how the ancient criminal penalty of severing the feet was later nullified by benevolent sovereigns. It was in this context of the search toward progress that he described the abnormal and inhuman treatment of the young and innocent child, whose limbs were so impaired that she had to ". . . get up by holding on to the bed and cling to a wall for support when walking." The poor with tiny feet were seriously inconvenienced in the performance of their many tasks, while the rich transmitted weak offspring as a direct result of their having been physically harmed.

> With posterity so weakened, how can we engage in battle? I look at Europeans and Americans, so strong and vigorous because their mothers do not bind feet and therefore have strong offspring. Now that we must compete with other nations, to transmit weak offspring is perilous.[14]

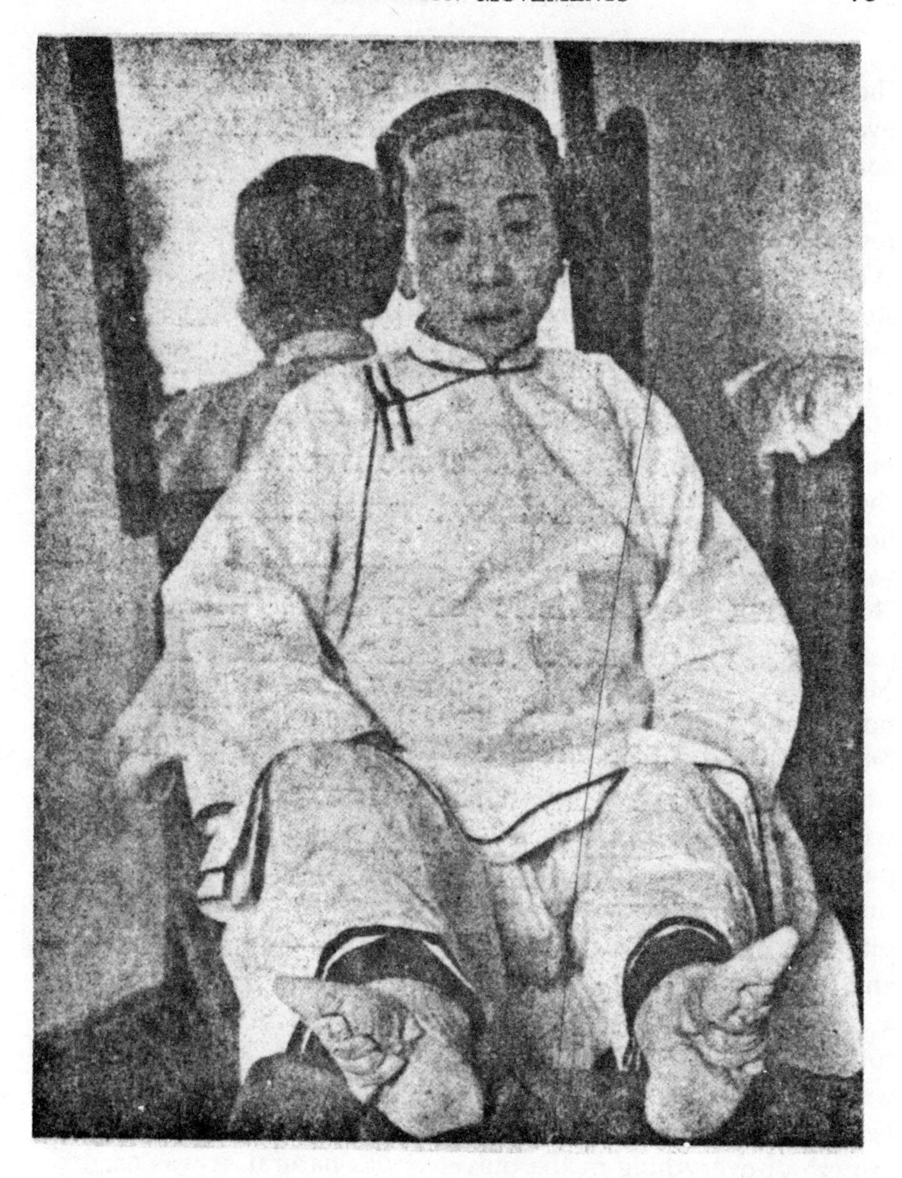

AN UPPER-CLASS LADY BARES HER GOLDEN LOTUSES

K'ang Yu-wei's association came to number more than ten thousand followers. Natural-foot societies began to spring up everywhere, with main quarters in the cities and branches in the countryside. Progress was slow at the start, with conservative opposition from the villages particularly stubborn. Abolition was resisted and interpreted as an alien idea imported from the West. In an effort to combat the natural-foot societies, malicious stories were circulated which maligned the leadership. The story was told, for example, of the supervisor of a Shanghai branch who publicly favored emancipation but had a bound-foot wife. He was in constant fear of her and was once punished by being made to lick her feet. The narrator, writing in 1897, said that the incident became known to outsiders. They nicknamed the henpecked husband "the Supervisor Who Licks Feet," a play on words, since the words sounded identical to those meaning "Natural-Foot Supervisor." [15]

Most of the natural-foot societies operated the same way. Members would vow neither to bind the feet of their children nor to allow their sons to marry girls other than with natural feet. The societies held mass meetings, published songs and tracts, and secured official support in getting their propaganda widely distributed. Every effort was made to influence the parents: "If the child's parents do not pity her but bind her feet unmercifully, how can she be expected on some future day to pity her own children?" [16] The tracts were easy to understand and were aimed at the masses. Footbinding was condemned as a profitless and injurious thing which meant lifelong pain and suffering. It made getting around inconvenient; a natural-footed woman, for example, could buy medicine for her sick parents in less than half the time it took the tiny-footed. Development and growth of everything in the universe was natural, it was argued, and the body needed a firm base just as a house did. A person who failed to grow would consult a doctor, but in footbinding medicines were used instead to stunt growth. The saying that without bound feet one couldn't find a husband was dismissed as being demonstrably stupid: "Even cripples and the blind find husbands; why can't someone who is perfectly normal?" Confucius was cited as having favored changing wrong to right, with the implication that he too would have joined the emancipation movement. A Christian point of view, that since God made man and woman the same parents should not try to make them different, was also emphasized. The drawbacks of footbinding and the delights of natural feet were summarized in easily remembered slogans:

Ten Sighs About Footbinding

1. Why was my natural foot ruined?
2. Kuanyin is barefooted; why did I have to have bound feet?
3. You can't get anything done with bound feet, and yet it takes great effort.
4. It is easy to get sick, because one's blood circulation gets stopped up.
5. Because of tiny feet I can't be filial towards my own parents, and I feel apologetic to my in-laws because I can't perform manual labor for them.
6. I get angry to the point of illness because of the pain, but my own mother won't let me loosen the binding.
7. The tiny-footed are prone to being deceived by evil men.
8. Poor women bind their feet. There is no food in the house, but they can't go out to get firewood and the necessities of life.
9. People feel that poorly-bound feet are ugly and not clean enough.
10. Don't make the younger generation suffer, but let out the feet in order to cause the family to prosper.

Ten Delights of Natural Feet

1. I can work easily.
2. I have freedom, and my parents don't worry about my foot size.
3. Convenience; Goddess Kuanyin is also large-footed.

4. I can visit my parents whenever I want, even though they live far away.

5. When my husband is away, I can take care of anything which occurs at home.

6. A large-footed woman is not easily deceived, and she has no problem in keeping her feet clean.

7. To eradicate the evil age of footbinding is to restore the intent of our ancient Sages, who elevated natural-footedness.

8. The natural-footed is stronger, more patriotic, and can achieve heroic deeds.

9. The nation benefits from her vigorous spirit and devotion to study.

10. She is unhampered by bad roads and can travel freely everywhere, both in China and abroad.[17]

The effect of the natural-foot societies was considerable. A ladies society which was formed in Shanghai in 1895 had a concurrent educational objective. A proposal was made two years later to establish a school for girls in which those with bound feet would gradually be refused admission. One school in Tientsin insisted that all girls entering it remove their bindings and introduced a song encouraging foot emancipation into the school curriculum. In 1909, it was still being taught to students there.[18] An orator proposed to the Shanghai society that fines be levied on the tiny-footed to promote national prosperity. If each of these eighty to ninety million women contributed a hundredth of an ounce of silver daily for a year, remarked a Mr. Hsü, the *likin* tax on goods being transported could be lowered and official salaries raised. "With one-tenth of the contributions, the Empress Dowager's flower gardens can be maintained, with one-half of the money we can train our soldiers, and with the remainder we can reward the women who don't bind their feet and the foot investigators."[19]

Foreign observers in China near the end of the nineteenth century were appalled by footbinding and made known their critical impressions. Circulation of these views abroad aroused international indignation and made the Chinese appear half-civilized to Western eyes. Chinese intellectuals realized this and tried to eliminate the practice by bringing about a national consciousness of the loss of international face and prestige which it caused. There must have been a common Western belief that footbinding was achieved through wearing an iron or wooden shoe, for this was often explicitly denied by experts on China. Bound feet were decried as useless; Swatow women, for example, were described as getting from one room to another by putting their knees on stools to avoid having to touch the floor with their feet. They threw their weight upon one knee at a time and alternately moved the stools forward by hand. One American wrote about a young girl treated in a Christian hospital for gangrene caused by footbinding who finally died of blood poisoning. Another girl died shortly after having had her leg amputated at the thigh. To Western observers, tiny-footed girls usually looked as if they were in pain, for instead of jumping about happily they needed help in walking, as if they were wounded. The victim of fashion was sympathetically portrayed. She was described as being forced to sleep only on her back, her feet dangling over the side of the bed, with the edge of the bedstead pressing on the nerves behind her knees to slightly dull the pain. "There she swings her feet and moans, and even in the coldest weather she cannot wrap herself in a coverlet, because every return of warmth to her limbs increases the aching. The sensation is said to be like that of having the joints punctured with needles." [20] Footbinding was denounced as an evil which crippled half the population, added to the misery of the poverty-stricken, increased infanticide, prevented women from support-

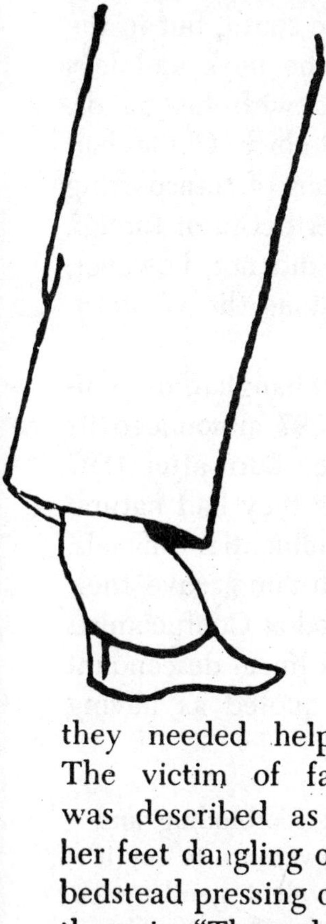

ing themselves and from caring adequately for their children, kept their homes filthy and cheerless, and confined woman and her thoughts to the narrowest of spheres.

American eyewitnesses in China in the eighteen-nineties reported seeing tiny-footed women being carried on the backs of servants. They were carried pickaback in the south, but in the north they were tied on, with arms around the neck and legs bent, while the servant supported the knees with his hands. Chinese writers explained that foreigners in north China had merely seen a northern custom in poorer regions of transporting prostitutes to places of assignation.[21] Chinese criticism of foreign comments as being prejudiced and one-sided did not, however, minimize the impact of criticism abroad or among the Western-oriented and liberal-minded at home.

There was a foreign natural-foot society in Shanghai, in addition to the Chinese organizations, which in 1897 announced its intention "to petition the Emperor that children born after 1897 should not be recognized as of standing unless they had natural feet."[22] Liberal Chinese intellectuals and influential officials, including prominent viceroys like Chang Chih-t'ung, gave their support to the emancipation movement. Orthodox Confucianists joined its ranks; near the turn of the century, a lineal descendant of Confucius named K'ung Hui-chung was quoted as having said:

> I have always had my unquiet thoughts about footbinding and felt pity for the many sufferers. Yet I could not venture to say it publicly. Now there are happily certain benevolent gentlemen and virtuous daughters of ability, wise daughters from foreign lands, who have initiated a truly noble enterprise. They have addressed our women in animated exhortations and founded a society for the prohibition of footbinding.[23]

Christian missionaries exerted a strong influence and were instrumental in accelerating change. Footbinding among converts was discouraged. In many cases, only pupils with natural or unbound feet were accepted into boarding schools; sometimes this was made a condition for entering the church. The zeal with which Gladys Aylward served as a provincial foot inspector was characteristic of the uncompromising and positive efforts by missionaries in the field to do away with the custom.[24] Foreign reaction against footbinding was international. In 1895, ten women of different nationalities formed a natural-foot society and, in order to request support from the Empress Dowager Tz'u-hsi, drew up a memorial to which "nearly all foreign ladies in the Far East added their names." [25] The memorial is believed to have reached the palace, and it may have influenced the Anti-footbinding Edict of 1902 which the Empress Dowager finally issued.

There must have been official discussion two years later as to whether still another edict was needed, for a news editorial appeared on September 10, 1904, commenting on a proposal by a Minister Chou to abolish footbinding by imperial decree. The writer took exception to the need for further legislation and

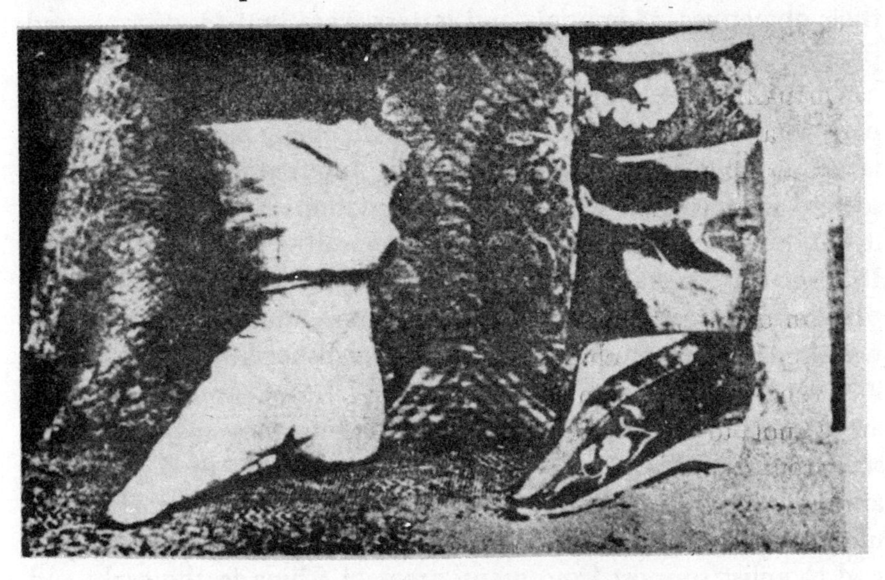

BOUND FOOT BARE AND BOUND FOOT SHOD

favored moderation. He noted that footbinding, which had existed for more than a thousand years, had been started by the upper class and imitated by the rest. He therefore proposed that eminent families renounce the practice to initiate a reverse trend. He advised that the youth of China be taught that woman was man's equal and not his inferior. By using persuasion from above and teaching at all levels, he concluded, the custom of footbinding would naturally end.[26] Opponents of coercive measures repeated these views in the two decades following the Revolution and criticized officials in charge of eliminating footbinding because they physically beat recalcitrants, levied harsh fines to increase their personal incomes, and used regulations as a pretext to amuse themselves with helpless women. The advantages of peaceful persuasion and education over blind coercion were stressed in news editorials throughout the twenties: "Use peaceful means to change this custom. Once the peasants understand its evils, they will change of their own accord."[27]

Natural-foot societies used various techniques to advance their objectives. Memorials and letters were sent to viceroys and provincial governors, and public meetings were held in provincial capitals and large cities. Over a million tracts, leaflets, and placards were sent out from Shanghai alone, in addition to a large number from other cities. The internationally organized society in Shanghai seems to have functioned until 1908, when it handed over its operations to a committee of Chinese ladies. It then stated that ". . . the custom has been abandoned by practically all people of the official classes and, though it is still widely practiced among the lower ranks, especially in the North, its extinction can hardly be far distant."[28] Mrs. Archibald Little, an influential leader in the anti-footbinding movement, was instrumental in organizing opposition near the turn of the century among both Christians and important officials. She described her unceasing efforts to found the natural-foot society at Shanghai and to enlist support from many areas of China in the early and formative years of the abolition movement, and she stressed the significant contribution made by Western missionaries.[29]

Liang Ch'i-ch'ao was another noted political reformer who wrote persuasively in favor of the abolition of footbinding. He approached the problem from a broader perspective and thought in terms of elevating the social status of women. His essays evoked a general response and may have influenced those who felt antipathy to ideas they believed were imported from abroad. Here is an example of Liang's argumentation taken from the Chinese press:

> The eyes, ears, nose, hands, and feet come from Heaven and our parents. If one is incomplete or mutilated, we call this being lamed and say that Heaven has harmed the people. The ancient kings, in determining punishments, cut off noses, ears, and legs in order to punish evildoers and awe others into submission. Benevolent persons sometimes criticized these sovereigns for having damaged Heaven by injuring mankind in this way.
>
> Men and women share equally. Heaven gives them life and parents give them love, treating them equally. . . . But the difference between strong and weak is most clearly marked in the difference between man and woman. Over the vast universe and throughout the ages, political edification from the sagely and virtuous was diffused like the vast seas, but not a word was said or a deed committed for the sake of woman. Women were treated in one of two ways: they either fulfilled a series of duties or served as playthings. They were reared like horses or dogs to satisfy the first need and adorned like flowers or birds to satisfy the second. These two methods of oppression gave rise to three types of punishment. In Africa and India they pressed a stone against a woman's head to make it level, a punishment like our tattooing; in Europe they wanted the woman to have a slender waist, and to accomplish this they punished her by pressing wood against her waist; in China the woman had to have her feet bound, a punishment like cutting off the lower legs. These three punishments produced imperfect women throughout the world. I don't know when bound feet started, but the originator must have been a corrupt prince, an immoral ruler, a robber of the people, or a despicable husband.
>
> Alas! Good things in the world are done only with the greatest

caution and hesitation, but evil things are transmitted very easily from one to another. These cruel, despicable, and frightening things spread their poisons everywhere and for countless ages! Parents force their daughters [into footbinding], while others make this the basis for selecting their sons' brides. And a man esteems his wife for this reason. The child is punished this way when it has still not lost its first set of teeth. Its bones are broken and its flesh deteriorates, with bloody pus scattered about and injury widespread. Parents ignore its sighs, do not pity its weeping, are cold to its entreaties, and deaf to its screams. The child cannot get up for several months, even with the aid of a cane; a year later, she can only get about by being carried in a sedan chair.[30]

Poems were used for propaganda purposes with perhaps even greater effect than the essays, for they were easy to understand and appealed to the emotions rather than the intellect. Poems in praise of the golden lotus had been legion in the days of its unquestioned popularity, but as the abolitionists gained momentum the tiny foot came under increasing poetic attack. Liang Ch'i-ch'ao's contemporary Lin Ch'in-nan wrote three poetic denunciations of footbinding under the title of "Tiny-Foot Lady." The poems, which resorted to practical arguments rather than theoretical or abstract ones, are translated below:

TINY-FOOT LADY

Tiny-foot lady, whose daughter are you?
Three-inch bowed shoes beneath her skirt.
She trembles in the blowing wind,
For she's durable above but unsteady below.
How hard for her to move one step,
As if she's gone ten thousand miles!
She leans on an amah to the left,
And a maid servant to the right;
If perchance you step on her foot,
She feels an excruciating pain.

When did you start the binding?
Why do you suffer such endless pain?
I do not know why, is her reply.
At five, when I could fill out my clothes,
Mother made shoes and ordered me to start.
My toes were pointed, my instep bent down,
And though I cried out to Heaven and Earth,
Mother ignored me as if she were deaf.
My nights were spent in pain,
My early mornings in tears;
I spoke to Mother by my bed;
How you worry when I'm ill,
How frightened if I fall!
Now the agony from my feet has penetrated
 the marrow of my bones,
And I am plunged into despair, but you,
You don't care a bit about me.
Mother turned to comfort the delicate child:
I felt just like you as a girl,
But I want your foot to be so small
That it earns you a social reputation,
And that is why I am willing
To devote such time to the binding.
How inconceivable, that in reducing the foot,
Her flesh and bones are so distressed
That she loses her appetite for food.
So much of her fragrant youth
Spent weeping by the fallen flowers;
She hears the chirping of the birds,
But her bowed foot is like a tiny grave.

The second poem:

TINY-FOOT LADY

The bright sun penetrates an old room,
Slipping in through broken rafters;
There is a wife seated within,
Chaste like a model of antiquity.

Busy daily cooking, carrying firewood;
But with each step, grievously she sighs.
If you ask why, she replies:
My feet are no good at all,
And whenever I look at them,
My silent tears begin to flow.
So tiny, an error of my childhood.
Seven years ago, living by the river,
A great flood came with a roaring sound;
My good man, away on business,
That night failed to return home;
My lovely children, absorbed in dreams.
In my left arm a boy, a girl in my right;
Where could we go in the thick of the night?
My tiny feet were easily pushed about by the water,
And I knew spring flood would take mother, son, and daughter.
There is nothing so pitiful as tiny feet;
What happened then still causes my heart to break.
The next move was to the outskirts of the city.
A bird sat on the rafters, portent of fire,
How the sudden flames nearby terrified me!
To avert disaster, barefoot I walked along the road,
My heels and toes were broken open and bruised,
My feet bled the color of a crimson camellia.
Please persuade all women to unbind their feet,
And if parental hearts remain as hard as steel,
Make them listen to my heart-rending appeal.

The third poem:

TINY-FOOT LADY

The mounted enemy comes,
The mounted enemy comes,
Bandits bearing down on us
Amidst dust and confusion,
Making the most of chaotic times.
Fighting men, both victors and conquered,

Join in the slaughter of the innocents.
Eight of every ten villagers have fled,
For there is butchery from door to door.
My neighbor, a healthy wife,
With feet bare and unbound,
Escapes to the valley, babe in arms.
Another wraps her turban like a man,
Rice in a bag, pot on shoulder,
Lucky she can hide femininity from bandit eyes.
A delicate lady nearby, lovely as jade,
Finding it so hard to travel on tiny feet,
Holds her head and weeps, afraid.
Bandits swoop down before the weeping ends.
They disgrace her so vilely,
Her heart turns cold within,
And her only choice is death,
Whether she accepts or rejects the shame.
Because her steps were so tiny, so hard to take,
Her husband's children share the bitter fate.
How pitiful the sight before our eyes,
But still they speak of tiny feet begetting lotus flowers!
Embroidered lovebird sandals, adorned with camellias,
So divinely elegant, but severed with one knife thrust.
Parents so often are deaf to reason,
Knowing that their daughter's feet
Are lovable only if tinily bound;
Bandits smash all to the ground![31]

The natural-foot movement in the eighteen-nineties was identified with liberal reformers and champions of women's rights. By the early twentieth century, powerful officials and influential statesmen were giving it increasingly open support. A major factor in bringing the evils of footbinding before a larger audience was the missionary community, which worked devotedly for this cause and gradually influenced public opinion against it. To reach the illiterate masses, simple and popular refrains were devised with a graphic and unmistakable message:

A five-year-old girl,
Bravely repressing bitter sobs,
Tearfully asks her mother:
You used to love me so tenderly.

Why do you now bind my feet,
As if you were binding a chicken?
The toes in my feet are broken,
And my heart breaks with them;
I can't walk by day nor sleep at night.
But the neighbor's girl, with feet unbound,
Walks to school to improve her learning.[32]

The French doctor Matignon, serving in a Peking hospital near the turn of the century, remarked that footbinding, while widespread, was more frequent in the town than in the countryside. Women living north of Peking all had this deformity, he added, with the exception of Christians. Missionaries were generally able to get their adherents to renounce it, but in certain communities in the south religious directors of orphanages were obliged to sanction the footbinding of young girls in their care to make sure that they could later get married.[33]

A few years before the Revolution, enthusiasm for the anti-footbinding cause began to develop in urban centers and in rural areas which were near cities or easily accessible to communications. The common sayings of earlier decades had exalted the manifold charms of the three-inch golden lotus, but these were now replaced by the critical catchword:

One pair of bound feet, but two cisterns of tears.

Once feet are bound so small,
Such effort to do any work at all!

Once feet to a sharp point are bound,
The woman's cries to Heaven resound.[34]

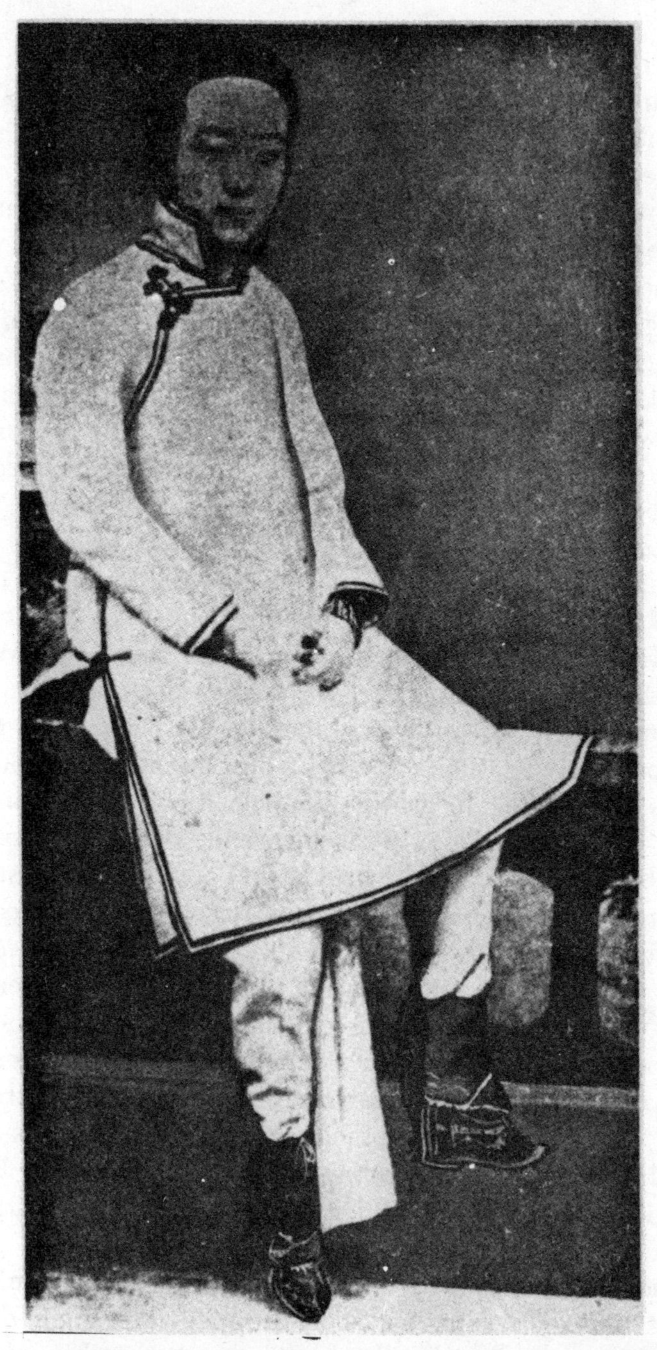

MISS CHIA YU-WEN, WHO AFTER 1900 BECAME AN ESPECIALLY FAMED TIENTSIN COURTESAN, NOTED FOR HER SUPERLATIVE TINY FEET

The anti-footbinding movement in China was part of a larger movement to emancipate woman and elevate her status. Progress was achieved in stages. In the late nineteenth and early twentieth centuries, natural-foot societies organized followers and distributed propaganda in town and village. This led the way to greater popular enthusiasm and participation in the years shortly preceding the Revolution. Before 1894 anti-footbinding was officially sponsored, but after that liberal intellectuals and enlightened missionaries took the lead. There came to be a widespread awareness that China could not go forward as a modern nation as long as vestiges of its outmoded past remained. The anti-footbinding movement, which achieved success only gradually, pressed forward unremittingly for several decades.

A satirical essay ostensibly written in defense of the custom appeared in 1915 in the *New Republic*, entitled, "In Praise of Footbinding."[35] The Chinese writer reminded his Western readers that, contrary to assertion, footbinding was not a barbarous custom, since it prevailed in the oldest and most mature of the world's civilizations. It was painful, he admitted, but then pain was one of the measures of civilization. It was only the so-called barbarians who allowed men and women to dress alike and to share equally. (Here he implied that the earliest stage of development in China and elsewhere was a primitive communism.) With the emergence of civilized nations, however, the status of women was lowered and they could no longer dress like men or participate in their councils. Footbinding therefore became an ultimate goal in the civilizing process, he asserted.

He spoke as a Chinese husband of the pains of footbinding and told of the experiences of his own daughter In his family girls had always started binding at the age of three, but he delayed it as long as he could in deference to the pleading of his wife. He cited a saying—"A barrel of tears for each pair of bound feet"—and remarked that it was exaggerated, for his little girl wept bitterly at first but soon dropped into silent despair. Perhaps the most original and revealing passage in his essay was one in which he described the psychological advantages accruing to the Chinese male:

> The bound foot is the condition of a life of dignity for man, of contentment for woman. Let me make this clear. I am a Chinese fairly typical of my class. I pored too much over classic texts in my youth and dimmed my eyes, narrowed my chest, crooked my back. My memory is not strong, and in an old civilization there is a vast deal to learn before you can know anything. Accordingly among scholars I cut a poor figure. I am timid, and my voice plays me false in gatherings of men. But to my footbound wife, confined for life to her house except when I bear her in my arms to her palanquin, my stride is heroic, my voice is that of a roaring lion, my wisdom is of the sages. To her I am the world; I am life itself.

Implying that footbinding and the spiritual bondage of women were synonymous, he caustically remarked that Western man was on the right track, since he denied woman the ballot, handicapped her in professional life, belittled her intellectual accomplishments, and minimized the value of her personality. But, he reminded his Western readers, there was still the danger of woman's rebelling against these artificial barriers in order to assert her independence. "What you need for the civilizing of women is a simple and radical strategy. Bind their feet."

The revolutionaries who overthrew the Manchu government were determined to eliminate footbinding from the Chinese scene, and from their seizure of power onward a series of decrees were issued which reached into every provincial town, hamlet, and village. The degree of success varied according to the ability of local officials and the degree of resistance to them; details on enforcement are given in Chapter Nine.[36] Some idea of the effectiveness of the abolition movement can be gotten by analyzing statistical surveys and scholarly observations.

When the Chinese National Association of the Mass Education Movement made a population study of Tinghsien in 1929, a rural area 125 miles south of Peking, it secured figures to show the extent of footbinding among 1,736 females of 515 families. These were discussed by Sidney D. Gamble in an article which appeared in the *American Journal of Sociology*.[37] As Mr. Gamble stated, "These figures, when correlated with the ages of the women, show very clearly how the cultural pattern changed in Tinghsien within thirty years and how foot-binding gradually disappeared, slowly at first and then with increasing rapidity, until it was completely discontinued about 1919." The Tinghsien villagers were representative of the rural population, except that there was a slightly higher proportion of families with large land holdings. It was estimated in the study that footbinding ordinarily started when the girls were about three years old, or about two years earlier than the national average. The study was made in 1929. Of women born before 1890, who were forty years or older when the study was made, almost all bound their feet (99.2 percent). Mr. Gamble raised a question as to why four women in this group had natural feet. The answer might lie in their having been very poor, orphaned, or in the lowest menial category. There was only a slight change in figures for those born between 1890 and 1899, a rise in the proportion of the natural-footed from .8% to 5%, indicating that reformist ideas were slowly catching on. It was after the turn of the century that significant changes occurred. The proportion of girls with normal feet rose to 18.5% from 1900 to 1904 and 40.3% from 1905 to 1909. Then came the Revolution and the elevation of woman's social status, for which the elimination of footbinding was essential. Statistics show the sweeping effect in Tinghsien, for 80.5% of the girls born from 1910 to 1914 had unbound feet. The percentage increased to 94.4% for girls in the 1915-1919 group; from 1920 on, there were no new cases. In conclusion, commented Mr. Gamble, "Knowing the general conservatism of the countryside, it is remarkable to see how this old and well-established custom, which had lasted for almost one thousand years and had successfully defied imperial authority, disappeared completely in these Tinghsien families in a period of about twenty years, or less than one generation."

The statistics for the Tinghsien study were as follows:

Tinghsien Females With Bound and Unbound Feet
515 Families, 1929

Age Groups	*Unbound Feet*	*Bound Feet*	*Total*	*Percent Bound*
Under 5	294	—	294	—
5–9	169	—	169	—
10–14	152	9	161	5.6
15–19	120	29	149	19.5
20–24	52	77	129	59.7
25–29	24	106	130	81.5
30–34	6	97	103	94.1
35–39	6	103	109	94.5
40 and over	4	488	492	99.2
Total	827	909	1,736	—

The Police Office in Amoy, a southern city on an island opposite the island fortress of Kinmen, issued census statistics in 1937 which included information on footbinding. The custom was practiced there from the Sung dynasty onwards. The move to eliminate footbinding started in Amoy before it did on the mainland. Bound-foot young married women there in 1937 were migrants from other parts of China. The total number of women in Amoy in 1937 was 71,332, of whom 3,288, or about 4.5%, still had bound feet. Their breakdown in ages was as follows: thirty and over, 3,082 (born in 1907 or earlier); over fifteen but under thirty, 202 (born after 1907); under fifteen, 4. Women in Amoy were called up for military training in 1937, but those whose feet were still bound or had been bound previously were excused. The local press reported incidents of fathers ordering daughters to bind their feet in order to avoid the military draft.[38]

The Tinghsien study was also noted by Nagao Ryūzo, the Japanese sociologist who was in China from a few years before the Russo-Japanese War to the end of the second World War. Nagao stated that when a population census was carried out in Shansi Province during 1932-3, the number of bound-foot women was also investigated. Shansi, incidentally, was a stronghold of conservative custom. The census figures for footbinding were as follows: under sixteen, 323,064; over sixteen but under thirty, 625,625. Not including the number over thirty, which was not revealed, there were almost a million young women in Shansi Province still observing the custom more than two decades after the Revolution. This was in sharp contrast to the Tinghsien and Amoy studies, which showed that by 1920 footbinding was already dying out in these areas. Nagao stated that Chinese government statistics in the thirties were extremely unreliable. However, the 1932-3 Shansi census probably erred on the side of understatement, since many with bound feet hid in order to avoid official censure. Nagao, traveling through Shansi in 1921, was impressed by the official posters outlawing footbinding which he found strategically placed throughout the capital city of Ta-t'ung and vicinity. Ta-t'ung was the most famous center of the "lotus" in China; Japanese medical units in North China after 1937 commented on the large number of tiny-footed, middle-aged women there.

It is evident that footbinding in the thirties among the middle-aged and older was still common and that the great success in eradicating it was with the young. My interviews in Taiwan (see Chapter Ten) showed that letting out the feet often resulted in bleeding or in such pain that walking became impossible. In such cases, binding had to be continued. The tenacity with which tradition-oriented women clung to this custom led to repeated legislation against it. A Peking daily in January, 1935, published a series of pronouncements by the Peking Municipal Government against footbinding, threatening punishment for violators. Issued more than twenty years after the Revolution, these directives must have been intended for the middle-aged die-hards. The press in the thirties still reported unceasing organizational efforts to eradicate this ancient practice. These frequent reports were evidence that it was a slow process to eliminate footbinding from the village centers of conservatism in which it was entrenched. Nagao wrote in 1941 of the influence of the New Life Movement which Chiang Kai-shek had launched. As one example, he cited a decree issued by the Provincial Governor of Shantung to the effect that women with bound feet would not be issued marriage permits. Such permits were to be granted only after each case had been investigated, to assure that the bride-to-be had natural feet as required by statute. However actual implementation depended on the attitude of the investigators, for it was reported that some Shantung women with bound feet were granted marriage licenses nevertheless.[39]

The progress of eliminating footbinding in an area as vast and diverse as China was uneven and varied. A Japanese encyclopedia article published in 1932 remarked that women in the large cities had all let their feet out, with resistance confined to the villages. But the writer added that women in the Honan city of Loyang had recently reverted to the custom of binding feet and admiring them for their beauty.[40] Gotō Asatarō, a less objective Japanese student of Chinese customs, in 1938 recorded his impressions of footbinding. He first confessed that he was prejudiced: "I have been in China for a long time; therefore, when I see a woman who has large [natural] feet, I have the feeling that she is not beautiful." He stated that an observer who restricted himself to Shanghai and Peking might conclude that footbinding had ended, but asserted that eighty to ninety percent of the women in the rural areas still practiced it. This figure which Gotō cited is undoubtedly exaggerated, and may be explained by his enthusiasm and personal interest in seeing that footbinding flourished. He stated the well-known fact that women in the Shansi provincial capital of Ta-t'ung had the tiniest feet in China, bound feet which were especially well pointed, took "lotus steps," and did not seem to touch the ground. Gotō did not attribute revolutionary motives to the anti-footbinding movement but rather thought it had come about to save China's "National Face." He doubted that it would succeed. In Shanghai, he said, some women still put cotton inside large shoes to conceal their tiny feet and to avoid criticism, secretly wishing that they could revert to the practice. He described rows of beauties in Chungking houses of prostitution: "Their faces and figures were concealed, and the only thing visible to the guest was tiny feet enclosed in shoes of flowered embroidery." According to Gotō, men made the choice of prostitutes on the basis of the lotus feet alone. He concluded his essay by saying that fewer and fewer prostitutes in Peking, Shanghai, and other large cities still bound their feet, but that in villages and especially in parts of Shansi and Szechwan, remote areas distant from centers of civilization, "the feet there are just as small as they were in antiquity."[41]

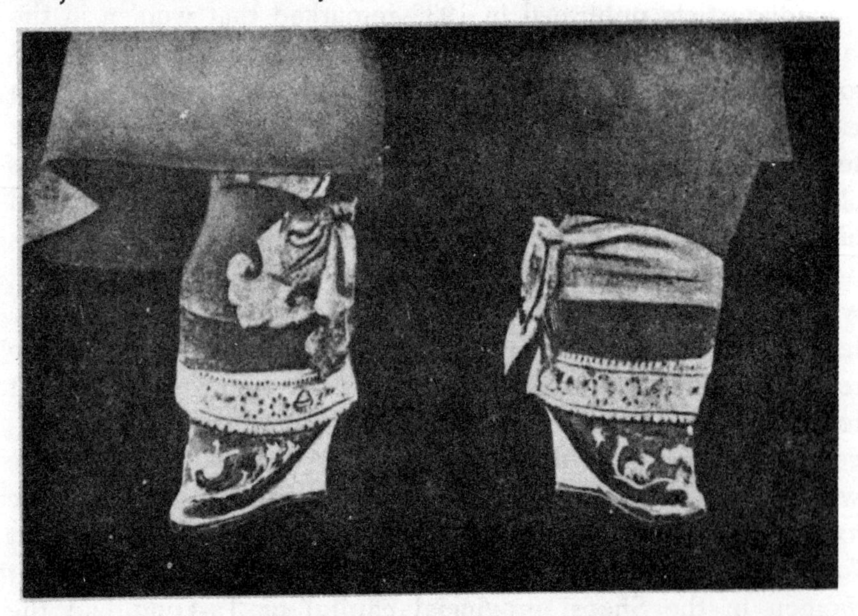

THE OLDEST KIND OF SHOE ORNAMENTATION

The movement to eliminate footbinding in Taiwan was closely identified with the Japanese occupation.[42] From the start, Japanese officials and intellectuals were critical of the Chinese habits of opium smoking, wearing pigtails, and footbinding. Colonial authorities felt that these customs were obstacles in the way of efficient rule. Opium smoking was injurious to the health and adversely influenced work output; pigtails and bound feet were looked down upon as ugly and unsanitary. But the Japanese also realized that they were just settling down in Taiwan, with their troops still busily engaged in putting down local rebellions. They knew that customs which had been practiced for centuries could not be eradicated overnight and were afraid that sudden implementation of a policy of total abolition might endanger their control of the native population. Unlike the mainland, anti-footbinding in Taiwan was not part of an indigenous revolutionary movement to extend women's rights but was imposed from above by foreign colonials.

The Japanese first adopted a policy of non-interference, shown in the way they allowed the wearing of pigtails. This custom was an old one, shared by the Hsienpi, Turk, Jürched and Mongol peoples. In the early twelfth century, Chin ruler T'ai-tsung ordered all Chinese to adopt the queue, but the edict proved only partially successful and was later discontinued. The Manchus who conquered China enforced the wearing of the queue as a proof of subjugation among inhabitants of occupied areas. Those who refused to obey were threatened with execution for disloyalty. This method succeeded, and in little more than a decade the policy of having Chinese men wear the queue had been enforced throughout the empire.[43]

The Japanese ridiculed the Taiwanese by calling them "pigtail Chinese," while the Taiwanese called their conquerors "opium heads," referring to the brisk opium trade which had been carried on before the official prohibition. About the turn of the century, a few Taiwanese advocated cutting off the pigtail because it was inappropriate for the modern age, but without effect. On January 1, 1902, a newspaper article in Taiwan noted that, fully eight years after the occupation, only twenty-eight men had cut off their queues out of a Taipei population of several tens of thousands. There was a small rebel uprising in the south in October, 1901, during which Japanese subjugation forces conscripted able-bodied Taiwanese and persuaded them to cut off their pigtails so that they could be more easily distinguished from the rebels. Later they forced the rebel leader and the five thousand men who surrendered with him to remove their queues. But in the early occupation phase some officials still felt that coercion was improper. On September 29, 1902, the Civil Affairs Chief issued a notification which advised subordinates to be cautious in interfering with this custom, since it was correct to have queues removed only if the masses acquiesced.

Some cut off their pigtails to avoid being mistaken for anti-Japanese rebels, but were looked down on by fellow Taiwanese. As on the mainland, influence towards change was exerted through the educational system, even though it was colonially controlled. This had increasing effect on Taiwanese youth attending Japanese language curriculum schools; by 1910, about half had given up the practice. The success of the Chinese Revolution in the following year, with its call for eliminating the queue and footbinding, also had its effect on changing the psychological outlook of mainland-oriented Taiwanese. Many intellectuals favored reform, and a society was organized for cutting off pigtails while retaining traditional dress. The society came into existence in 1911, not to commemorate the overthrow of the Manchus, but to celebrate the anniversary of the founding of Japan. Its leader, Huang Yü-chieh, made this statement during his inaugural address:

> Law-abiding citizens must realize that after the Meiji Restoration all Japanese, including the Emperor himself, cut off their long locks. We Taiwanese bound our hair during the Ming dynasty and adopted the pigtail during the Ch'ing dynasty. But

圖一

（下）同前

內著「軟底鞋」所謂「換脚鞋」也鞋外套以「靴登子」夠是「褲腿兒」竝意最外著「靴子」則又「褲腿兒」與「套鞋」連爲相聯式者也 「靴子」上部曰「靴腰（讀去聲）子」下部曰「靴襻子」而上「月亮門」中貫用布或緞色尚白「靴口」與「腿帶」之間微彰起者即「靴登子」也「靴登子」多用所謂紅藍色（較湖色微偏藍）布製

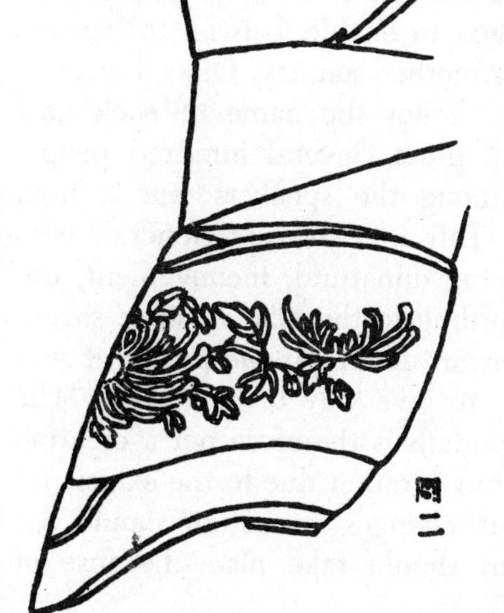

（上）淸光緒二十年時天津纏足外觀式

「套鞋」所謂複底鞋以「褲腿兒」綁有「弓鞋」連意「套鞋」有「木底」以便行鞋內或尚有「軟底鞋」或無之無者晚間去「套鞋」易「軟底鞋」所謂「睡鞋」是也

其時長裙委地微露鞋尖

足面穹起 足底凹 尖微向下

上束「腿帶」「褲腿兒」邊「鑲狗牙」

TIENTSIN FOOT APPAREL

Taiwan is now a part of Japan; it should therefore adopt Japanese customs. The Japanese are much more benevolent than were the severe Manchus. Though we are really Japanese, it is difficult for us to enjoy first-class treatment as citizens of Japan because we look like Manchus when we go abroad. Many peoples, like the Koreans, have recently cut off their pigtails. And compared with Korea, we enjoy the relationship of an elder brother to a younger brother. So it is hard to understand why the Taiwanese are still unwilling to abandon the pigtail. Some say: "Cut the pigtail and change the dress," but this is not economically feasible. The Japanese who cut their hair in the Meiji era kept their old dress; we should do the same until our clothes wear out. The Manchus have already cut their hair, so the fate of the queue is sealed. This custom, which affects our personalities and our cultural response, is unsanitary and inconvenient.[44]

The society stressed in its regulations that its sole objective was removal of the queue. At each meeting, any number of participants in excess of ten could have their queues cut off together. The underlying aim was to enable Taiwan to become as one culturally with Japan, its mother country. Official encouragement was given, and as an honor the name of each new member was listed in the local press. Several hundred people attended the first meeting. Among the speakers was a high official from the office of the Taiwan Governor-General, who publicly attacked pigtails as being unnatural, inconvenient, uneconomic, and unsanitary. According to the official, since seventeen years had passed with Taiwan under Japanese rule, it was really time for the old customs to give way to new ones. "The opposition to footbinding and pigtails is therefore not a creation of official government pressure but is rather due to the exigencies of the present. To be successful, changes in custom should not only be effected externally but should take place because of inner conviction."[45]

During this meeting, eight barbers cut off the pigtails of more than a hundred members. Some were so emotionally affected by the removal that they put the pigtail in paper and took it home as a remembrance. Others had photographs taken "before and after." This event of 1911 was imitated elsewhere in Taipei, which led the rest of the island in organization and procedure. Within a few months, hair-cutting ceremonies had taken place throughout Taiwan. In September, 1913, 2,500 out of 4,200 men in a village near Taichung cut off their pigtails, and by November of the next year only thirty-eight boys of a total of 9,800 in Taichung public schools still kept their queues. But adults and elders from the villages did not take to this liberalization quite so readily. In 1915, the twentieth year of the occupation, the Japanese authorities decided to order that pigtails be removed, with official action to be taken by the seventeenth of June. Without waiting for the deadline, almost one and a third million Taiwanese cut off their queues, leaving only a die-hard remnant estimated at eighty thousand.

The drive against footbinding was launched earlier than the moves against the queue, with similar leadership. Huang Yü-chieh, mentioned earlier in connection with anti-queue organization, was the first Taiwanese in Taipei to advocate publicly that footbinding be eliminated. Huang, a practitioner of Chinese medicine, often said that the bound-footedness of Taiwanese women was unnatural. About the turn of the century, Huang and his friends organized a natural-foot society[46] and applied to the Taipei County Office for formal registration.

The natural-foot society wanted to accomplish two things: eradicate the footbinding habit, and lead fellow Taiwanese in making the transition towards a more enlightened culture. It functioned like similar mainland organizations, with members vowing not to let their sons take bound-foot brides. Certain members were appointed to propagandize among the masses and try to persuade them to renounce binding. If membership in any one area totaled one hundred or more, branch societies were to be established. The society was granted a formal permit to operate in February, 1900; from this time on, local intellectuals joined, and its active membership increased. A meeting of about 250 members was held on March twentieth, attended by the Taiwan Governor-General and other high dignitaries. Huang Yü-chieh, in his inaugural address, criticized footbinding as an unhealthy practice which prevented a woman from fulfilling her duties. He informed his audience that it was often ridiculed and laughed at by foreigners.

> Now Taiwan has become a part of the Japanese empire, and the government is carrying out reforms. The Taiwanese are also a people of reform, but it will really be shameful if they are not made aware of the evil customs of the past. The natural-foot society was formed with this objective in mind. . . . We must continue striving forward, hoping that women can keep their Heavenly endowments. [Natural-footed] women can pound the mortars, draw water from the wells, and sew garments diligently in the service of their in-laws. Going one step further, they can enter schools to study the Japanese language, embroidery or calligraphy, and perhaps specialize in arithmetic, accounting, science, or other fields. If successful, they will create a worthy livelihood and greatly help society by assisting men who are too busy to accomplish certain deeds.[47]

Huang's principal argument was traditional rather than liberal, as he did not advocate social equality for women but wanted them to be able to perform menial household tasks with increased efficiency. His criticism of footbinding because it prevented women from working harder was widely supported. Many Taiwanese had originally migrated to the island from Fukien Province, and it was in Fukien that the following anti-footbinding ditty was popularly known:

> I rise with the dawn,
> Binding my feet;
> Bed and cover soiled,
> Soiled by unwashed feet.

Binding my feet,
Combing my hair,
Hidden in a bedroom;
Household tasks unattended.[48]

Even though it was an officially encouraged organization, the natural-foot society faced many difficulties. Many privately admitted that footbinding was a bad thing, but few, including intellectuals, were willing to pioneer by openly directing their wives to remove the bindings. The general tendency to make fun of women with natural feet brought about a type of inertia against radical change and a social compulsion to keep things as they were. Transfer of the Taipei county chief in November, 1901, weakened the society, since he was one of its staunchest supporters. The Japanese bureaucracy went through many administrative changes at this time, causing lessened official concern with the movement. There was little activity in 1902, but 1903 saw a revival of interest. The Taiwan county chief held a meeting that August, informing his subordinates that footbinding should be eliminated, and instructed them as follows: natural-foot societies were to be established throughout Taiwan, with the main office at Taipei; members were not to bind their daughters' feet if more than six years old; boys over ten could not contract to be engaged to marry bound-foot girls; boys in the society could marry outsiders only if they had natural feet; society members would be fined from five to one hundred yen if they let their children revert to this practice, and members were to be fined like amounts if they sold their natural-footed daughters. (This may have referred to the Taiwanese custom of selling daughters, which, though illegal, is still practiced.) While branch societies were set up as ordered, the effect was negligible.

The unbound foot was still a popular butt of ridicule. To counteract this, society leaders decided that its members should be given congratulatory medals. These were officially sanctioned in September, 1903, and were in the form of a lotus, inscribed with the words, "Glorious Medal of Taiwan." [49] Those who had let their feet out had a blue ribbon attached to the medal; a red ribbon meant that the wearer had natural feet. Each medal holder was presented with a silken sash by the Governor-General, on which he personally wrote the Confucian maxim that filial piety began with our not daring to injure our persons.[50]

In the early years of the twentieth century, a major obstacle to success of the abolition movement on Taiwan was the inability of the Japanese to pacify every segment of the population. As late as 1909, the chief of the Civil Affairs Bureau indicated in correspondence with the branch chief of Keelung that local bandits were present everywhere, keeping the masses in a state of unrest. He advised that it was premature to end such evils as opium smoking, pigtails, and footbinding, and said that the Japanese "would have to be very careful not to injure public sentiment by their remarks about the local customs." In April, 1911, regarding whether Taiwanese should be granted Japanese nationality, the Governor-General officially said that such recipients would be ridiculed if they went to Europe and America wearing pigtails and dressed like old-style Chinese. This was considered detrimental to the national face of Japan, and as such was officially deplored.

In 1914, the Taichung Office Chief invited prominent people to discuss the problem of revising outmoded Chinese mores. One outcome of the discussions was organization of a Society for Improvement of Our Island's Customs. That spring, a Society to Let Out Footbindings was organized by the influential Lin family of Wufeng, located near Taichung. More than six hundred women let out their bindings, and others began to imitate their example. The Taiwan Governor-General realized that the time was opportune. In 1915, on the occasion of the twentieth anniversary of Japanese rule in Taiwan, he decided to end footbinding once and for all. On the fifteenth of April, an official order of prohibition was issued. The decree was effective, and by August more than 763,000 women had obeyed. Recalcitrants were forcibly dealt with, more and more Taiwanese complied, and the custom virtually disappeared, owing to strict government prohibition and the development of public feeling against it. The bound-foot elderly lady in Taiwan has today become an increasingly uncommon sight.

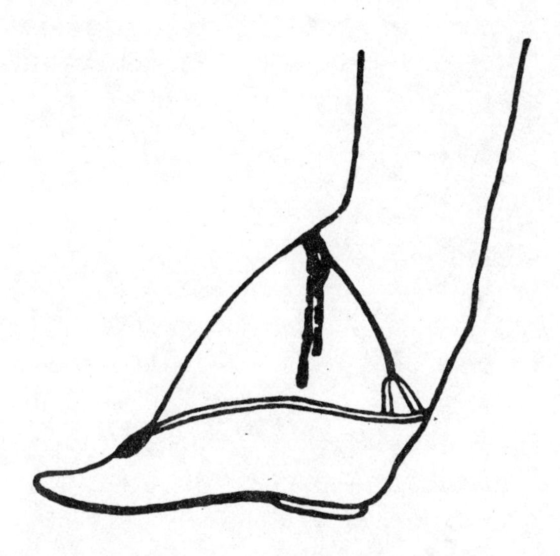

Part Two

CURIOUS

CHAPTER FOUR

Lotus Lovers

The elimination of footbinding in the first half of the twentieth century resulted directly from the drive to emancipate Chinese women from an age-old inheritance of social inequality. Chinese reformers and Western missionaries made unremitting efforts to destroy the custom. They enjoyed official as well as private encouragement and presented their cause with conviction. The fact that the "golden lotus" had once been an inextricable part of Chinese culture was disregarded; the outcries of the opposition drowned out the voices of footbinding's apologists.

In the earlier ages, when the view of the enthusiast was virtually unopposed, footbinding had its proud proponents. There were Peking families, for example, who looked upon it as a matter for rejoicing. At the start of binding, congratulatory visits were made by women who were either close relatives or intimate friends. They would pay a formal call to put the parents' minds at ease by praising the form of the child's foot.[1]

Well-known essays praising footbinding were composed two or three hundred years ago by an aristocrat who wrote under the name of Fang Hsün, probably an alias. This self-styled "Doctor of the Fragrant Lotus," lyric in his exaltation, listed the necessary aesthetic components of the praiseworthy tiny foot, added critical comments, and analyzed drinking games in which shoes played a principal role. Fang Hsün ostensibly imitated the thematic arrangement of a botanical work called *Qualities of Plum Blossoms;* the result was "Classification of the Qualities of Fragrant Lotuses," the essay for which he is best known.[2]

Fang Hsün enumerated fifty-eight varieties of the human lotus, including feet which were properly bound and gloriously favored as well as those which were either ugly or shameful looking. Lotus petal, new moon, harmonious bow, bamboo shoot, and water chestnut were the euphonious names given to principal styles. The three precious qualities were plumpness, softness, and fineness, for a thin foot cooled the ardor of the onlooker, too much strength detracted from its femininity, and the common look gave it a liability which no medicine could cure. Plumpness implied voluptuous beauty, softness an enticing skin texture, and fineness a mystic elegance. The plump and the soft might be appreciated visually, but the quality of fineness had to be grasped through spiritual understanding.

Fang Hsün did not include diagrams in the monograph, but some idea of foot contour may be derived from the way in which he described dominant types. He stated that the Lotus Petal on All Sides was perfectly narrow and arched, three to four inches long. The Lotus with Silk Linen Sides was correctly bound but about an inch longer, preventing the wearing of sharply pointed shoes. The Long Hairpin Lotus, while shaped like a bamboo shoot, was too long and thin to satisfy critical aesthetic standards. The Buddha's Head Lotus had a very full instep, hunched like the knot on the top of the head of Sakyamuni. "Two-headed lotus petals" depicted the feet of a woman who walked pigeon-toed, toes turned in like the Chinese numeral eight 八. Toes pointing outwards were called "double flowers," calloused heels were euphoniously termed "interwined hearts," and the body bent forward in an effort to walk was a "bound branch lotus." Morning Lotus walked on her heels, with the big toe pointed upwards, because the bent-under toes were too painful to press down upon. Tibetan Lotus, symbolized as a large flower, constituted the foot which was first bound but then let out. This was inferior but still preferable to the Lotus of the Jade Well, referring to a natural foot disguised by wearing a pointed sandal.

Fang Hsün set forth nine gradations of excellence, comparing them to the nine official ranks. Divine Quality (A1) was neither plump nor slender but as perfect in size as the ancient beauty Hsi Shih, who looked superlative in every posture. Wondrous Quality (A2) was weak and slender, like a willow branch leaning for support and bending in the breeze. Immortal Quality (A3) was straight-boned, independent, and not of the common herd. She was like one who lived in the mountains and partook of natural foods, liable to run away if you angrily tried to seize her. The other six grades were marred by imperfections. Precious Article (B1) was as conspicuous and brilliant as a peacock, but the back of her foot was too wide and disproportioned. Pure Article (B2), too long and thin, looked like the neck of a goose with outstretched throat crying aloud or a duck with its neck elongated in flight. Seductive Article (B3) was fleshy and short, relatively wide and round. Frailty was the mark of femininity, but a woman with this foot shape could easily withstand a blowing wind. Excessive Article (C1) was narrow but not smooth, slender but insufficiently pointed, reminding the beholder of a landscape painting with one strong rock but crumbling clouds and precipices. Ordinary Article (C2) was plump and almost common, looking like one so troubled at heart that she remained hunched over. False Article (C3) had such a large heel that she gave the impression of a climbing monkey. Even though from a good family, she moved in a way which gave the onlooker an uncomfortable feeling.

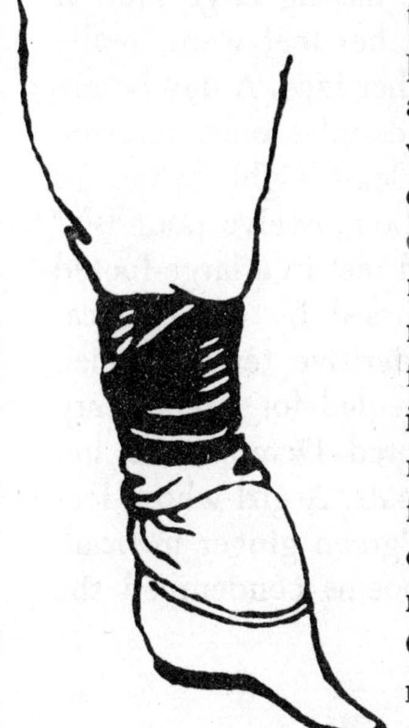

Regardless of how the foot varied, it looked best under the following circumstances: when placed in the palm of a man's hand; perched on a swing; revealed under the bedcovers; silhouetted by a lantern; leaving an imprint in the snow; glimpsed through a screen, partition, or bamboo fence. There were four taboos to be observed:

1. Don't walk with your toes pointed upwards.
2. Don't stand with your heels seemingly suspended in mid-air.
3. Don't move your skirt when sitting.
4. Don't move your feet when lying down.

Fang Hsün stated that women were ashamed to hear whispered criticisms behind their backs about having large feet. If the groom said on the wedding night that her feet were "really large," the mortified bride dared not show her face. A day before the wedding, a line in a congratulatory couplet once referred to the bride's large feet as weighing at least eight *catties* (a Chinese weight in this context equal to about twelve pounds).[3] If one criticized servants for having natural feet in a large-footed woman's presence, the latter felt embarrassed by the implications of the remark. There was a set of derisive terms applied to the large-footed. The girl might be ridiculed for having carp or herring feet or be called a Large-Footed Demon, and her shoes might be referred to as Crow-like Boats. A girl whose feet were poorly bound might be satirized as "green ginger in front, a goose egg in back." Folk ditties and poems condemned the large-footed:

Her face is passable,
But those big feet, laughable!

A large-footed woman tarries,
For no one wants to marry her.

You say they resemble feet?
They look more like twin boats in a fleet.
You there, with the two large feet,
You've nothing to lose;
Wear your husband's old tattered shoes.

My large feet repelled my wedded mate;
But how can I begrudge Mama,
Who knew my childhood dread,
My fear of binding for the lotus gait.
My foot-long extremities,
Not only twice the bound variety,
But growing with each passing year.
An epidemic took my husband from me,
And I can't even squeeze into his shoes;
what ignominy! [4]

Fang Hsün felt that the human lotus was superior to the loveliest flower, for it understood human speech, persevered in overcoming pain, and resisted seasonal change. The tiny foot was comparable in quality and perseverence to the plum blossom, bamboo, and pine, and the poems in praise of it were legion:

Mother, Mother, it's her I must wed,
Her flowered high heels are unparalleled.
While I'm penniless, it's true,
To have her I'll sell all we've held.

Twin red shoes, less than inches three,
With pretty flowers for embroidery.
Wait till I tell the folks at home;
I'll mortgage the house, give up the land,
And wed with tiny feet as planned.

Her powdered pink face,
Prettier than a peach;

Her twin golden lotuses,
Perfect fit for my hands.
Wait for the fine harvest next year;
I'll take you home as my bride,
In a colored sedan chair.

A beauty in her bedroom
Binds the golden lotus.
A handsome lad walks by;
Miss, oh how tiny they are,
Like broken winter bamboo shoots,
And like dumplings in May,
But more fragrant and sweeter in every way;
Or like the fruit of June, Buddha's Hand,
But more sharply defined and elegant.[5]

Women who believed in the beauty of bound feet took care of them diligently, like a fastidious gentleman in the service of his lord. Fang Hsün advised men with concubines, whom he called Masters of the Golden Rooms, to be polite and proper to ladies whose feet were so finely bound that they seemed to give rise to lotuses with every step. "Do not remove the bindings to look at her bare foot, but be satisfied with its external appearance. Enjoy the outward impression, for if you remove the shoes and binding the aesthetic feeling will be destroyed forever."

For genteel lovers, the tiny foot provided endless amusement. The woman enhanced her attraction by allowing it to protrude slightly beyond the skirt. She stimulated her partner by extending the feet daintily outside the loving bird coverlets. With pretended pique, she kicked the lover's foot with her own, while he conveyed intimacy by touching her foot surreptitiously. He also wrote a character on the foot, holding it in his palm. On other occasions, he rubbed it in his palm in amorous play. The smell of the unwashed foot had its charms for some, who referred to it as a "fragrant bed aroma."

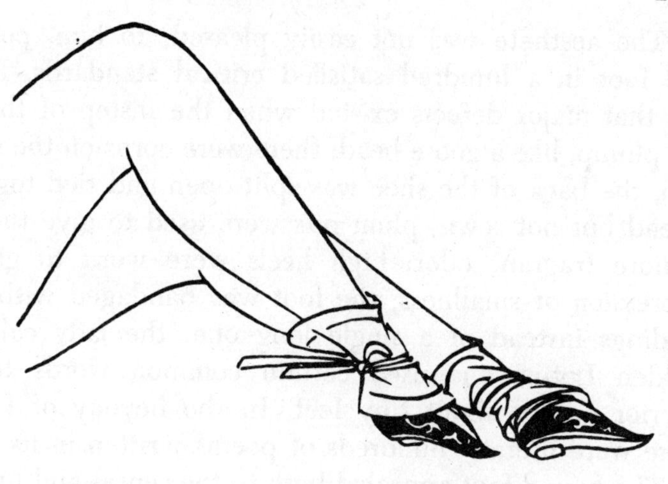

Last night's wild love-play loosened the lotus roots;

On arising, layer upon layer are tightly rebound.

As she binds, fleecy cloth entangles her slender fingers;

She sprinkles perfume, achieving greater fragrance.

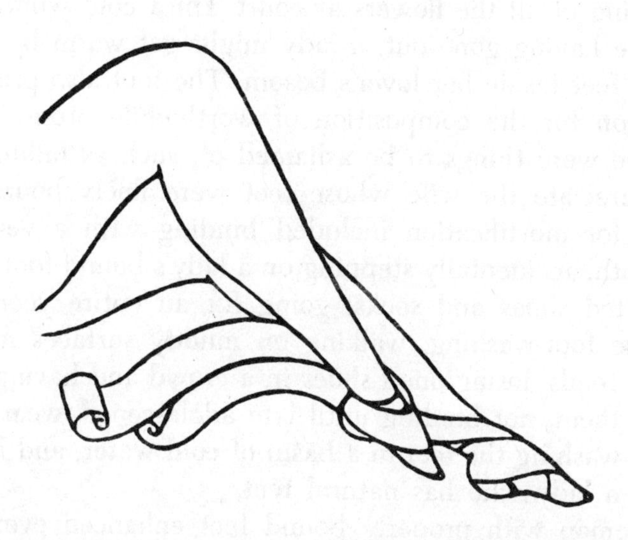

A POEM BY *TS'AI-FEI LU* EDITOR YAO LING-HSI BASED ON DRAWINGS BY TS'AO HAN-MEI

The aesthete was not easily pleased; to him, perhaps only one foot in a hundred satisfied critical standards. Fang Hsün felt that major defects existed when the instep of the foot was too plump, like a goose head; there were corns on the side or bottom; the back of the shoe was split open and tied together with thread but not sewn; plum pits were used to give the stockings a more fragrant odor; high heels were worn to give a false impression of smallness; the foot was bandaged with two short bindings instead of a single long one; the lady called herself Golden Lotus; one used certain common words to compose inferior poetry about tiny feet. In the heyday of footbinding, there were literally hundreds of poems written in its praise.

The bound foot appealed both to the senses and to the imagination. A man solicitously rubbed the foot of his beloved because he felt compassion for her discomfort from the binding. A shape of the foot was sometimes placed inside books, ostensibly to prevent insects from devouring the pages. To the initiated, the sight of a lady about to wash her feet was likened to the sudden blossoming of all the flowers at court. On a cold winter's night, the stove having gone out, a lady might get warm by inserting the tiny feet inside her lover's bosom. The foot also provided an inspiration for the composition of worthwhile prose.

There were things to be ashamed of, such as failing to love and appreciate the wife whose feet were finely bound. Other sources for mortification included binding with a very coarse linen cloth, accidentally stepping on a lady's bound foot, wearing dilapidated shoes and socks, going for an entire year without even one foot-washing, walking on muddy surfaces instead of the best roads, losing one's shoes in a crowd and having to walk without them, not binding until late adolescence, wearing grass sandals, washing the feet in a basin of cold water, and having to wait on a lady who has natural feet.

A woman with properly bound feet enhanced every scene. It was especially pleasing to watch her bind, wash, make shoes or try them on, tie shoelaces by the balustrade, or pare down

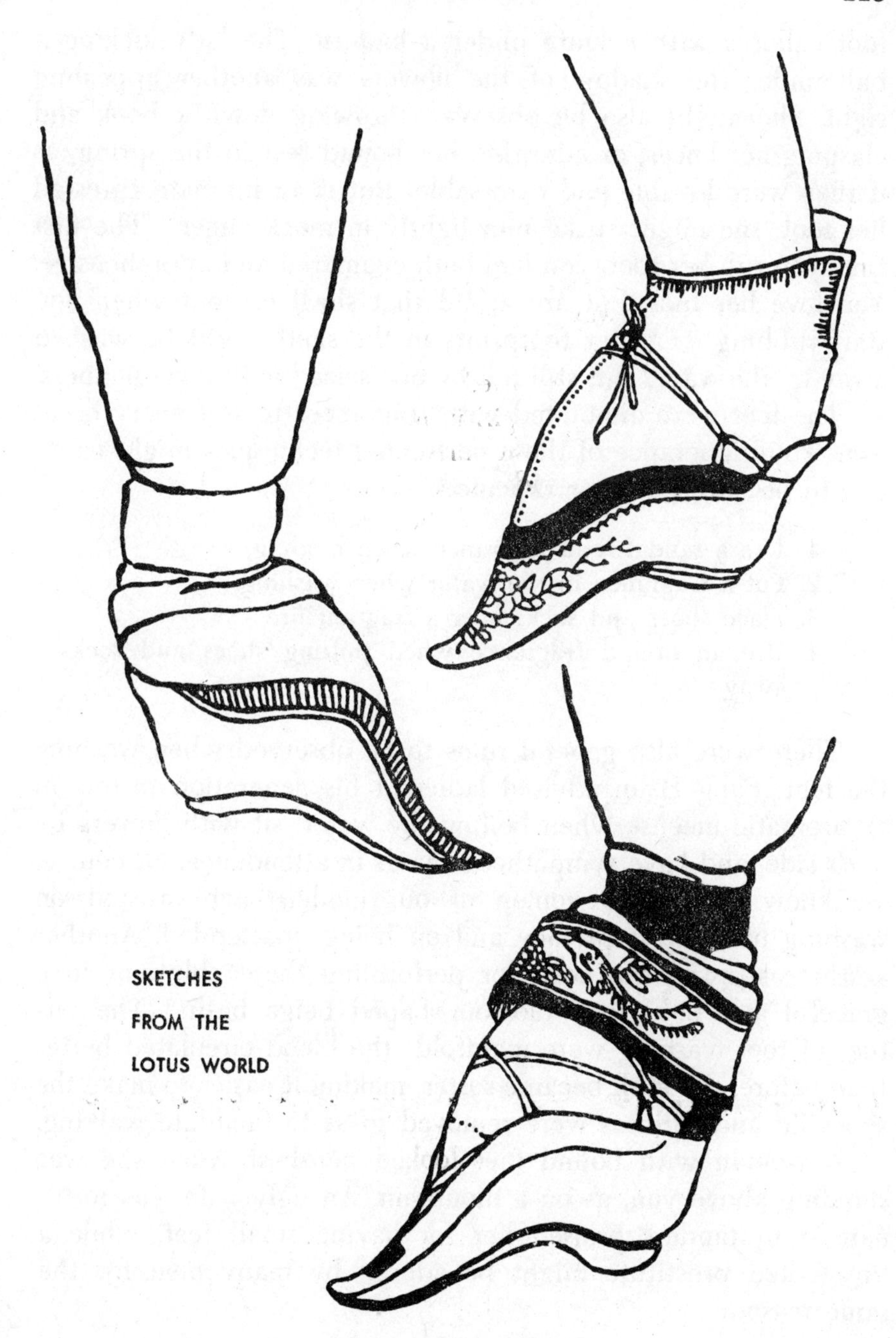

SKETCHES
FROM THE
LOTUS WORLD

foot calluses with a knife under a lantern. The lady kicking a ball under the shadow of the flowers was another appealing sight. She might also be observed throwing down a book and clasping her knees, or admiring her bound feet in the spring, as if they were lovable and caressable. But if an intimate caressed her foot, she might strike him lightly in mock anger. "The first time you rub her foot, you feel both enamored and apprehensive. You love her foot, but are afraid that she'll cry out when you start rubbing it."[6] Her footprints in the sand might be washed away by the waves but still felt by one seized with love madness.

The feet were annointed with fragrances to suit every occasion. Total ignorance of these perfuming techniques might cause one to be laughed at or ridiculed:

1. Use a sandalwood fragrance when binding.
2. Put a fragrance in the water when washing.
3. Place shoes and socks over a fragrant fire.
4. Use an orchid fragrance when putting shoes and socks away.

There were also general rules to be observed when washing the feet. Fang Hsün advised ladies of his generation to mix in an aromatic incense when boiling the water, sit with flowers by one's side, and have sympathetic maids in attendance. Of course, we know that most women of our modern age insisted on washing in strictest privacy and on being unattended. Another aesthete stressed the need for performing these ablutions in a graceful and light lotus-blossom-shaped beige basin.[7] The virtues of foot washing were manifold: the blood circulated better than before, the flesh became softer, making it easier to make the shoes fit, and calluses were removed so as to facilitate walking.

A woman with bound feet looked her best when she was standing above you, as on a mountain. An ugly wife was fortunate if bystanders praised her for having small feet, while a tiny-footed prostitute might be adored by many men for the same reason:

A tiny foot can atone for three-fourths of a woman's ugliness.
One never selects a large-footed prostitute.

A large-footed woman, when walking, sounds as thunderous as the combined noise of more than ten households.[8] But unlucky indeed was the lady wedded to an uneducated village boor, having to let her dainty feet be grasped in his coarse hands. Still more hapless was the low-grade prostitute who, night after night, was pawed about by drunken customers and had her tiny feet lifted on to their shoulders.

Fang Hsün supplied the above comments in *Qualities of Fragrant Lotuses,* and in a second monograph called *A Golden Garden Miscellany* supplemented the orderly presentation in *Qualities* with random remarks and subjective impressions.[9] These were arranged by subject:

Things which never happen—waiting for a woman to claim her lost shoe, since she is too embarrassed to do so. Asking a famous artist to paint a flower on your sandal, since no one of repute will paint by order. It is bad luck to have your shoes painted this way, and also an ill omen to get rid of shoes or give them away to someone else.

Inappropriate—a large foot in red shoes.

Ashamed to go out—the bride whose husband has just complimented her for having such extraordinarily large feet.

Fear of being discovered—the woman who lightly touches a man's foot with her own to communicate love feelings.

Never averse—to wearing someone else's old shoes. The country bumpkin is never averse to choosing a wife with big feet so she can help with the work.

Slow—a girl trying to walk after her feet have first been bound.

Inevitable—the bride trying to force small shoes on her big feet to avoid being criticized by the groom.

Analogies—the small foot which, like silver money, is universally liked. The large foot in a high heel, making a noise like a croaking frog.

To be avoided—tapping one's foot on the ground to keep time with music; lifting one's legs in order to kick a ball.

Slight displeasure—the mother who loves her daughters but still has to bind their feet.

Bothersome—new shoes chewed by a rat.

Sarcasm—damning a large-footed woman with faint praise by saying that her lower extremities are as good looking as those of the natural-footed goddess Kuanyin.

Unhappy—the wearer of new shoes who inadvertently steps in dog faeces.

Can't bear to hear—the cries of a young girl as her feet are bound for the first time.

Wasted childhood—she was not diligent in footbinding as a child and now, because no one wants her large feet, she has to marry a poor man and go through life wearing straw shoes and cheap stockings.

Unbearable—painful corns; smelling the awful odor when the binding is suddenly removed.

Ludicrous—the large-footed woman who criticizes a tiny-footed lady for having bound her feet excessively in order to attract the opposite sex.

Inner thoughts—wondering who left the small footprint by the side of the road.

Befuddled—the big-footed lady who wants white flowers painted on her shoes, since these will accentuate the largeness of her feet.

My mad contemporaries—who adopt the Manchu style of natural feet through fear of footbinding.

False accusation—to revile an ugly woman who, nevertheless, has tiny feet.

Inevitable impoverishment—one who wastes an entire piece of cloth merely to make the sides for a pair of tiny shoes; one who makes great noise on the ground with the heel of her foot.

Inevitable wealth—one whose shoes still display freshly embossed flowers even after the soles have been worn out.[10]

Capable—the woman who makes her own shoes and stockings, producing new and elegant styles.

Improper—washing her feet in the same basin where she has washed her face.

Acting like a servant—putting shoes and stockings away in front of others.

Easy to get—a prostitute's shoes.

Unattractive—the moving buttocks of one with large feet.

Annoying—canceling an appointment because your feet suddenly hurt; about to wash your feet, when a distant guest arrives.

Untrustworthy—you give shoes away as a love token, but the lover displays them as proof of your love and you hear about it from others.

Pitiful—a beauty with large feet.

Difficulties—descending a steep slope in high heels; wearing tiny shoes when you suffer from painful corns.

Too late—to start binding when you're old enough to wed.

Incongruous—secretly pleased at hearing someone refer to you as Madam Large Feet.

Can't stop—anytime during the binding process.

Unendurable—itching between the toes; not being allowed to cry out when the foot is first bound.

Meaningless—to pay a call on a large-footed prostitute.

Disagreeable—stepping on a frog with your embroidered shoes during a heavy rain.

Silent endurance—being criticized by a big-footed peasant mother-in-law because of your slow tiny-footed walk.

Coercion—the servant who has to rub her mistress's foot to make it more comfortable; the prostitute who, though suffering from corns, has to accompany an important guest in roaming about the mountains.

Distressing—to see someone with small feet having to pound with a pestle or thresh the rice.

Can't trust—the women of Suchow and Yangchow who become prostitutes at sixteen, go to Peking and other northern areas, earn money, and return home to marry in their twenties. The literal phrase is "Suchow face, Yangchow feet," implying that they are too beautiful to be trusted. [Suchow women were renowned for facial beauty, Yangchow women for their tiny bound-feet.][11]

Especially pleasant—to marry a woman whom you know through hearsay is a beauty, first remove her veil, and later place her tiny feet in your hands.

Motherly encouragement—to the daughter who complains about having her feet bound.

Speechless—trying to remove a corn but piercing it with a needle instead; losing one's shoes in a crowd; the priest who secretly collects tiny embroidered shoes, only to discover that someone has stolen his collection.

To be discarded—corns; the water in which you wash your feet; the bindings.

> May this red satin shoe, my love,
> Worn only once,
> Resolve your lonely melancholy.
> Place it under your bedcovers,
> Caress it to your heart's desire,
> Enjoy it in my absence.
> When will it rejoin its mate?
> When we are as one.[12]

The bindings were generally discarded, but a Hunanese physician once allegedly used them to cure illnesses, with wondrous effect. If the sickness was brought about by the presence of evil spirits, relief was obtained by wrapping the bindings of young girls around the patient's waist. For the treatment of cholera, the doctor stirred boiling water with the bowed sole from an old shoe of a footbound young girl until the water thickened. The patient then drank the water as a palliative. Fevers were reduced by placing the old shoe of a footbound young girl on the patient's navel. As the shoe heated up, it was replaced by another one, causing the temperature gradually to subside. To restore consciousness, a young girl's tiny feet were washed in boiled water which had slightly cooled. The patient was made to drink this, and immediately came to his senses. The remedy for relieving extremely sore throats consisted of tiny-foot toenails, flat spiders, lamp wick ashes, frankincense, cow bezoar, and elephant tusks, ground together in prescribed amounts. Sufferers from malaria, blurred vision, or dizziness could get immediate relief by smelling the tiny foot, but the cure was ineffective if the foot was either old or lacked the addition of alum.[13]

There were many drinking games during the Yüan and later dynasties in which tiny shoes figured prominently in the overall festivities. This type of drinking probably originated in the Sung and was not done directly from the shoe but from a cup placed in it, sometimes called the Cup of the Golden Lotus. One story was told of a Yüan official who enjoyed removing a prostitute's tiny shoe to drink from it in this way. The official, Yang T'ieh-ai, so infuriated a meticulous friend that the latter left in disgust whenever Yang drank from a shoe, feeling that the habit was extremely unsanitary. Until the early twentieth century, Chinese men might still be excited by the chance to drink out of a wine cup placed in a courtesan's tiny shoe. The Cup of the Golden Lotus habitué revered Yang T'ieh-ai as the patron saint of tiny-shoe inebriation.[14]

We are indebted to Fang Hsün for detailed descriptions of how drinking parties were conducted. At one banquet, pretty prostitutes spurred on the drinking by playing a game in which small fruits and seeds were tossed into a tiny shoe, delighting both winners and losers. The shoe was first passed around from hand to hand and was widely admired. It was compared to a mythical raft which revolved like the moon and was so referred to in play.

The Raft was played according to a fixed set of rules. The prostitute with the prettiest and tiniest feet had both of her shoes removed, A wine cup was placed in one shoe, while the other shoe was placed in a basin. The shoeless prostitute became Recording Secretary. It was her duty to hobble about, basin in hand, before each guest in turn and hold the basin about one and a half feet away. The guests took lotus seeds, red beans, or similar objects from a bamboo box, held them parallel with the basin and tried to throw them into the shoe. The tosses were made by grasping the seeds or beans with the thumb, forefinger, and middle finger. Each person made five tosses and, after all had taken turns, the Secretary prescribed drinking penalties for those who had gotten the fewest throws into the shoe.

The Raft might take as long as four to six hours to complete. There were different names for the ways in which throws got into the shoe. A direct throw into the shoe was called a Passing Star, while five successful throws at one turn were called Five Pearls. The most difficult achievement was to have the seed or bean hit the point of the shoe and then go in. If this happened, it was rewarded the same way as were five good throws. If a throw hit the basin first and then entered the shoe, it was counted twice and called a Flying Star Entering the Moon. It was considered an offense to make a throw outside the basin area or cause the shoe to move or turn over; the offender had to take additional drinks, by order of the Recording Secretary. If a winner had five good tosses but a loser only two, the latter had to take three drinks. But no one had to drink more than five cups at any one time, and this, according to our author, removed the danger of intoxication. "The winner allows the loser to drink as a sign of politeness to him. The game is conducted by gentlemen according to the rules; there is no boisterousness or undue emotional display."

There was another game besides the Raft which featured drinking from a cup placed in a prostitute's shoe. The actual shoe was handed from one participant to another, and as it was received each counted one day until the thirtieth day was reached. Each person had to hold the shoe in a certain position, which differed with the day. The shoe might be held up, down, by the toe or heel, level or raised on high, or even concealed under the table.

This complex way of playing was described in song:

> For the even days, speak in a high voice, but for the odd days in a low voice. On the third day, hold the shoe like a new moon; on

FAMOUS PROSTITUTES OF NEARLY A CENTURY AGO, NOTED FOR FACIAL BEAUTY AS WELL AS TINY FEET

> the eighth day, reverse the shoe like a man facing downwards; on the fifteenth day, point the shoe outwards and on an incline; on the twenty-third day, hold it level; on the last day, turn the glass over, but on the first day turn it up again.

The player who moved the shoe incorrectly according to the specific day represented had to drink as his penalty, and then repeat the procedure correctly. If he were sufficiently intoxicated or simply forgot what had to be done, he probably repeated the error over and over again. These games, usually joined in by relatives and close friends, might last from noon to night. Ladies of leisure in the Republican era might amuse themselves by playing other drinking games in the boudoir, to which men were not invited. A typical penalty for a loser was to have to imitate a dog by crawling about on all fours. A woman who once had to do this caused an uproar by barking at the participants, biting as many tiny feet as she could.[15]

The Lotus Gathering Boat was a dice-throwing drinking game which also made use of tiny shoes. The theme was ancient history, and players represented the beautiful concubine Hsi Shih, the Prince of Wu, his villainous Prime Minister, a eunuch, palace ladies, and the Envoy of the Boat.[16] The Envoy of the Boat, who removed the shoes of the prostitute selected for the role of Hsi Shih, had the pleasure of rubbing her feet in the process. Drinking was determined by throws of the dice and their color, either red or black. Both shoes might be passed around at once, with one to two cups in each. On one call of the dice, the evil Prime Minister had to kneel before the beauty Hsi Shih, take one drink from the wine cup in her hands and four others from the two shoes. Certain dice throws required the participant either to sing or play musical instruments. Those who failed to do so had to take additional drinks. If the prostitute excused herself from the game because of the demands on her time from other quarters, she drank one large cupful as a penalty. The Envoy returned the shoes, which she put on herself, and the game awaited her return. When she reappeared, ten large drinks were ordered for her if she had inexcusably gotten her shoes dirty in the interim.

There was still another drinking game in which the players drank according to special throws of the dice, but the determining factors were social occupation and personal inclination or idiosyncrasy. For example, if a certain number was thrown the following persons had to drink:

> One whose concubine had just given birth to a son; one who bragged about his drinking capacity; a new official; a spendthrift; a metal carver; a literatus; the person with the most servants; a profligate; one with a flower, tree, or number in his surname or given name; an owner of attractive servants, handsome youths, or wondrous prostitutes; one praised by his wives and concubines.

Another number:

> A man with new shoes and socks; one who liked to adorn himself; one whose name in characters contained the grass or water elements.

Another number:

> An antiquarian; an accountant; one suffering from hernia; an owner of gold or jade; one with the five metals in his name.

Another number:

> A local gossip; a friend of prominent officials; a good fighter and rider; those whose surnames were the same as the twenty-eight ancient heroes [twenty-eight generals who distinguished themselves militarily in the restoration of the Later Han dynasty].

Another number:

> One who had a handsome male servant [a probable reference to pederasty]; one in mourning for a deceased wife; one

who owned singers and actresses; one who had thrown out a concubine.

Another number:

One whose wives and concubines were frequently pregnant; one whose cheeks got red from drinking; a bald man; one with protruding teeth; one whose prostitute was then menstruating.

Another number:

An expert in determining auspicious grave and building sites; one adept in bedroom techniques; a drunk; a henpecked husband; a large landholder; an intimate of the imperial family.

The last number:

A matchmaker; a nearsighted person; one with a scarred face; a private tutor; one about to take a concubine; an aging egotist.

The last drinking game mentioned by Fang Hsün was played on a surface resembling a checkerboard but having 216 squares. The board could be made of paper, but the finest ones were of bamboo and sandalwood. A woman was entrusted with moving about a tiny shoe on the surface of the board; to do this, she sometimes actually sat on the table which supported the game. The dice represented the ancient southern warring kingdoms of Wu and Yüeh, which had fought lengthy wars against one another prior to the unification of China in 221 B.C. The object was for one side to vanquish the other. Participants had to drink while trying to accomplish this, with the number of drinks depending on tosses of the dice. The maximum number of drinks taken at any one time was ten, propriety was observed, and the losing side was given a toast by the victors.

Fang Hsün lived in an era in which the social custom of footbinding was virtually unquestioned. But as China approached the modern age, voices of protest began to be increasingly heard.

The male enthusiast was placed more and more on the defensive, and by the twentieth century he was forced to rationalize why footbinding flourished in civilized Chinese society. The apologist of the thirties admitted that the custom was in its last stages and that there would be no place for it in China's future. He conceded that it was lewd and cruel to advocate footbinding, but asserted that it was dictatorial and oppressive to prohibit it. Its decline was regarded as a reflection of a changing aesthetic view unrelated to progress or barbarism.

While the Manchus legislated against binding, some of their leaders privately conceded the superior merits of the tiny foot. The renowned statesman Li Hung-chang, for example, once covered his mother's feet with his sleeves in audience with a subordinate because he was ashamed of their largeness. To the critic who commented on the loss of natural beauty caused by footbinding, the apologist brought out the fact that hair-dos, eyebrow plucking, and confining of the breasts were all violations of the natural order. "Permanents and plucked eyebrows were imported from abroad. If China were now the greatest power in the world, wouldn't every foreign women today be studying footbinding?"

The rationale behind the practice was woman's desire to please. By changing the shape of the foot, it was argued, an interest in the bizarre was added with which to attract men. The binding served as a sort of matchmaker intended to increase male desire, and the flesh which it concealed remained a mystery. The woman of imperial China was taught to esteem chastity, and the golden lotus was regarded as an exclusive possession of her husband. Even close relatives avoided the woman's tiny feet; their being rubbed by a man was regarded as an act of ultimate intimacy. If one other than her husband rubbed the foot or stole her shoes, the properly-reared woman felt extreme embarrassment and shame.

Not allowing binding in childhood was advocated as the humane way to eliminate it. The coercion of grown women led to such unhappiness and bitterness that the means in effect defeated the end. Moderation was proposed so that binding would die out naturally and without causing undue social upset. Women were willing to endure all sorts of physical suffering to be considered beautiful, and the hypothesis was set forth that they and not men were responsible for the origination of binding.

> Later Ruler Li did not have his concubine start this, but she did it herself and endured the pain to excite the sovereign's interest. How could she have known that this would influence countless numbers of posterity? . . . The one to blame is not Ruler Li but the concubine. He probably only said that he approved in order to compensate her for the suffering she had gone through in order to please him. Even the concubine was guiltless, for she did not purposely encourage others to imitate her.

The writer concluded that footbinding had nothing to do with imperialism, feudalism, private and public possession, or economic dependence, but was a manifestation of the difference in man and woman. Since it was instinctive for women to use adornments to win the male, binding served this instinct. By destroying a part of their bodies women caused men to love this part even more, to the point of madness. The way it rose and declined was predictable: "The poor copy the rich; the rich copy the courtesans." With both courtesans and the well-to-do favoring natural feet, it was only a matter of time before the masses would follow their lead; the end of footbinding was inevitable. "Why disturb the peace and interfere? If we say that binding must be eradicated because foreigners ridicule us for doing this, it must be admitted that they ridicule us for other reasons as well."

The tendency of contemporaries to divorce tiny-footed wives was deplored as a barbaric act, out of keeping with a civilized and compassionate society. For how could a person cruel enough to cast aside his wife because she was old fashioned talk about improving the nation and the general welfare?

MISS YANG TSIUI-HSI, RENOWNED IN THE TIENTSIN AREA FOR HER LOVELY FACE AND TINY FEET, PICTURED AT THE HEIGHT OF HER BEAUTY

> I have heard of highly educated, modern young girls who tempt their lovers to divorce bound-foot wives so that they can take their places. This conduct is both inconsiderate to their own species and thoughtless. Because one should realize that the man who is irresponsible to his first wife will act the same way towards his second one. A girl cannot always be fashionable; how can she fail to think of the day when she is out of fashion and must give way to a more modern successor?[17]

The sexual attraction of footbinding was noted by the occasional Western observer. In 1928, a German scholar named H. Laderland wrote that the fundamental meaning of this injurious practice was the arousing of male lust. With the feet bound to an excessively small degree, he went on to say, the section from knee to ankle became stunted in growth; as a consequence, when walking weight had to be placed on the thighs and hips. And as the woman walked, the outer folds of the vagina rubbed against one another. Laderland stated that a footbound woman could press her hips together forcefully during sexual intercourse and therefore had greater sexual desire than the natural-footed. His thesis supported the assertion that the tiny-footed woman was eagerly sought after as a bedmate because she gave the same sensation to the male as a virgin (due to the pressure which she was able to bring to bear upon the male member).[18] The French doctor Matignon, writing on the subject about thirty years before Laderland, dismissed as groundless the hypothesis that deformity of the foot led to further development of the thighs and the Mount of Venus. But the fact which particularly interested him was the way in which the foot sensually excited the Chinese male. He had seen many pornographic drawings in which the male was voluptuously manipulating the woman's foot, and he felt that the foot in the hands of a Celestial affected him as much as the caressing of young and firm breasts did the European. The Chinese gentlemen whom he questioned were unanimous in their praise: "Oh! The small foot! You Europeans can't understand how exquisite, agreeable, and exciting it is!" Matignon mentioned that during his stay in China (about 1895), he often heard about Chinese Christians who had admitted during confession to having thought evilly about a woman's foot. The caressing of the foot by the woman to stimulate the male was also mentioned in a modern Chinese short story, which described how a man, who was forced into an arranged marriage by his parents, was seduced by his spouse when she took his feet, held them close to her warm breasts, and started to rub them with her hands. This gave him a feeling of such tenderness and warmth that his repugnance toward his arranged bride was overcome and he had relations with her for the first time. Tanizaki's short novel about sexual passion, *The Key*, describes in some detail attractions felt by a Japanese man who desired ardently to lavish caresses upon his wife's feet.[19]

An American lotus lover who had lived in China for twenty years always elected tiny-footed prostitutes for his pleasure. As the custom dwindled and approached extinction in the thirties, the American would sigh and complain to his Chinese friends that it was inconceivable for vast China to be utterly devoid of tiny-foot areas. Upon being queried, he confided that footbinding's wondrousness was "in the wondrous place," leading the commentator to conclude:

> It used to be said that Westerners detested tiny feet,
> And yet today a Westerner adores them. . . .[20]

It may have been a young monk turned profligate who left behind a treatise on how to manipulate the tiny foot as an aid to love-making. The story was told of a southern monk named Ti-ming,[21] who lived in a temple along the lower reaches of the Pearl River. He was attractive in appearance and a persuasive speaker. A youth with whom Ti Ming had had homosexual relations once told him about the pleasures to be derived from tiny-footed maidens, saying that they were kinder to men than the Buddha. Ti Ming invited a young lady to the temple and, as the story goes, grasped her feet, feeling that their warmth and softness were unforgettable and unique. The fragrant foot aroma fascinated him, and he felt that she was an immortal to whom he could entrust his life. The woman proved adept in love-making and, while he put her tiny toes in his mouth, she placed his jadestick in hers. They did not arise until noon of the following day. Ti Ming built special rooms within the temple and had them elegantly furnished. He consumed aphrodysiacs and had relations with seven or eight women a night. Rubbing the tiny foot helped him forget fatigue and prepared him for the next encounter. Ti Ming claimed that the tiny foot was the best aphrodysiac of all. He made love at all hours and seasons, and in spare time recorded his experiences. He was finally poisoned by a gentleman who resented his having seduced several concubines. By this time, Ti Ming had had relations with over a hundred women, with as many as ten in bed at once, wearing different colored shoes. Ti Ming's favorite before he died was a tiny-footed woman named Hsü. She attended him in his dying days and inherited his writings. His parting words were that the visual attraction of tiny feet was minor when compared with its emotional appeal. Miss Hsü instructed ten prostitutes in the sexual advantages of the tiny foot, using Ti Ming's writing as a manual to be understood thoroughly and memorized. The course was completed in three months, after which brothel training commenced. A few years later, the trainees were all intimate favorites of the influential and wealthy.[22]

A Chinese editor asked if readers might supply him with a certain book in vogue at the start of the Republic, which described in detail ways in which tiny feet could be manipulated during the sex act. Variations in technique depended on the size of the male member. This corroborates one statement by the monk that prostitutes studied a special training manual for the tiny-footed.[23]

A manual for men instructed one how to correctly hold the lotus. Massaging, squeezing, and caressing were left to individual preference and specific circumstance. Here are some of the orthodox techniques of grasping the narrow three-inch handful:

Normal hold—with her right lotus in your left hand, or her left lotus in your right hand, have the point of the lotus face upwards. Tightly grasp the side of the lotus in your palms, press

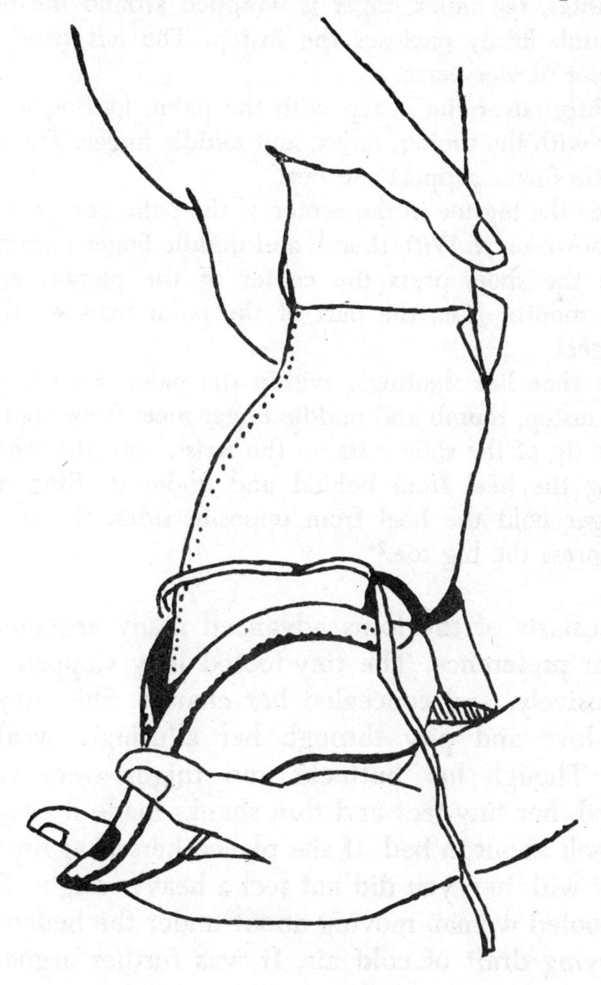

the thumb and forefinger on the toes, and jointly cover the instep with the other fingers.

Reverse hold—press with your palm and four fingers on the tip of the lotus and the instep, with your thumb across and under the center of the plantar. Grip tightly, and twist your wrist around so that it faces outwards.

Tightly hold the tip of the shoe between the lower palm, ring finger, and little finger. The middle finger presses the center of the plantar, the index finger is wrapped around the heel, while the thumb firmly encloses the instep. The left hand grips the right foot or vice-versa.

Tightly cover the instep with the palm, locking it under the plantar with the thumb, index, and middle finger. The ring finger and little finger support the heel.

Place the big toe in the center of the palm and press the little finger down on it. With thumb and middle finger forming a circle around the shoe, press the center of the plantar against the "tiger's mouth" [i.e., the part of the palm between thumb and forefinger].

The shoe lies slantingly within the palm. Four fingers press on the instep; thumb and middle finger meet from opposite sides.

The tip of the shoe rests on the wrist, with the middle finger hooking the heel from behind and under it. Ring finger and forefinger hold the heel from opposite sides, thumb and little finger press the big toe.[24]

Enthusiasts of the lotus advanced many arguments to support their preference. The tiny-footed lady stepped lightly and apprehensively, and concealed her charms. She aroused a mixture of love and pity through her alluringly weak feminine posture. Though her buttocks and thighs were voluptuously developed, her tiny feet and thin shanks made it easy for her to turn herself about in bed. If she placed herself against you when you slept with her, you did not feel a heavy weight. By contrast, a large-footed woman moving about under the bedcovers caused an annoying draft of cold air. It was further argued that tiny shoes were the only attractive part of otherwise drab village dress, that tiny feet were much more economical than large ones, since shoes could be made for them from only a remnant of dress material. The tiny foot had the beauty of the entire body: it was glistening and white like the skin, arched like the eyebrows, pointed like jade fingers, rounded like the breasts, small like the mouth, red (with shoes worn) like the lips, and mysterious like the private parts. Its odor was superior to that from armpits, legs, or glands, and it also had a seductive power. "When I loved a woman, I went all the way and wished that I could swallow her up. But only the tiny feet could be placed in the mouth." [25]

Rubbing a woman's foot stimulated and aroused her. One lotus admirer who frequented houses of prostitution requested that the tiny-footed remove stockings and bindings and reveal the bare flesh, but this request was consistently refused. The excuse varied with the season; in winter it was because of the cold, in summer because the woman was used to wearing foot apparel. He became an intimate friend of one prostitute who, after considerable hesitation, confided that play with the foot increased sexual desire. Rubbing the arch of the bared tiny foot deepened feeling and enhanced the sexual act. But prostitutes avoided this because they did not wish to become overly stimulated during the course of their daily work. He finally persuaded his confidant to remove her bindings.

> A white lotus root revealed itself before his eyes. The five toes were distinct, rouge-like red in color. The size was just right, as was the degree of plumpness and whiteness. He closed his eyes and rubbed; it was like a ball of white jade. . . .

Another prostitute insisted that customers rub her tiny feet vigorously. The more amorous she felt, the harder she wanted the feet rubbed. The mere scratching of her plantar caused a vaginal flow. A woman living with her lover in Peking in 1927 told him that when sexually excited, she wished only to have her tiny feet tightly grasped. Otherwise, she felt frustrated. She also derived pleasure from rubbing her own feet when washing them or changing socks. She became most excited if her feet were grasped during the climax of intercourse, saying they were useless if not pressed vigorously by a man five or six times daily. She felt that the firmness of a man's grasp was proof of his feelings towards her.[26]

The euphonious terms used to describe the foot, the shoe, and its appurtenances were many and varied. There was one popular saying that the Golden Lotus was three inches or less, the Silver Lotus four inches, and the Iron Lotus longer than

that. The carmine of Carmine Water-Chestnut and Carmine Lotus referred to the color of the shoe, water-chestnut and lotus to its shape. Phoenix Head implied that the tip of the foot was small and pointed like the head of a bird. New Moon depicted the elegant, slender, and pointed bound foot enclosed in silk stockings. Jade Bamboo-Shoots honored the tiny foot which was as warm, glossy, and soft as jade, with its sharp tip likened to a bamboo shoot. Twin Bows referred to the tiny feet successfully formed like the ancient bows used in archery. The bowed shape was also called a hook, and this was the derivation of the terms Lotus Hooks and Fragrant Hooks. Twin Wild Ducks applied to natural as well as bound feet; like ducks traveling in pairs, the feet were always together. Tiny feet might also be called Dumplings, because of their shape, or Red Cocoons, because the same sort of tireless energy had to be spent on tight binding that the silkworm devoted to spinning its silk to form the cocoon.[27]

The use of art names by courtesans and prostitutes was a Chinese custom spanning two millennia. One enthusiast listed the names of tiny-footed prostitute acquaintances in Peking, with addresses, for fellow lovers of the lotus. The commonest names were Moon Immortal, Phoenix Immortal, Red Treasure, and Golden Bell. Golden Bell referred to the bell concealed in the shoe which tinkled as the woman walked. Gold formed the most popular first half of the name and was used in Golden Bell, Golden Phoenix, Golden Pearl, Golden Treasure, Golden Flower, and Golden Jade. Jade was next in popularity (Jade Youth, Jade Treasure, Jade Vase, Jade Phoenix, and Jade Pavilion). Treasure was the most common second character (Golden Treasure, Jade Treasure, Kingfisher Treasure, and Red Treasure).[28]

The prostitutes who were available to all comers were most prone to sexual license in which the tiny foot played a major role. But for women of respectable upbringing, concealment of the foot was a canon of behavior rarely violated. This outlook was a product of moral training and the inner conviction that the weird shape was unaesthetic. Unavailability served to increase the craving of the lotus lover. "Things hard to get are comforting to acquire, like eating when you are starved." Proper women kept their feet a secret, and they were mortified if ever touched or played with by the vulgar or rustic. This was particularly true in the north, where women remained in concealment and were apprehensive about going out alone. There was one account of a young girl who was so mortified at having her feet rubbed by a stranger, who had crawled through to her in a crowd, that she took to her deathbed. A popular form of entertainment in the villages was the evening play. Women enjoyed going to these plays, but the more prudent sewed socks and shoes together to prevent theft. There were still admirers who stole the shoes by cutting the threads. One young girl reputedly lost her shoes while absorbed in watching a play, and she was

SHANGHAI PROSTITUTES, ABOUT 1915

forced to swallow poison by an enraged and humiliated mother. In general, girls of modest means tried to catch the shoe thief and make their annoyance known, but upper-class families hushed things up and merely ordered a servant to bring another pair of shoes. The accounts about shoe purloining which follow indicate male sexual aberration.

WHITE DEW IMMERSING THE RED CHESTNUT

There was an old woman who had only one daughter, famed for her beauty. The girl drew shoe patterns for neighbors and showed them how to embroider flowers on the shoes. She had tiny bowed feet and walked with elegance. She was admired for a long time by several shiftless youths, who found her bowed shoes most lovable. But they had no chance to touch her feet, as she was zealously guarded by the widow. One day she attended a village play with a few girl friends. It was a dark night in winter, and the weather was so cold that her lower limbs became numbed. When the play ended, she discovered the loss of one shoe. She had to endure the pain of walking home leaning on walls for support. She said nothing to her mother and went to sleep beside her. Suddenly, something was thrown through the paper window in the bedroom. The widow awoke in fright and noticed the object, her daughter's missing shoe. It had been lewdly saturated with semen. The girl wept with shame, but the understanding mother comforted her without a word of scolding. Culprits spread the news around until it became public gossip.

THE RED CHESTNUT SOAKED BY WHITE JUICE

There were a certain male actor and an actress in a Tientsin troupe. The actor admired the actress for her tiny and beautiful feet and wanted to become intimate with her, but he was rejected. He therefore stole her shoes, discharged semen into them, and put them back in their original place. The actress discovered this only when she was about to go on the stage and was extremely embarrassed and annoyed, but she had to maintain silence. The actors circulated the story, and it was published in several newspapers.[29]

Ku Hung-ming, a conservative Chinese writer and intellectual, was the leader of a post-revolutionary hard core of opposition to the elimination of footbinding. Ku felt that the tiny foot was an integral part of Chinese culture and that its advantages outweighed other considerations. He once noticed a young lady who to him appeared about twenty years old. Discovering that she was thirty-two, he remarked that preservation of youthfulness was characteristic of the pre-Republic woman. Because she had bound feet and spent her days secluded in the bedroom, he explained, she was not exposed to the sun and wind. In this way, she kept her youth and facial beauty. Ku asserted that the modern woman, with her daily tennis playing, aged prematurely and looked old before thirty. He contrasted the European practice of confining a woman's waist with the Chinese one of footbinding, stating that a woman's gracefulness resulted from the way in which her figure impressed the observer. Foreign women emphasized small waists to make their hips protrude and accentuate the beauty of their curves. But pressure on the waist injured the internal organs. Footbinding, however, did not interfere with well-being, but naturally broadened a woman's hips and enhanced her femininity. Rather than imitate Westerners and tamper with the waist, a region which contained the source of future generations, Ku asserted that it was much better to bind the feet instead.[30]

Ku was representative of the educated Chinese who, in spite of having lived abroad, never wavered in preference for tiny feet. There was a diplomat named Sun Mu-han,[31] for instance, with tiny-footed concubines. Sun was assigned to Russia; he transported a trunk filled with their shoes and privately amused himself with them. He traveled without dependents and took along only two tiny-footed maid servants. Most of Ku Hung-ming's concubines had tiny feet. He was an ardent advocate and would tell people that footbinding was one of China's national treasures. When he met a woman socially, he would first look at her feet and then her face. Before going to sleep, he had his bed partner change into bright red sleeping shoes. One of his conversations on the subject was recorded in the Shanghai press:

> The smaller the woman's foot, the more wondrous become the folds of the vagina. [There was the saying: the smaller the feet, the more intense the sex urge.] Therefore, marriages in Ta-t'ung [where binding is most effective] often take place earlier than elsewhere. Women in other districts can produce these folds artificially, but the only way is by footbinding, which concentrates development in this one place. There consequently develop layer after layer [of folds within the vagina]; those who have personally experienced this [in sexual intercourse] feel a supernatural exaltation. So the system of footbinding was not really oppressive.[32]

Ku also asserted that binding caused the blood to flow upwards and produced more voluptuous buttocks and that women wore high heels for the same reason. Chang Ching-sheng supported Ku's theories, saying that footbinding had its wondrousness. The difficulty of walking caused strength to be concentrated in the buttocks, which became larger. The vagina also became developed, Dr. Chang remarked, so ". . . . from the viewpoint of sex, footbinding was very profitable."[33] It was also believed that tiny feet not only made the buttocks more sensual, but concentrated life-giving vapors on the upper part of the body, making the face more attractive.[34]

Rubbing, smelling, chewing, licking, and washing the feet were popular pastimes of lotus lovers, varying according to individual preference. There were stories circulated about an official who forced his concubines to let him use their plantars as human ashtrays, while another insisted on immersing a tiny-footed concubine's foot in a basin of tea, which he then drank as a nightcap.[35] Love-intoxicated tiny-foot admirers might put the feet in their hands, on their shoulders, or hold them up to their nostrils. This partly explains why women were so particular about decorating shoes and stockings, filling the inside of the shoe with fragrance. Love under the bedcovers partially consisted of caressing the toe portion with lips and tongue and the heel with tongue and teeth. Sleeping shoes might become covered with tooth marks. At a moment of high passion, the dirt of the shoe was forgotten. But when that moment passed, the lover might feel that the shoe was tasteless and the smell of alum repugnant.[36]

A Nanking official who had a concubine with slender lotus hooks personally washed her feet nightly. He told his friends: "You gentlemen know how much time I spend in washing Little White's feet, but you don't know how often I bend down to smell them. I alternate between washing and smelling, sometimes taking as long as forty-five minutes; and I don't let the servant re-enter until the water is cold." When asked about the flavor of the foot, he replied that it was "the greatest flavor of mankind, beyond sweet and sour, un-nameable."[37] Another official liked to visit prostitutes early in the morning, remove their bindings, and smell the bare feet. This was one of his chief pleasures. Ku Hung-ming shared this craving, and in old age stated that only the tiny foot which could be inserted halfway up the nostrils could be considered beautiful. Some men were offended by an odoriferous foot, but others craved the odor of the flesh or the perspiration. Licking the foot during washing was once called, "Eating Steamed Dumplings in Pure Water."

> Every night I smell her feet, placing the tip of my nose in the deepest recesses of her plantar. I am extremely excited by the smell, which is like no identifiable aroma of perfume. I only regret that I cannot swallow down the white chestnut with one mouthful. But I can still place it in my mouth and chew the plantar. Much of it has already been "swallowed"; the use of my tongue is, naturally, subsidiary.[38]

A writer revealed that the plantar and tiny toes of his beloved were the most sensitive parts of her body. Because she was more responsive barefooted than when wearing shoes, rubbing the shoe required greater effort on his part. First he held the tip of the shoe in one hand, and rubbed heel, arch, and sole with the other. Then he inserted one finger inside the shoe and rubbed with it. Finally he massaged the whole shoe area vigorously and methodically. He not only rubbed the bare foot, but smelled, licked, and sucked it. He first rubbed the flesh near the tiny toes, then the arch, big toe, heel, and area under the heel. Both greatly enjoyed his playing between the toes and his rubbing the toes one after the other. One man of wealth never had relations with a prostitute, but insisted instead on smelling the foot and removing dirt between the toes and in the plantar with his fingernails. He was careful to remove every speck, made a tablet out of it with his hands, and swallowed it as if it were a delicious tidbit. There were others like him who lost interest if the foot were either cleansed or perfumed.[39]

The odoriferous foot may have substituted for smelling salts in helping one to revive. There was an early-twentieth-century newspaper report about a man in Ch'ang-ch'un who suffered from epileptic fits. Whenever he was about to lose consciousness, his wife restored him to normal by hurriedly removing the bindings and placing her bare feet over his face. This technique always succeeded. He was once in town, felt convulsions coming on, and staved off insensibility by having a prostitute in the street remove her bindings and let him smell the bared flesh.[40]

One woman delighted in urging her feminine boudoir companions to use their tiny feet in place of the male member, and was not satisfied unless she changed partners seven or eight times in the course of the evening. There were also women who liked to fondle the male member with their tiny feet. When intoxicated, they would remove the bindings, place the organ between their feet, and rub it back and forth until the aroused male scattered his sperm about in profusion. This delighted the woman. One commentator believed that the sole of the foot may have been so extremely ticklish that this rubbing sensation gave it relief. "Touching of the genital organs by the tiny feet provokes in the male thrills of an indescribable voluptuousness. And the great lovers know that in order to awaken the ardor, far too cold, of their old clients, to take the rod between their two feet is worth more than all the aphrodysiacs of the Chinese pharmacopeia and kitchen. . . ."[41]

Footbinding also appealed to the male whose main interest in sexual relations was to inflict punishment on the woman. A love of woman reduced to a piteous state was a perversity, like the chewing of flesh, burning it, or beating someone with a whip. A stepmother or aunt in binding the child's foot was usually much harsher than the natural mother would have been. An old man was described who delighted in seeing his daughters weep as the binding was tightly applied. In an age of male dominance, the master of a household of concubines could give unlimited rein to sadistic impulse. In one household, everyone had to bind. The main wife and concubines bound to the smallest degree, once morning and evening, and once before retiring. The husband and first wife strictly carried out foot inspections and whipped those guilty of having let the binding become loose. The sleeping shoes were so painfully small that the women had to ask the master to rub them in order to bring relief. Another rich man would flog his concubines on their tiny feet, one after another, until the blood flowed.

One writer stated that he was in a bandit area in east Kiangsi, about 1931, where bound-foot women unable to flee had been taken captive. The bandits, angered because of their captives' weak way of walking and inability to keep in file, forced the women to remove bindings and socks and run about barefoot. They cried out in pain and were unable to move on in spite of beatings. Each of the bandits grabbed a woman and forced her to dance about on a wide field covered with sharp rocks. The flesh was broken open, and the field was stained with their blood. Although the women requested death in preference, the bandits sang, danced, and refused to let up in the slightest. The harshest treatment was meted out to prostitutes. Nails were driven through their hands and feet; they cried aloud for several days before expiring. One form of torture was to tie up a woman so that her legs dangled in mid-air and place bricks around each toe, increasing the weight until the toes straightened out and eventually dropped off. One woman lost two toes in this way before her relatives finally ransomed her life with gold. In 1900, Russian troops were accused of committing atrocities against women in areas which they crossed along the Pei-ning Railroad. They violated women and then strung the tiny shoes around their necks as a source of amusement. Villages near the Yellow River region during chaotic civil conditions in 1933 suffered far worse atrocities. Tiny-footed women had their bindings forcibly removed; some were stripped naked and used as human tables of flesh on which mahjong was played and wine was drunk.[42]

The rationale in favor of footbinding survived the centuries and is still echoed occasionally today by the older male generation. Chinese college professors and intellectuals of note on Taiwan informed me in 1961 that Ta-t'ung ladies during the bound-foot era had layer upon layer of fleshy folds within the vagina, and cited a saying about "gates and doors, one after another."[43] Footbinding survived countless centuries in China and was toppled only by revolution; it had snob appeal as a mark of gentility and evoked an instant sexual response during an age in which women were spiritually as well as physically bound, regarded mainly as male possessions and playthings. As scholars have pointed out, the claim of influence on the sexual organs was scientifically invalid,[44] but nevertheless Chinese men believed in and spread stories from one generation to the next about the delights of caressing the bound foot and its wondrous effects on the feminine form; this was instrumental in ensuring its perpetuity.

CHAPTER FIVE

Wondrousness of the Lotus

This essay by a writer from Nanking discusses the way in which the tiny foot added interest to sexual relations. Our apologist counters the arguments of natural-foot advocates and never questions the superior beauty of the three-inch standard.

Like writing about brush and ink, that which is wondrous is unexplainable, for it arises from our sense impressions. The lotus-loving scholar has been a phenomenon for more than a thousand years. While sexual intercourse represents the extreme of bedroom delight, it is rather vulgar simply to lie down and enter battle in naked embrace. How many times a day can this be done without getting fatigued? One is at a loss for what to do the rest of the time and feels an isolation in the midst of Warm-Soft Village. And there is no describable sweetness in what has occurred.

Now, before and after the act, one must extend warm affection, imitate intertwined roots, and make many sensual sounds together. Later heart and spirit become so oblivious to the mundane and so immersed that the pleasures of intercourse are multiplied and limitless enjoyment known, apart from the act itself. The husband's spiritual expression consists of his smiling facial appearance; physically, he kisses his wife's cheeks and hand-manipulates her breasts. Love feelings thus transcend the norm, and desire becomes intensified until intercourse itself becomes a sign that an irrepressible peak of passion has been reached. Even the delights of gods and immortals fail to surpass this.

This is the order of the sexual life, common to mankind. Our race shares in it and yet has added a point of dissimilarity, the three-inch golden lotus, which affords endless pleasure. The achievement of the golden lotus, difficult to attain, is to be treasured. People are afraid to imitate it because of the difficulties of production. Left out in a corner, they have to seek another path to beauty, so they change their views and reject it. The ancients who rejected it, like the Taoists, advocated simple dress and austere living, appealing to morals rather than to the senses. Today's advocates of human rights favor a similar "style of dress." They obviously want to eliminate seductive and misleading postures of either sex towards the other; however, the feasibility of their doctrine has already caused doubts.

Their theories give rise to a natural aesthetic contradiction. There are two reasons for beauty being conceptualized as such, one its being rarely seen, the other the difficulty of obtaining it. For example, a piece of flawless jade by its very nature is rarely seen, and it is carved into a sceptre by a skill which is difficult to obtain. Today, footbinding is Heaven-sent and then adorned, like beauty added to beauty. There is nothing laughable about it. Those who reject it know this and change their tone, saying: "It makes a plaything of woman." They look austere and grave, like advocates of human rights.

In actuality, the ancients restricted their playing to the deepest recesses of the inner apartments. Modern couples leave home arm in arm and amuse themselves in villages and large cities, by famous mountains and rivers, amidst gatherings of hordes of people. They have beautiful slogans—sowing the seeds of women's rights, equality of the sexes, etc. Women ignorantly fall into the snare and come to hate intensely the fact that they are playthings. Now men definitely shouldn't regard women as playthings, and vice versa. But when exchanging pleasures, they must play with one another. After they undress and touch and move as sexual desire dictates, they throw off all restraints of propriety. Things which they ordinarily couldn't bear to do physically are then done to a degree which seems beyond human indulgence. Many great scholars corroborate this.

So the word "play" cannot be obliterated with a mere brush stroke. There were educated ancient women who not only didn't oppose the male view in books written about sensual pleasures, but followed it. Women restrained by the teachings of propriety had to accept masculine ideas as their source of enjoyment. But women are now largely emancipated. If treated improperly, they demand apologies and submission from the opposite sex. Still, if man today regards something as beautiful, women willingly waste time and money or destroy hair and skin so that each can find joy, without calling this "play." Many worldly pleasures come from other people. In eating and living together, one may deprive oneself to see that one's mate is amply provided for. In achievement and scholarship, there is also this factor of deriving satisfaction from pleasing others. When exchanging pleasurable sensations, the woman is stirred by the man's greed for love, while he is stirred by her alluring, seductive postures.

At this moment, the woman fears only one thing—that he won't play with her! How can she feel annoyance because he regards her as a plaything? The three-inch golden lotus represents an additional plaything, extremely well liked by the man. The woman wants it to be perfect, and endures endless pain to achieve it. Though we say that it is something for the man to play with, she actually relies on it in order to be able to play with the man.

To consider bound-foot women as playthings is really silly, for viewed historically all women are playthings, not merely the footbound ones. Each part of a man's or woman's body secretly serves to spur on sexual desire. The delight of kissing is not equal to that of rubbing the breasts, as kissing is common to both and can be seen. The breasts are sometimes concealed, sometimes seen, and differ in size for each. Rubbing the breasts is not equal to playing with the sex organs, which differ in shape for each sex. The organs are usually concealed and not easily seen, and so unusual thoughts can be imagined about them. At one viewing, sexual desire becomes stimulated and intense, and a wish for direct contact arises. For every race of mankind enjoying sensual pleasures, the dissimilarity is the same. But since our race has the added wonder of being able to play with the Golden Lotus, the order of preludes to the sex act is increased and desire blazes up that much more intensely.

The pleasure of grasping the golden lotus is not inferior to that of sexual intercourse; in other words, one aids the other. The woman's tiny foot is probably more mysterious than her private parts. The man lusts to see her privates; though difficult to see, they are often exposed in young girls. If one has wives and concubines, their sexual organs can be sought out and

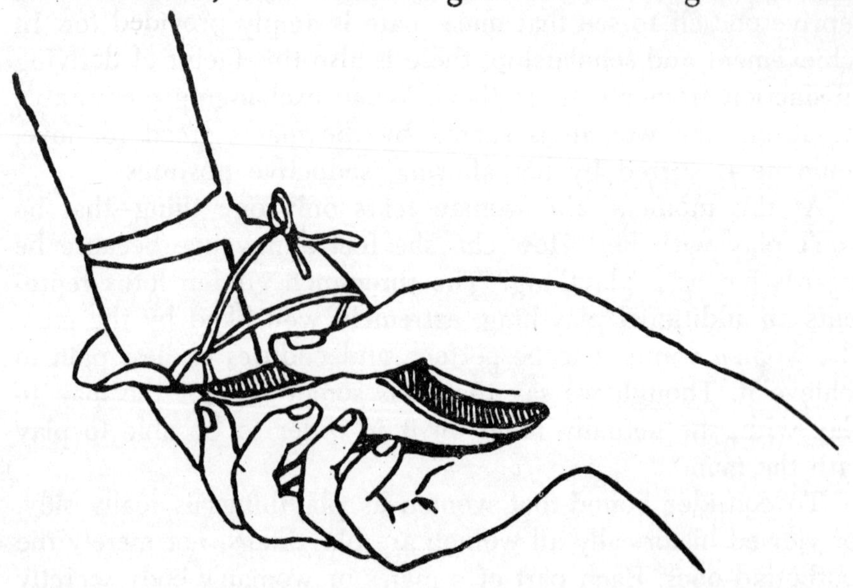

rubbed at all times. But once binding starts, even the young girl must keep the foot concealed. She is as apprehensive about this as if it were an untransgressable and divine law ordained by the Holy Sages. With the possible exception of having intercourse with her husband, she is never willing to let a man remove the binding, inspect the foot, and rub it. So the man looks at the tiny foot with more interest than the natural one, for he wonders how small it really is and how much its flesh has diminished. His curiosity is intensely aroused; if one day he can really see it, his mad, intoxicated joy knows no bounds.[1]

One rub was therefore enough to excite. The foot, moreover, was at the end of the lowest extremity, and after rubbing it one's hand easily extended upward towards the private parts. When playing with the breasts, by way of contrast, special preparation was needed to attain the objective. As to why a woman considered this part of the body most excitable: it was ordinarily concealed and regarded most sedately, even hidden from a servant's view except possibly when binding. And then one day, rubbed and played with in a man's hands, the sexual effect was like an electrical charge between them. While the world commonly regards the woman's foot as dirty, it was so favored and liked that it was placed in the palms, lifted to the shoulders, and even kissed and smelled. As a stimulus and comforter, it was unparalleled. These moments of joy compensated the woman sufficiently for the eight to ten years of pain which she had previously suffered. Through the golden lotus, she won the man's complete love and secured unlimited good fortune.

Binding the feet to a small size caused the private parts to become tight and narrow because of the pain which was felt. The buttocks became full and large, and immeasurable wondrousness was added to bodily beauty. Because it was difficult for her to walk long distances, the tiny-footed woman lived an uncomplicated existence in the inner boudoir, with sexual desire developed to a fullness unattainable by the natural-footed woman.

If there were no footbinding, then her foot would merely be the same as the man's. Grasping a natural foot during sex play may excite, but only to the extent that grasping the hand does. It cannot compare to the wondrousness of grasping a golden lotus. Styles in dress change every ten or several tens of years, but the bound foot remained unchanged for a millennium. Its beauty goes without saying, and its wondrousness has become increasingly apparent. It has been unaffected by the importation of European customs and the increased variety of sex play.

Those who reject it often say:

> The tiny foot is very smelly. What is so wonderful about it? Those who crave it are addicted to its odor and are of the lowest and most common class. The fact that famous men like Ku Hung-ming and his followers advocated this was really shameful.

These critics are unaware that the special craving of Ku Hung-ming and the others was similar to the lustful tastes of the ancients. The objective was to inhale its natural aroma. If the foot had no odor, they were unwilling to smell it even if it were tiny. Those who describe this interest state that they became disaffected if the feet were washed. Those who oppose footbinding take the strange cravings of a few and make a sweeping generality to cover everyone. How can we submit to their sarcastic verse?

That the foot has odor comes about not from its being small but from a failure to wash it. Any foot, bound or not, will smell if it is not washed. This includes both sexes. If a man delights in the tiny feet of his wives and concubines, how can they bear to let them smell? They must frequently wash them and change shoes, stockings, and bindings. It is as if one is making up her face and is just as clean. If she is meticulous, she washes the foot in fragrant, heated water and spreads a perfumed powder over it. She extracts the juice of flowers and immerses her toenails in it. The term Fragrant Lotus was no exaggeration. This was a treasure women were proud of, for with it they could get a man's love and protection. When they were about to go to sleep or wake up, or were idly drinking wine, the man might want to unravel the bindings for them. Even a lazy woman had to wash. How could a woman who naturally liked cleanliness and beauty fail to have paid attention to this?

If a natural-footed woman fails to keep her feet clean because they are not objects to be played with, her feet are worse than small feet, which have bindings to cover the odor. The binding was rarely removed, out of fear that the foot might grow larger. The defect of undue perspiration was overcome by wearing sleeping shoes in bed. These not only suppressed odor, but fascinated men with their beautiful embroidery and hidden fragrance of perfume. Men loved to go to bed with women wearing red sleeping shoes. If a natural-footed woman tried to imitate this by wearing high heel leather shoes or flat brocaded shoes in bed, she would only be laughed at. So the woman whose feet smelled was lucky to be small-footed. The fact that certain men

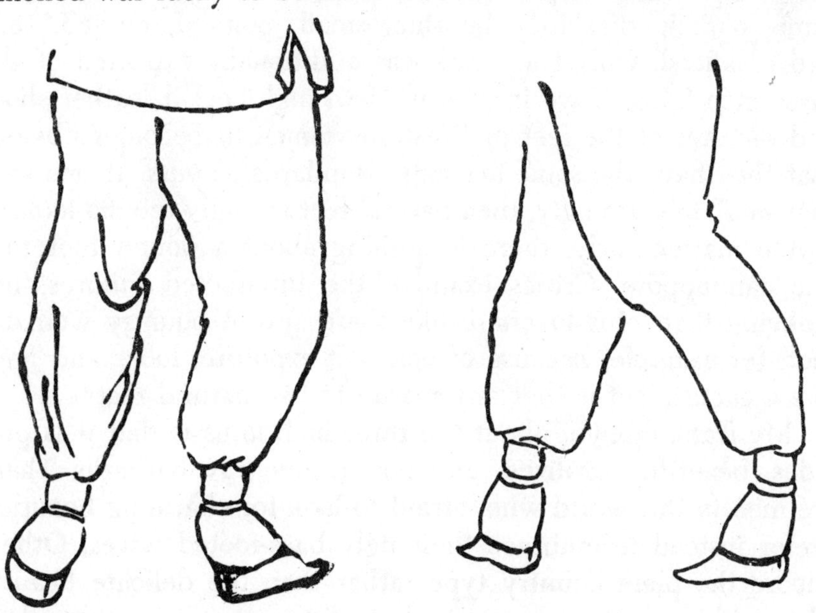

love bound feet does not mean that they are indiscriminate. The tiny and narrow lotus is vastly preferred. Those with the best specimens walked lightly; I always found this to be true. Conversely, poorly bound feet were associated with ugly posture and walking difficulties. For example, the woman who walked on her heels stuck her head forward, raised her shoulders, stiffly shook her breasts, and swung her hips with heavy steps. Women in certain areas of Anhwei, Kwangtung, and Fukien always walked like this. But in cities where footbinding was famed, women walked lightly with toes first touching the ground. How soft their bodies looked! Footbinding opponents often unfairly criticize the worst examples. Besides, the benefit of binding was not in the walk but in the way it increased desire. And desire was a matter for the bed, not the street.

Someone said that small feet were unnatural looking. This was only true of those poorly bound. The best examples not only preserved nature but through artificial means added beauty to it. The standards for praiseworthy tiny and natural feet were the same, namely that they be thin, small, pointed, curved, soft, and balanced. Only fragrance was additionally expected of the three-inch lotus. If we inspect modern high-heeled leather shoes and pictures of the feet of Western women, it becomes obvious that they have the same aesthetic standards as ours. If one says that small feet are ugly, then natural feet are ugly too. So looking at the matter fairly, there is nothing about a bound foot that one can oppose. Critics examine the tiny-footed failures, not realizing that lotus lovers dislike these also. A country woman's foot, for example, because of constant exposure, looks and feels like a cactus. But is that any reason to like natural feet?

My frank opinion about the three-inch lotus is that it is precious, beautiful, civilized, and not in any way barbaric. There are men in this world who, afraid to look for charming beauties, prefer instead to embrace their ugly bare-footed wives. Others choose the plain country type rather than the delicate beauty. They either want to be praised as virtuous or are resigned to their situations. But this doesn't mean that they are insensitive to beauty or fail to realize that what they have is ugly.

My aesthetic and sexual points of view are frank, unlike those whose words never reflect their true thinking. I am getting old and have seen much. Southern lotus; northern lilies; I have tasted them all and know well their charms. Now I often hear the talk of novices, based on pure imagination. To appreciate the wonders of the lotus, one must first understand its beauty.

People like to follow fashion. When bound feet were fashionable, every woman bound her feet and every man esteemed them. Now changing fashions have caused people to change too. But if the medical world can invent a medicine which will reduce the foot in three days and later return it to its original shape, then the golden lotus will become popular again, not only in China but throughout the world.[2]

CHAPTER SIX

Secret Chronicle of the Lotus Interest

The anonymous writer of this essay, who signs himself Lotus Knower, addresses his remarks to lotus-loving gentlemen and describes in detail eighteen positions of sexual intercourse in which the tiny foot is manipulated. While the writer recognizes the inhumanity of footbinding and its incongruity in the modern age, his essay preserves for posterity insights into the sexual attractions of the lotus as a thing-in-itself.

It is human nature to eat and to desire. While sex is universal, its desires cannot be unrestrained nor its pleasures without limitation. The ancients clearly directed that sexual indulgence be limited to bedroom intimacies enjoyed by husband and wife. These bedroom delights were achieved through sexual stimulation by both sexes and were the antithesis of the satisfaction derived by profligates from every chance pursuit and encounter. True lovers of beauty delight without lewd indulgence and do the ordinary things without losing their aesthetic sense.

Human and lower beings devote prolonged study to beautification and sexual amusement. Our country, with the most ancient culture of all, has made especially varied and unique contributions in the fields of food and sex. The search for progress is a tenet of philosophy, as is the search for beauty. Artificial means were devised to make up for sexual deficiencies in natural beauty and enhance the pleasures of the pillow; the footbinding which was practiced for a millennium was but one example.

The third volume of *The Record of Gathering Radishes (Ts'ai-fei-lu)*[1] explained in detail the connections of the lotus with sex. To the refined gentleman of antiquity, these were synonymous terms. The relation of sex to lotus was like that of mouth to taste. Lovers of the lotus penetrated the profoundest mysteries, mysteries which can be recaptured not in words but only through experience. It was the psychological and not the visual effect which really mattered. Oh, Lotus, Lotus! With a three-inch tininess and a bowed hook, you have the seductive power to lead souls astray. You aid stimulation and nocturnal pleasure, representing the acme of mystery and delight. Nothing beyond the lotus can embellish the arts of love, and only one who has tasted of it can describe its flavor. I was born rather late, when the fate of the lotus was on the wane. But my liking for it had already become a craving; looking back, I feel that something was gained from my lifetime of amusement with it. I moved to another area to avoid chaos, living alone and at leisure. There I conjured up the past, recorded what I could remember, and now present it systematically in the form of eighteen explanations. I have written honestly, not preoccupied with literary elegance, and have revealed innermost secrets. My descriptions are unavoidably vivid, and perhaps verge on the indecent. But my thought in compilation was only of the considerable number of lotus-loving gentlemen who still exist. Our comrade in the Lotus Club, planning to edit the fourth volume,[1] requested a manuscript of me, and I had to oblige with whatever I could for the amusement of fellow lotus lovers.

While the lotus is lovable, it heavily injures the limbs and goes counter to humanity. It should vanish. Since that which is rare is precious, I have taken this opportunity in a period of transition to appreciate the vanishing lotus. Perhaps lotus-loving gentlemen will enjoy my narration, which is intended for them and not for outsiders.

I. Wild Duck Alighting on Both Shoulders

Husband and wife find coolness in the garden, in midsummer. The moon shines above the willows; there is silence everywhere, for it is deep night. A refreshing breeze brings cooling relief to the couple. The man takes out a long piece of cloth, and ties its two ends to the branch of a tree, so that it looks like a semi-circle. He has her sit in the center of this contrived swing, her jade arms holding to either side. She swings back and forth, supported by his hands on her thighs, with her "wild ducks" on his shoulders. She wears bowed shoes embroidered and red, slender, pointed, and graceful, causing him to become mentally intoxicated and spiritually lost.

II. Slender and Pointed Bowed Sole

The bedroom furnishings are elegant and refined. On a couch under the window the man lies on his back, head on a pillow, and the woman lies on top of him. She supports herself on her knees, raising her feet so high in the air that he can clearly see the soles of her shoes. Her shoes are slender, pointed, and well curved, like a pair of red water chestnuts. He holds them in his palms appreciatively, and his heart and eyes rejoice.

III. Grasping Twin Bowed Shoes Behind His Back

On a cool day in autumn, desires are intensified. There is a fashionable round table in the room. She sits on the table, while he stands facing her. She encircles his waist with her legs, crossing her ankles together. He grasps her two feet behind him. Clasping her arms around his neck, she raises her head and bites his tongue. Her tiny and lovely red shoes are a mere handful, and her heels rhythmically move back and forth.

IV. Lotus-Petaled Buddhist Devotee

They drink in the bedroom; the wine is green, the lantern red. She becomes slightly intoxicated and enters a state of meditation. The man sits upright, with trousers slightly loosened, while she removes her silken sash. She sits on his lap, cross-legged like a

Buddhist devotee, with her lotus petals curled upwards. He grasps them with both hands. She is intoxicated, tottering like a jade hill about to fall. Her hands are clasped together as in prayer, her eyes are closed, and muttering sounds come forth as he grasps her tiny pointed ones. The depth of the man's emotion goes straight towards her. I dare not speculate whether its flavor is in the realm of fairy immortals or of the Buddha.

V. Lifting the Left One, Holding the Right One

A bed in an orchid boudoir is covered with embroidery. Awakened from a noon nap, she sits up in bed, binding her feet. The man pushes aside the drapes at the entrance, delighted by the sight. He goes to grasp her twin lotuses and, with desire swiftly aroused, has her sit on the edge of the bed. She leans backwards, supported by her hands behind her, and spreads her legs upwards and apart. He stands facing her, puts her right foot on his left shoulder, and grasps her left foot in his right palm. She wears soft-soled embroidered shoes; one foot feels as soft as cotton in his hand, while the other on his shoulder is as tiny as a water chestnut.

VI. Twin Peaks Fixed at the Waist

Having taken a perfumed bath, she washes her feet by the bed. Her jade bamboo shoots are delicate and fine, charming and lovable. He turns around and, delighted, leans on a pillow and enjoys the view. She finishes washing, binds tightly, and changes into silk stockings and new shoes, achieving a wondrous and elegant effect. Moved by her beauty, he urgently embraces her before the bed, and they engage in intercourse by a mirror. In a semi-reclining position on the bed, she spreads her legs and positions her feet at his waist, while he stands and bends forward slightly towards her. He keeps her feet in place by pressing them in with his arms, held close by his sides. The narrow and painted red hooks look like twin peaks fixed at the waist. He turns his head to look at the mirror and times the frequency and vigor of his movements with the upward and downward movements of the lotuses. The pleasure is indescribable.

VII. Delicate and Graceful Silk Stockings

It is a hot summer's night; he quietly gets up and lies down on a long bench under the window. She awakes and urges him to return to bed. Her body is semi-nude, while she is wearing tiny phoenix-head shoes. Desire is suddenly aroused, and he orders her to sit, straddling his stomach. He supports himself with his hands, elevates his stomach so that it is inclined slightly upwards, and forcibly raises his thighs. This causes her twin lotuses to be suspended in mid-air; he holds one in each hand. Her delicate and graceful silk stockings, in his palms, reveal their charm. Bowed and wave-like, tiny, and resembling a full moon, the twin-petaled autumn lotus is as light as a falling leaf and lovely as it moves to and fro in mid-air. How can this view and the feelings aroused fail to cause a man to lose his soul?

VIII. A Penetrating Grasp With Left and Right

In the quiet of the boudoir depths, they lie pillowed together. She lies on her left side, with her left arm and foot stretched outward and her left lotus behind his back. He lies facing her, with his head resting on her arm and his body pressing on her left thigh. They kiss and bite each other's tongue. She draws up her right leg so that he can hold her lotus with his right hand (from behind his back). He also grasps her left lotus with his left hand, extending it behind the back. Her tiny feet under the coverlets are tightly bound and suitable for holding. There is limitless delight as he penetratingly grasps with left and right. They are mouth to mouth with limbs entangled, electric charges flowing freely between them. With such bodily comfort, how can anyone fail to be thoroughly satisfied?

IX. Encircling Twin Lotuses

In one corner of a beauty s red chamber, which is elegantly decorated, stands a Western-style dresser. It has a long mirror in the center and individual chests on either side. She sits on one of the chests, smiling radiantly, while he stands by the mirror, facing her. She tightly clasps him around the back, with her legs encircling his waist, and her tiny hooks press his back and signal him to move as she desires. She wears either red-embroidered soft shoes or white silk stockings; her tiny feet resemble twin spring bamboo shoots when parallel and twin lotuses when crossed. He clasps his right hand around her neck and kisses her, while with his left hand he plays endlessly with her feet from behind his back. They look into the mirror and see both lotuses and lovers paired. The paradise they enter is as indescribable as the pleasures they enjoy.

X. *Bright Flower, Concealed Willow*

Preparing for sleep, she has just removed make-up and clothes. He sprawls on the bed, half reclined on the pillow, facing

inwards. One foot is stretched out; the other hangs beside the bed. She sits, resting her thighs on his stomach, and turns her head to look into his eyes. Her left thigh traverses his knee, with the tiny shoe curled upwards. It is shaped like a new moon, but dazzlingly bright. Her right thigh crosses her left, with her knee drawn up to place the bare lotus in his left palm. He grasps the beautiful hook and gets the sensations of its being pointed, slender, soft, and tiny. Twin lotuses, twin delight; the bright one for visual pleasure, the bared one for playful palm manipulation. Intercourse in this position leads to a continual increase of excitement, verifying the saying about bowed shoes being a soul destroyer.

XI. Lovebird on One Foot

It is a cool mid-autumn night, with a soothing moon shining overhead. He sits on a stone stool; she stands enticingly before him, bending her head towards his. Clasping his neck with her right arm, she balances herself on the right foot only. Her left foot, enclosed like its partner in embroidered red bowed shoes, is drawn upwards. She takes off her left shoe and places the revealed lotus in his left palm. He enfolds her tiny waist with his right arm and raises his head to kiss her as she leans forward. They bite each other's tongue. Their souls are assured a sublimity beyond Heaven, with tongues caressing, one lotus touching earth, looking like a red pepper, and the other in his hand like a spring bamboo shoot.

XII. Heavenly Hooks in Palms

She is nude in a room illumined by electric light. She lies in bed on her side, thighs drawn up towards her chest and spread apart. She lies across the bed and he lies at the edge of it, lengthwise. With buttocks joined together, their bodies in union look like the letter "T." He holds her lotuses tightly, and rhythmical movements are easily regulated. Sometimes she kneels on the bed, on her knees, with body bending downward but ankles inclined upward. He stands to the rear of her and has intercourse from behind while holding the twin lotuses. This reverses the first technique mentioned. Whether the lotuses are stockinged or bared, desires are aroused with a single touch. The feeling of softness and smoothness is beyond description; pleasure is increased by holding them tightly and fiercely.

XIII. Embracing Soft Jade

On a snowy night, they talk intimately by the stove. They feel desire rising and go to bed hand in hand, facing one another under the lovebird coverlets. He lies on his side, while she bends her left arm to support her cheek with the palm. Her legs are drawn up towards the chest, with ankles crossed. She puts her bare lotuses in his embrace, and he presses them to his bosom. Their love is tender, the lotuses soft and fine, and her twin rising peaks rich and full. Fragrant, warm, smooth, and soft; spring is everywhere.

XIV. Twinfold Joy of Bamboo Shoots

Two nudes lie down, inside hibiscus curtains. She removes the bindings to please him with the bare lotuses. He lies on his side, half reclining on a pillow, and presses his chest tightly against her back. His right hand reaches under her right armpit to caress her breast. His legs clasp her right thigh as well as one bare lotus. She draws up her left thigh in order to place the bared left lotus in his left palm. The jade-like bamboo shoots are pointed and fine, glossy and flawless. In his palms, they feel warm and as soft as silk, with the skin as slippery as grease. Twinfold pleasure is created from either playing with the plantar or from squeezing the entire lotus. How can you describe the delight of lotuses which overflow with fragrance?

XV. A Head Inserted in Lotus Petals

Inside a silk curtain filled with the ardor of youth, she lies on her back, head pillowed on forearm and thighs spread apart. He supports himself on his arms as he crouches over her, with head raised and knees bent. She lifts up her bare lotuses and places them on his shoulders in such a way that they tightly press against his cheeks. They play with his face and touch his nostrils; their fragrance overflows his lips and teeth. And this jade bamboo shoot contemplation so satisfies the five senses that all other flavors of life are obliterated.

XVI. Jade Claws Touching The Cave

They sleep on floor mats on a hot summer's night. The cool midnight air awakens in him a superabundance of desire. He relaxes limbs and lies on his back, legs bent in such a way that the plantars join one another. She crouches over him, supported by her arms, with her legs stretched out so that the tips of the bare lotuses touch his plantars. He fondles her breasts with his hands; pleasure is felt in every limb, with hands on breasts and feet touching lotuses. As the jade claws move up and down, the plantar is scratched in its most ticklish spot. The satisfaction and thrill are indescribable.

XVII. Two Dragons Playing With A Pearl

The moon shines through a window; it is in the depths of the night. Waiting for his return, she has fallen asleep from fatigue, and the red tips of tiny shoes emerge slightly from the corner of the bedcovers. He returns and is delighted by the sight. Drawing down the curtains, he eagerly grasps and plays with the phoenix tips. He is still not satisfied, so she removes embroidered shoes and bindings. Her white lotuses are pointed and fine, beautiful as polished jade or a mound of powder. She lifts twin hooks and caresses his sex by rubbing them up and down against it, and they bull it about like two dragons playing with a pearl. It finally becomes as soft as if a mere breeze could blow it down; the intense delight is such as he has never before enjoyed. This marvel is still another special benefit accruing from the lotus.

XVIII. Upside Down Lovers

It is an old scholarly platitude that lovers make love side by side, but that to turn upside down is unusual. On a splendid sprir night, pillows separate accuser and defendant. He lies on his back in a reclining chair, legs stretched out and pillows under the waist. She kneels and sits on his stomach, facing in the same direction. Her ankles are lifted upwards but the lotuses recline downwards to fit into his palms. He can play with them any way he likes. There are three stages in the playing process. First he plays with the tiny three-inch embroidered shoes she has on, which are red, pointed, thin, and narrow like a water chestnut. They are brightly colored and cleverly designed, with beautiful needlework, rivaling nature in artistry. Then the shoes are removed, revealing silk stockings shaped like a new moon. Her feet have pointed tips and slender heels. They are beautifully curved and are unmarred in contour from instep to plantar.

The last stage is the removal of the bindings. The bare lotus, like a bamboo shoot, gradually and completely reveals itself. Its skin is white as frost, its flesh tender and smooth. Its fullness does not hurt the eyes, nor does its thinness expose the bones to view. The heels are well balanced and the toes close to one another. Four toes are thin like bean halves, and the big toes curve upward diminutively like young ginger. Her feet are lukewarm and soft as cotton, but once caressed they become smooth and slippery. Treasure them as you might large jade tokens, love them so that parting with them becomes unbearable, so that you can't help smelling, kissing, biting, and chewing them. The soul wanders to the Great Beyond, ignoring the beginning of dawn.

It is difficult for me in writing these rare words to avoid the criticism of having been lewd. But I had to do this to depict the interest of the lotus. Wasting little ink, I tried to make it as expressive as possible; may the reader understand and forgive. One can discuss the lotus interest inexhaustibly, analyze its details from start to finish, and arrive at these conclusions:

Woman adorns herself for the beloved, and love of beauty is ingrained in her nature. This is true both past and present, in China and elsewhere. Every woman considers beauty glorifying and exalts it as she might a second life. To achieve a beauty's reputation, she willingly endures starvation and cold, injures her skin and impairs her limbs. Our women anciently regarded as beautiful a broadened forehead with side-locks of cicada-like transparency, silkworm moth-shaped eyebrows, soft fingers, and glossy skin. Their views included the pain of breaking the bones and destroying the veins to acquire the tiny bowed-foot effect. This was considered a dazzling mark of distinction and a competitive quest among beauty lovers. But lewdness was unavoidable, and grasping of the spring bows caused lost souls. Was there divine merit in this?

It cannot be criticized as improper. It was an integral part of orthodox upbringing shared by everyone and an essential aspect of nuptial delight. There was no reason for a pair of lotus hooks in and of themselves to feel shame at being an instrument for exciting lust. When lotus feet flourished, they provided the only "matchmaker" for private meetings between man and woman. The qualities they had for affecting man were those of being thin, small, pointed, bowed, warm, soft, pretty, and elegant. They could be appreciated visually and could bring on feelings of sympathy. She was willing to let him play with them in his hands; who would not find this lovable? Lotus feet were everywhere suitable, in the palms, on the shoulders, by the pillow, or under the coverlets.

But, by way of contrast, how could the foot-long Lotus Boat be held in the palm of one's hand? And how could one bear to have a heavy pair of ducks alight on one's shoulders? An encounter with natural feet meant disinterest, for they could not conceivably cause one to lose his soul.

Things which are rare are esteemed. That which is tiny and cleverly contrived is always looked upon as superior. Therefore, while not binding the feet was one alternative, once bound tininess had to be strived for. Tininess was not sufficient in and of itself, but the reduction had to be balanced. This balance was supernaturally achieved and not attainable through human striving. The wondrous lotus was very hard to obtain. Ancients often poetically praised the three-inch golden lotus, but in reality only one in several hundred met this standard. The perfectly

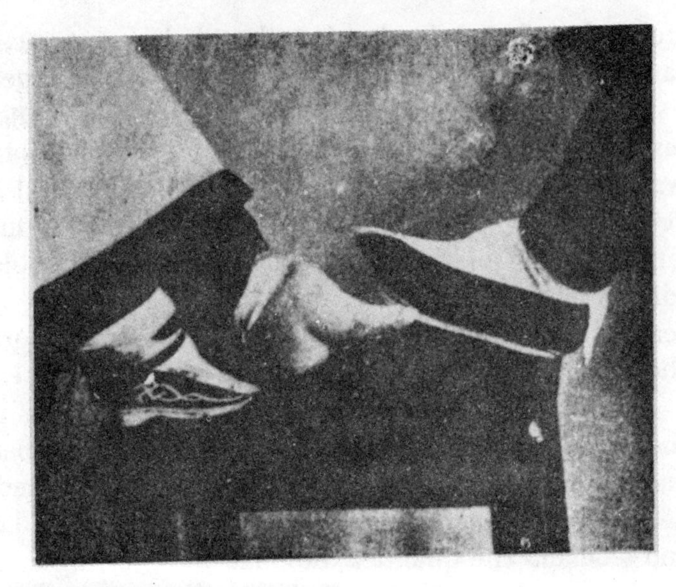

A WOMAN'S NATURAL FOOT AND ANOTHER WOMAN'S FEET BOUND TO SIX INCHES

A WOMAN'S NATURAL FOOT AND ANOTHER WOMAN'S FEET BOUND TO FOUR-AND-ONE-HALF INCHES
(from *Intimate China*, 138 and 139)

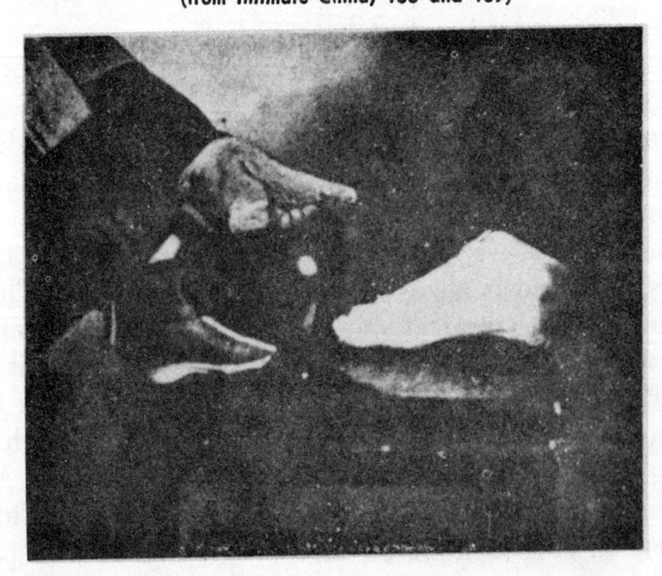

proportioned and incomparably elegant tiny foot was a rare worldly treasure, like finding a phoenix hair or a unicorn. It might be accidentally seen but was never a common sight.

I feel that the preciousness of a tiny foot is in its diminutive elegance, which causes the beholder to find it lovable. But a small shape is sometimes clumsy looking. Three to four inches (about four to five Western inches) is considered proper, over four inches is rather looked down upon, while less than three inches is inevitably too small.[2] The three-inch type is first class if the thin and pointed foot has bones, flesh, and surface in harmonious proportion. Women of antiquity regarded the tiny foot as a crystallization of physical beauty; it was not a product of lewd thinking.

Someone asked: "Why not restrict amusement to only playing with the lotus? Why must it be connected with sex?" However, it is only through sex that satisfaction reaches its fullest extent. The lotus has special seductive characteristics and is an instrument for arousing desire. Who can resist the fascination and bewilderment of playing with and holding in his palms a soft and jade-like hook? Who can resist the temptation to try, heart leaping with excitement? Lotus and sex have a reciprocal effect on one another. Lotus depends on sex for its form, while sex depends on lotus for its use. If lotus playing doesn't culminate in sex, its delight is inexhaustible. If sex doesn't include the lotus, there is no way in which to reach the extremes of pleasure. The two are vital to one another and each profits accordingly. And there is a strange mystery between them.

Women in the past had good reasons for seriously preventing their lotus hooks from being seen. How could this devotion have been in vain? Yet if every man preferred bound feet, the modern woman would be completely ignored. But this is not so, for tastes change. Today's natural feet are sought after as much as bound feet were in the past. Preferences vary with the times; beauty or ugliness, right or wrong as invariables are non-existent. Liking becomes a craving which must be shared to be appreciated. The lotus style has become insignificant, and its shadows are suddenly obscured. Old village ladies let out their feet in order to be fashionable, but the swollen limp increases ugliness. How can beauty result, and how can one discern lotus truth through such specimens?

From now on, women will be large-footed immortals, and the spirit of the lotus will be relegated to the historical past. How will a world ignorant of the lotus be able to appreciate the elegance of its shadow and the gracefulness of its walk, or the pleasures that were derived from playing with it? Tiny and bowed shoes will be regarded by posterity as a useless type of shoewear.

To indicate their eminence, wealthy families must have a profusion of dishes at the table when they eat. But the poor villager, ignorant of wealthy tastes, is better off if he fills himself up on pork alone. Knowledge leads to beauty, beauty to love, and love to craving. Craving comes from such depths of love that the source of initial attraction is forgotten. This is true of all things; the lotus is no exception. I am asked: "Do you advocate the lotus foot?" Customs do not spring up overnight, but have deep roots and a hidden strength. But once they change, the rapidity in affecting man is like a swift wind bending the grass. Even a mighty power cannot stop this.

In the former age of autocracy, when our gates were closed to the outside, the lotus custom remained unchanged for a millennium. Even awesome emperors couldn't eliminate it. Now our form of government has changed, and European ways have come to the East. The natural foot is elevated and flourishes. The change in custom follows our revised aesthetic viewpoint. The golden lotus will never again be mentioned in a discussion of beauty. Only the six-inch rounded foot is considered modern, and it is now universally imitated. How can the lotus still be advocated when its extinction is unpreventable?

Our country's footbinding has become a type of backward practice in world history. Nowhere was woman confined more severely than through this. It should naturally be annihilated and become an unheard of phenomenon. But I did not mind using my energy and words to write this in order to indicate something of the utilities of the lotus and its holy mysteries, which survived a millennium. I have discussed it boldly, without regard for my own person, and spoken of things men dare not speak of and consider trifling, in order to bequeath a true record of the history of the lotus and indicate its true manifestations.[8]

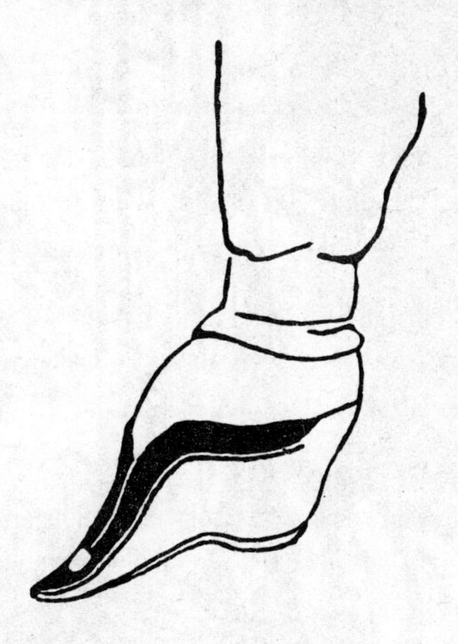

CHAPTER SEVEN

Reckless and Cruel Treatment of the Drunken Lotus

This allegedly true story concerns the sexual aberrations of a widely traveled and well-to-do lotus enthusiast. His sadistic treatment of concubines and infliction of pain on the tiny feet are recorded in convincing detail.

This is about a friend whom I shall refer to by the assumed named of Green Crane, since he is still living. He lost both parents in his youth and was reared by his grandmother. He was attractive-looking, discerning in intellect, and well-versed in poetry, history, classics, and philosophy. He grew up to be an extreme lotus addict, one who naturally inclined towards sexual indulgence. He was first engaged to marry a beautiful maternal cousin; however, her feet had already been let out because of educational influences. Green Crane felt this defect keenly and was spiritually overwhelmed everytime he saw the tiny and superlative hooks of his fiancée's cousins Moon Resplendent and Moon Beauty. He finally made this proposal to his fiancée: "If the two Moons became your reinforcements, your virtue in allowing this would far exceed that of Emperor Yao's daughter in antiquity, who had no objection when a sister joined her in wedding Shun." When Green Crane's wife-to-be revealed his intent to her uncle on the day of their marriage, the uncle was vehement in his opposition: "Green Crane, enjoying his present good fortune, now wishes to take away the other daughters of my household! If this is his real sentiment, he is wasting his time in speaking about it." The two Moons were forbidden to see him again, causing him almost to perish from sorrow. A few days later, he left his bride with these parting words: "There are many beautiful women under the Heavens, and I vow to get them all." He ranged north and south and one after another visited the provinces of Hopei, Shantung, Honan, Shansi, Shensi, Kansu, Chekiang, and Szechwan. He immersed himself in lotus and wine and upon satisfying his pleasures moved on. He returned after two years, during which time he had possessed more than a hundred women. There were eight virgins among them, two each from Suchow and Shensi, one each from Chekiang, Honan, Kansu, and Shansi. They were all satisfying tiny-footed beauties.

Green Crane took in the virgins as concubines, bought three more Suchow maids, and returned home. His imposing family domain included a large house and spacious, well-landscaped gardens and pavilions. A hall named Concealed Spring had utterly luxurious embroidered curtains and innumerable paintings of love. He and his concubines were depicted in every one of them, in a variety of appealing poses. The women might disclose their tightly confined breasts, have their lotuses raised, be wearing sleeping shoes or silk stockings, or have unraveled their bindings. The man might be smilingly grasping the lotuses while the woman looks at him sensually as she lies either under or on top of him. Green Crane probably had these paintings made in Peking from actual photographs.

Green Crane practiced Taoist breathing exercises[1] and was addicted to manifold sensual pleasures. His tool was superlatively imposing, and he could only be satisfied by having intercourse with several women nightly. He treated his women very strictly and cruelly. He said that a man should behave towards women as a great general might towards his favorite horses.[2]

And every day a general had his horses cleaned meticulously and readied for combat. His theory was that because men were generally too lenient in controlling women, they found it difficult to secure meritorious feminine valor in front line battle. He also said that a horse's might could not be displayed unless it were subjected to pain and that this was why spurs were pressed against its belly. Women likewise had no way to display their beauty except through suffering pain. The use of aphrodysiacs and lewd instruments made women pliable, and the acme of pleasure for both partners was to be sought in the tiny foot. Every one of his concubines and maids walked with the elegant lotus step. When he had intercourse, he always grasped the lotuses tightly and bit them, not desisting until he had caused extreme pain. The bound foot was of first significance, for through it was effected a compliant and elegant feminine attitude.

Green Crane also said that the bashfulness of a virgin could cause a man to lose his soul.[3] At the moment of defloration, he tightly grasped the twin hooks in order to make her suffer a twofold pain. She cried and begged in a persuasive tone, her eyebrows knitted, her tears flowed, her lotuses kicked about in vain, and her willow waist twisted as she tried to escape. This certainly excelled having intercourse with a non-virgin, who could be aroused merely by lightly scratching the plantar with bindings removed and who might giggle and become dissipated. But since the pleasure from a virgin lasted only briefly, he advised that one concentrate on this amusement and not let the pleasure go by without gaining from it.

It was Green Crane's conviction that only through bound feet could one get a virgin-like pleasure from a non-virgin. Order the woman to adorn herself, he said, have her bathe in perfumed water, and have her feet washed. Then have another woman bind her feet most tightly, ignoring her frowning or even sobbing. After this binding, her feet will feel as if they are on fire and will gradually become numb. Then order her to wear soft-soled red embroidered shoes, and tell her to have two used binding cloths ready for use. Now she will know that suffering is near but will have no way to escape. She will become timidly fearful, like a child about to have its feet bound or a virgin about to be deflorated. At this time the man sprawls naked on the bed, with male member exposed, intimidating her with his fierce laughter. She tremblingly offers her bound feet, while he orders her to remove her clothing and await his pleasure. But when she has only removed her skirt, he unbuttons her blouse so that two chicken heads can be seen from within. They are so slippery that they elude one's grasp, hampered by a dazzling red-embroidered brassiere placed between her golden armor. He then takes the used binding cloths and ties her ankles and shins to the curtains so that they are suspended in mid-air and penetrates her slightly-opened vagina. The blood flows upwards towards her thighs and accumulates in her private parts, which become extremely full and tight. During intercourse, he grasps her golden lotuses, lightly kisses her fragrant breasts, embraces her tiny waist, and holds her fragrant tongue in his mouth. Everything is exactly according to his wishes. Even though it is hard to insert his member through such a tight obstruction, he receives the overall sensation of slippery smoothness and a comfort like that of a babe nursing at its mother's breast. His swollen member resembles a frozen snake boring into a hole, the center of which is sealed off tightly. The beauty of this experience is unparalleled, and it is not like that of the virgin's single attraction, namely a tight obstruction. After the woman had intercourse as described, she had to rest for three days before she could resume relations. This was one of the strange punishments used for subduing women.

Green Crane spoke of the wondrousness of the bowed foot, saying that Shensi and Shansi models were best. The southern foot style was usually fragrant and soft, the northern style slender and small. The women from Ch'ang-an and San-yüan (in Shensi) had feet which combined both styles, for they were pointed, small, slender and trim, fragrant, soft, and perfectly proportioned. And they were truly rare to behold.

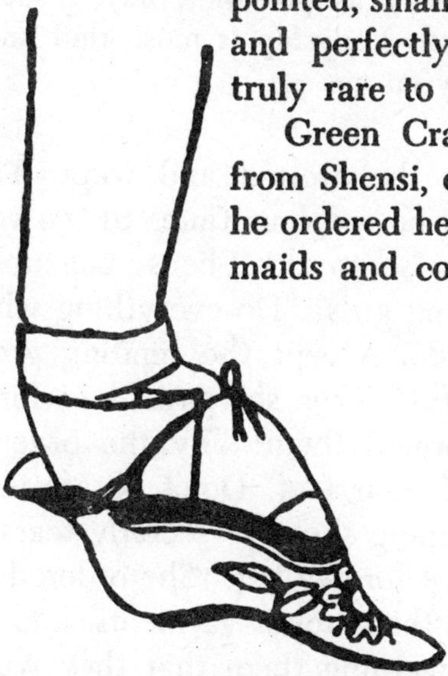

Green Crane had a beautiful concubine from Shensi, especially skilled in footbinding; he ordered her to supervise the binding of his maids and concubines. He also set up many regulations. A painting of the tenth-century consort Lovely Maiden, who was the first to bind her feet, was hung in the Lotus Cultivation Room. (This room was used exclusively for binding the feet of young girls.) A small whip was placed beside the painting, signifying that those who disobeyed would be punished. There were pictures on the walls of tiny-footed women singing and dancing. There were also three chests inside the room filled with bowed shoes, silk stockings, binding cloths, alum powder, various fragrances, scissors, cotton, medicine, and needles. A special footbinding chair was constructed so that when a girl sat on it her forearms were fastened immovably on either side. However, she could still move the part of her arms above the elbows in order to wipe away tears. There was a footstool in front of the chair to facilitate her placing both feet on it to have them bound. The day a girl's feet were bound, Green Crane's main wife sat on the chair in the room which was considered to be in the most honored position. The Shensi concubine stood to one side, and she and the wife led the young girls whose feet were to be bound to worship Lovely Maiden. The girls were ordered to kneel and say this prayer:

> I, *so and so*, begin to bind my feet on this day. May Your Ladyship protect me and lessen my pain and assist me in getting

> three-inch golden lotuses as quickly as possible. May I soon secure the love of a husband. Your Ladyship is most kind and compassionate; please have mercy on me.

After praying, they knelt on the ground and wept. They brought their hands together and bowed four times to the wife, who ordered them to bow likewise to the Shensi concubine. Then the wife instructed the young girls: "Do everything which your older sister wants you to do. Accept the binding gracefully; be neither lazy nor neglectful." Then she gave the whip to the Shensi concubine, who informed them: "By the order of our mistress, I am going to bind your feet. Don't be afraid. If anyone stealthily loosens the sleeping shoes or secretly tears off the stitches on the binding, I'll not forgive her." She ordered the girls to kneel down and take off their upper garments, and she whipped each one three times, warning them that they would be whipped this way again if they did not strive to be good. Each girl put a pair of binding cloths prepared beforehand on a plate, and in fixed sequence kneeled and offered the plate to the Shensi concubine, saying: "Older sister's commands will not be disobeyed; younger sister will endure pain and accept the binding." The concubine gave each girl a silk embroidered handkerchief, to be used for wiping away tears.

The girls accepted the handkerchiefs and bowed in gratitude. They were then ordered to sit on the footbinding chair, one by one, removing shoes and socks by themselves. There was a red wooden box in front of the chair, filled with clear water. The concubine first washed the girl's feet, paying especial attention to the plantars, which would become creased later from the binding. After the washing, the girl's forearms were bound to the chair, and one foot was pressed down on the footstool. Both needle and scissors were used. The girl's pretty face became lifeless, and she wept bitterly and cried aloud until she lost her voice, but she couldn't move an inch. Her feet were then tightly bound, with fragrant powder generously sprinkled first on all the creases and then between the layers of the binding cloth. The footbinding was soon completed. The feet were pointed and curved upwards, with a pleasant fragrance striking the nostrils. Green Crane was often present to enjoy the scene. He would say to others: "Everytime I see a girl suffering the pain of footbinding, I think of the future when the lotuses will be placed on my shoulders or held in my palms, and my desire overflows and becomes uncontrollable." This story dates back twenty years.[4]

CHAPTER EIGHT

The Tiny Foot in Truth and Fiction

There are aged Chinese gentlemen today who still consider bound feet more attractive than natural ones, but they are usually reticent on the subject, hesitant to express opinions which seem inconsonant with the present age. They may also be embarrassed to try to justify footbinding to an unsympathetic and hostile Western audience. The desire of the Chinese to conceal the custom from curious but condescending eyes is illustrated by the following incident, which took place in Paris about 1936. A bound-foot Chinese woman took her two children to France about that time and tried to earn a livelihood by charging Parisians one franc each to look at her golden lotuses. She did this on public street corners and had her children collect the contributions. We are not informed as to how much money she made, but overseas Chinese in Paris became indignant and protested to the Chinese Consulate that her behavior was an affront to national honor. The lady was consequently expelled from France and sent back to China.[1]

The tiny foot was a popular theme in poetry, fiction, and essay as late as the first third of the twentieth century. The lotus enthusiast generally avoided foreign confrontation, but presented an eloquent defense of footbinding to the domestic audience:

There are many good points about tiny feet, but I will talk only about the best ones. A tiny foot is proof of feminine goodness. Women who don't bind their feet look like men, for the tiny foot serves to show the differentiation. It is also an instrument for secretly conveying love feelings. The tiny foot is soft and, when rubbed, leads to great excitement. If it is touched under the coverlet, love feelings of the woman are immediately aroused. The graceful walk gives the beholder a mixed feeling of compassion and pity. Natural feet are heavy and ponderous as they get into bed, but tiny feet lightly steal under the coverlets. The large-footed woman is careless about adornment, but the tiny-footed frequently wash and apply a variety of perfumed fragrances, enchanting all who come into their presence. The tiny shoe is inexpensive and uses much less material, while the large foot by way of contrast is called a lotus boat. The really tiny foot is easy to walk on, but the large tiny foot is painful and inconvenient. The natural foot looks much less aesthetic in walking. Everyone welcomes the tiny foot, regarding its smallness as precious. Men formerly so craved it that its possessor achieved harmonious matrimony. Because of its diminutiveness, it gives rise to a variety of sensual pleasures and love feelings.[2]

Literary references usually depicted the tiny-footed as demure and yielding. But an occasional vixen reminded the reader that the Chinese woman, while perhaps preserving a subservient social image, often ruled the family with a firm hand. There was one story, for instance, of a tiny-footed but hot-tempered Szechwanese who tyrannized her timid spouse. If he returned home at night even slightly late, he had to kneel before her as punishment. She would box his ears, slap his face, and in general humiliate him. On one occasion, the husband was drinking wine with friends and did not return home until well after midnight. The maid servant let him in, and he furtively entered, looking uneasily from side to side. Suddenly he encountered his wife, who had removed the bindings and was washing her feet in a basin. He thanked the Buddhist god Amida under his breath, for he knew that she could not possibly strike him while in this pose.

"What are you doing at this hour, like a devil with his tongue hanging out?"

"Afraid of disturbing your sleep, I refrained from moving about or making noise."

"Stop your devil's tongue and come over here!" He did as commanded, like a criminal before a judge or an official in the presence of an emperor.

"Merciful wife, let me wash your feet for you."

"Get out of here, faceless one. Who asks you to wash for me?"

"Give me face, I beg of you."

"Answer me this. What devil's haunt did you frequent this evening?"

"My friends enticed me to drink. It was all their fault."

"Well, I'll give you the 'face' that you want and let you have another drink besides. Bring me a wine glass." The husband brought a glass at once, as compliant as if he had been commanded to do so by a sage. The wife scooped a glass of water from the basin in which her feet were immersed:

"Empty the glass and let me know how it tastes!" He hesitated for a moment but then, in obedience to her command, gulped down the contents.

"How does it taste?"

"Sweet!"

The storyteller went on to say that Szechwanese friends of his vouched for the tale's authenticity, insisting that if you ask for sweet wine at a Szechwanese banquet, the response around the table will usually be one of amused laughter.[3]

There were also stories about smelling the tiny foot, generally favorable in tone. Whether the odor pleased or offended depended on whether the individual was an impartial observer or a lotus enthusiast. A Japanese visitor to Shanghai in 1919, for example, said that bound feet, usually washed only once every two weeks, smelled most unpleasant. But he admitted that the

Chinese male was pleased rather than offended by the aroma.[4] During his student days in Kwangtung, a Chinese writer made a similar observation. He met a studious scholar there named Kuan, who lived with his wife in perfect harmony. When they slept together, Kuan placed his head by his wife's feet, so that the couple resembled two steamed and salted fish. Kuan slept this way in order to smell the aroma of his wife's bound feet, for only then was he able to sleep soundly. Mrs. Kuan once got ready to visit her parents, expecting to be away for about ten days. Just as she was putting her bags in order, Kuan made the following proposal:

"Wife, leave a pair of your shoes and bindings behind."

"Why?"

"You're really not very bright. Do I have to go into explicit detail to make you understand?"

His wife, grasping the implication, left behind one pair of shoes and two bindings which she had just been wearing. On the first night of her absence, Kuan tossed and turned about in bed, feeling so lonely and restless that sleep was out of the question. Finally realizing what he had to do, he took out the shoes and wrappings, placed them by his head, inhaled deeply, and calmly went to sleep. Our narrator stated in conclusion that this story was not fabricated but was told to him as the gospel truth by a fellow villager.[5]

Chinese storytellers commonly created fiction from a basis of fact by building their plots around famous historical figures They depicted charms of the tiny foot by conjuring up suggestive and mildly erotic bedroom scenes. Nan-kung Po, a master of this technique, is a well-known contemporary Chinese historical novelist. He once wrote a fictional adaptation of Sung dynastic episodes called *The Lady of An County* and included incidental remarks about the sensual delights of footbinding. A few of these passages have been translated below because of their relevance to our study, as they indicate how the attractions of the tiny foot were described in widely-read popular works.

The plot centered about the love affair of Han Shih-chung, a Southern Sung general, and a courtesan with the art-name of Carmine Jade. The first scene describes how they met:

It was an early hour, with few guests present. More than ten courtesans were seated at tables, idly chatting. Shih-chung's army friend nudged him with his elbow:

"Look how tiny their feet are! They must be only an inch long!"

"An inch? You silly fool, the smallest golden lotus is three inches; I've never heard of one an inch long."

"I was really referring to their width."

While the courtesans couldn't hear what was being said, they seemed to have guessed the topic of conversation. They displayed their tiny feet, forming a sort of Bound Foot Exhibition.

"Look," said Shih-chung in embarrassment, "they seem to know what we're talking about."

"They're all purchasable, so why shouldn't we first look over the goods?"

Shih-chung failed to reply, for he was staring at a pair of tiny feet in startled appreciation. They were the most beautiful he had ever seen. Though the shoes were not pretty, being an ordinary black color and lacking ornamentation, the foot itself was slightly over four inches long and about three fingers in width. Viewed in its over-all dimensions, the foot was unusually lovable. It narrowed from heel to toe, and about halfway towards the tip narrowed so suddenly that it was as slender as a long pepper. The tip curled upwards slightly.

A foot that long was a common sight in the capital, but it was rare to see one which narrowed as this one did. Most feet were unavoidably puffed up at the ankle, with the instep shaped like a dumpling, looking very much like a horse's hoof. Such types, no matter how small, were not aesthetic in the slightest.

Only this pair of bound feet led the viewer to think of rubbing them in his palms. Han Shih-chung imagined that her feet must be as soft as a ball of flour; otherwise, how could they be so delicate and tender? Shih-chung suddenly resolved to take them in the palms of his hands and knead them furiously with his fingers.

"Ouch!" The lovable pair of bound feet suddenly jumped up. Shih-chung was startled, thinking that he must have hurt her by the very thought of kneading her feet. This of course was not true, but "lovely feet" had cried out in actual pain. There had been a glass of boiling water at her table. When she turned to look at Shih-chung, the courtesan beside her deliberately spilled it over her and accused her of having done it herself. The women quarreled, spurred on by the words of the other courtesans, who were envious of "lovely feet," and began fighting furiously. This alarmed Shih-chung, who realized the tiny feet of the courtesan whom he admired were the object of widespread jealousy. A ponderous five-inch foot suddenly stamped down on "lovely feet." Shih-chung bellowed out in rage and rushed to her side, causing her adversaries to flee in panic.

"It must be very painful; I hope that you did not suffer serious injury."

"They tried to break my feet," she murmured, pressing her tiny feet with both hands."

"What is your name?"

"Carmine Jade . . . and your name, sir?"

For the general and the courtesan, it was love at first sight. In the bedroom scenes which follow, the ways in which the tiny foot enhanced sensation are clearly suggested:

Carmine Jade's bed was spotless; Shih-chung threw himself on it, stretched out, and beckoned to her:

"Why don't you come closer?"

She blushed, but slowly approached the bed and sat down, leaning on the bedpost. Shih-chung looked her over greedily, from tip to toe, until he felt satiated. He finally fixed his glance upon her thighs and raised her skirt in order to inspect her tiny feet.

Carmine Jade felt giddy; she reclined, extending her feet. Shih-chung, who was very strong, placed her foot in his palm, where it fitted perfectly. He pressed the foot with his fingers, causing her to cry out involuntarily.

"You press my foot till it hurts, without feeling tenderly towards me," complained Carmine Jade, struggling to free herself . . .

A pair of tiny feet, encased in red sleeping slippers, was outlined by the bedcovers. Her legs were crossed and entangled under a single coverlet, with the curve of her thighs enticingly revealed. Shih-chung was amazed that her thighs were so voluptuous and large. He stared at them thinking: "How hard it must be for tiny feet to support those thighs!" He couldn't help feeling compassion for her lower extremities. Compressing the feet in order to thicken the thighs must have been the invention of a genius. And of course the inventor must have been a woman. . . .

She felt at ease with him and, without thinking, extended her feet across his stomach. Shih-chung was just then reflecting on other matters, but when she placed her feet there he conveniently

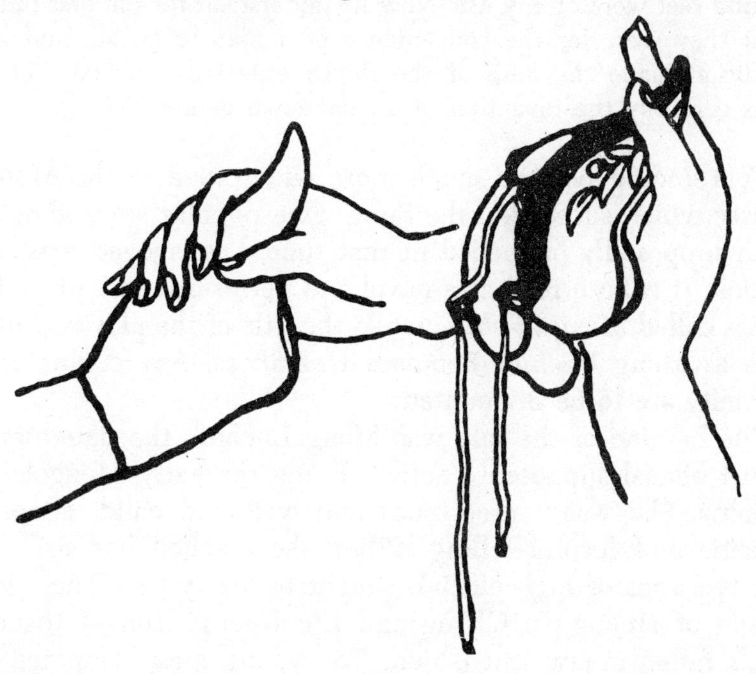

> grasped them and rubbed them in his palms. He had very powerful hands and grasped and rubbed her feet so that she became more excited with each passing moment. For her it was a mixture of suffering and pleasure. The more it hurt, the more intense became her feelings of delight; she moaned, unable to bear the excitement any longer . . .
>
> She usually felt pain in her little feet, bound so tightly, whenever she walked around. But when her feet were held in Shih-chung's palms and powerfully rubbed, though she cried out, this pain was really delightful. Not only was she unafraid, but she hoped that he would apply even greater pressure . . .
>
> He rubbed her feet as usual; she cried out as usual. She thought: "If I hadn't made my feet so tiny through binding, perhaps Shih-chung couldn't enclose them in his palms so tightly." . . . Shih-chung had previously doubted that women's bound feet were of any use. Now he understood for the first time that they were for the convenience of a man to knead, and in addition made the flesh of the thighs especially sensual. "This was certainly the invention of an unknown genius!" [6]

Footbinding became much more widespread in the Mongol dynasty which succeeded the Sung. One popular story about it, which supposedly happened at that time, has enjoyed mass circulation. It is both read as a novel and performed as a play. The story is called *Meng Li-chün,* while the title of the play is usually given as *Meng Li-chün Removes Her Shoes.* Any claims as to historicity are to be discounted.

The heroine of the tale was Meng Li-chün, the daughter of a court official supposedly active during the early Mongol rule of China. She was a precocious and well-read child, adept in medicine and fortune-telling. When she reached her sixteenth year, two sons of high officials sought to marry her. They were the son of Huang-p'u Ch'ing and Liu Kuei-pi, son of the emperor's father-in-law Liu Chieh. The young men competed for her through an archery contest, which Liu Kuei-pi lost when one of his three shots missed the target. Liu bitterly resented the defeat and asked his father to find some means to incriminate the clan of Huang-p'u Ch'ing.

Bandits in Shantung were then a menace to public order. Liu Chieh petitioned the emperor to appoint Huang-p'u Ch'ing to lead a subjugation campaign against them. This was done, but he was taken captive in the fighting. Liu Chieh falsely informed the emperor that Huang-p'u Ch'ing had capitulated, and as a result his clan was incarcerated. Only the son Huang-p'u Shao-hua managed to escape.

Meng Li-chün evaded an order that she marry Liu Kuei-pi and went to the capital in male disguise. She placed first in competitive examinations because of her brilliance and erudition. The empress later contracted an illness which only she could cure; as a reward, she was given the highest military rank. Shantung rebels were still active. To combat them, Meng Li-chün convinced the emperor that the nation should recruit its talent through impartial testing. Huang-p'u Shao-hua achieved top honors and took charge of the troops who crushed the rebellion.

He returned as a military hero, to a court where Meng Li-chün was now serving as minister. She was afraid to reveal her disguise to the emperor, for fear of punishment. However, the emperor had his own doubts as to her sex. He deliberately got her drunk at a banquet and ordered a palace lady to inspect her feet. Uncertainties about her sex were dispelled, for the carefully-concealed bound feet which were revealed fell into the three-inch golden lotus category. The emperor, concludes our storyteller, compassionately let Meng Li-chün resign her post, resume feminine dress, and marry her beloved Huang-p'u Shao-hua. Another version of the story had Meng Li-chün joined in heroic acts by two other young ladies, who also married the hero.[7]

Bound feet played a more important part in another popular tale of love which, however, may have originally had some foundation in fact. The story was already known in the T'ang and Southern Sung dynasties, but depiction of the tiny shoes probably represented a post-Sung amplification. A popular Chinese movie in operatic style based on this theme was shown in 1963 to packed audiences in Taiwan, Hong Kong, and overseas Chinese centers.

A Chin dynasty (ca. 4th-5th c.) scholar named Liang Shan-po was a good friend of a fellow classmate named Chu Ying-t'ai, who was really a woman in disguise. Miss Chu concealed her identity in order to pursue studies away from home which were available to men only. Liang and Chu got along so well together that they shared the same bed, though the heroine, as our version of the story goes, placed a pan of water between them.

One day Miss Chu had to return home to her parents. She had become emotionally attached to Liang and took leave of him with regret. Under the bed, she left behind a pair of tiny shoes; the moment Liang saw them, he realized that his charming bedmate had been a woman, a woman with whom he was deeply in love. He rushed to her door, only to be told that three days before she had gone to marry a Mr. Ma. The distraught Liang took sick and died.

When Miss Chu heard of the death of her beloved, she went straight to his burial place. There she spoke these words: "If you have a spirit presence, open the doors of the grave; otherwise, I shall have to become a member of Mr. Ma's household." No sooner had the words been uttered than the doors opened. The overjoyed girl stepped inside, after which the grave closed as before. While astonished onlookers were exclaiming on what had happened, two butterflies flew out from the grave and soared off together towards the heavens. This story is so well known that certain yellow and black butterflies are still respectively called Liang Shan-po and Chu Ying-t'ai.[8]

The reference to butterflies is reminiscent of a more general superstition concerning death. There was a belief that women who had bound feet and long fingernails would, when they died, be treated in the nether world like members of the upper class.

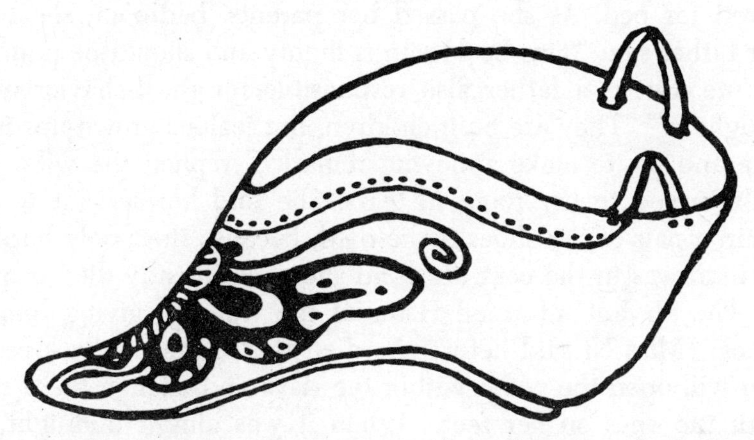

Due consideration was to be given them because they enjoyed the attributes of the wealthy.[9]

There was another theme of unrequited love in which the paths of frustration led to the grave. The wife of a merchant from Nanhai bore a son when the couple was more than forty years old. The child showed strange tendencies; he would insist on only eating food placed on the tiny toes of his mother or wet-nurse. This annoyed the merchant, but his wife reminded him:

> Our child was born because you liked to smell my feet nightly and kiss my private parts. His preference for the tiny foot is hereditary. We should pray for the birth of a girl somewhere who achieves lovable little feet, so that she can marry him and satisfy his special desire.

The husband's face reddened, but he had nothing to say in reply.

The boy as a teen-ager liked to search out tiny feet in women's bedrooms, like a hungry rat in search of food. His father's friend, a Mr. Ni, had a daughter who was a year the boy's senior. They met at a large party, exchanged admiring glances, and murmured phrases of love. While their elders were busily occupied, the boy rubbed Miss Ni's feet and received a smiling response. The guests finally departed, and Miss Ni prepared for bed. As she passed her parents' bedroom, she heard her father say: "This boy Hsün is flighty and should be punished by me. But is a father also responsible for the behavior of his daughter?" "They are both children, but jealous grown-ups interfere and try to make annoying remarks," replied the wife. Miss Ni returned to her room in tears. She told her servant to give Hsün a pair of her shoes if she died, because their only hope for reunion was in the next life. And she consequently died of grief.

The servant informed Hsün of the tragedy, giving him the shoes: "Miss Ni said before she died that if you really love her, you will open the coffin within ten days and change these shoes with the ones on her feet." When it was almost midnight, the servant escorted him to the coffin. He forcefully opened it and looked at her, lying as if she were still alive and in a deep sleep. He changed the shoes for her and then kissed her passionately. The eerie scene was illumined by moonlight above and candles at her side. Miss Ni's feet moved, and she came back to life. Her mother embraced them both and said it was Heaven's intent that they be paired. Wedding day guests thronged about to get a glimpse of her superlative lotuses, and bride and groom drank wine from tiny shoes in which wine-cups had been placed.[10]

It has been mentioned previously that men also preferred to have small feet. About 1906, in the capital of Peking, it was customary for boys of the upper class to compress their feet with binding cloths so that they could wear the narrow shoes then in vogue.[11] One major reason for male footbinding in China was superstition. If an astrologer determined that the rearing of a boy in a particular family would be inauspicious, the parents might attempt to deceive fate by bringing up the child as if it were a girl. The story was told of a Hunanese soldier who took a concubine after his wife died, early in marriage. When he was over fifty, she finally gave birth to a son. However, he followed the advice of an astrologer and reared his son as a girl in order to prevent calamity. He had the infant's ears pierced, presented it to his relatives as if it were a girl, and called it Lovable

Treasure. He had its feet bound at the age of one year, kept the child at home, and dressed its hair like a girl's. The child's bound feet were perfect and regular. His father revealed what had happened on his deathbed, and asked his son to revert to male attire, which he did, wearing larger shoes filled with cotton to accommodate his tiny feet.[12]

Male footbinding may have been known as early as the Sung dynasty. A certain official at that time was alleged to have had slender and bowed tiny feet, exactly like a woman's, which he proudly displayed.[13] One reference described young men in about 1465 who, with bound feet and in feminine guise, entered into marriage arrangements with uninformed male victims. When the wedding was about to take place, they would flee to freedom, undoubtedly getting away with the dowry which the unsuspecting groom had already provided. And a Ming writer wrote in convincing detail about an episode in 1480 which involved a footbound male. There was then a young and attractive widow in the capital, skilled in sewing and embroidery, who had tiny feet less than four inches long. She was on excellent terms with the wealthy and eminent, who employed her to teach their daughters how to sew. Whenever she saw a man, she would shyly withdraw from his presence. She also refused to respond to questions addressed to her by men, implying that to do so was improper. She was strictly correct in her demeanor and, when night fell, insisted on locking the bedroom door and on sleeping together with the young lady whom she was instructing at the time.

Because of her moral behavior, everyone regarded her highly. A certain Mr. Yang admired her and wished to have her for his own. He had his wife invite her to their home, pretending that she was her husband's younger sister. That night the wife obeyed her husband's instructions by opening the door of her room, under the pretense that she wished to go to the latrine. Mr. Yang extinguished the candle, throttled the widow's cries, and was about to rape her, when he discovered that "she" was a man. The female impersonator was interrogated by the authorities on the following day. He was twenty-four years old and had bound his feet in childhood as a device to become intimate with daughters of wealthy families. He had already enjoyed sexual relations with several of his unsuspecting customers.

Footbinding by male actors who impersonated tiny-footed women was mentioned during the Ch'ing dynasty and the early years of the Republic. At the end of the eighteenth century, a young actor in his teens from Anhwei named Hu Yao-ssu was well known for looks and talent. Hu's feet had been bowed in childhood like a girl's. When he took his place on the stage, fully made up, he looked extremely charming and attractive.

A certain official from Kweichow had lewd relations with him. When the official was transferred, Hu abandoned his acting career to accompany him. When the official went into mourning for one of his parents, less than two years later, Hu had already amassed considerable wealth. In order to conceal his plebeian background and the fact that he had formerly been an actor, Hu changed his surname to Ho and pretended that he was from an area near Peking. He made a donation to the official salt administration and in exchange was assigned a post in the Huai River region. When Hu discovered that the Kweichow official had received an important promotion upon completion of mourning observances, he paid a formal call and once again became a trusted intimate.

One day, someone had a letter sent in to him; Hu got so angry after reading it that he ordered the letter bearer expelled. Soon after, to celebrate his mother's birthday, he assembled numerous entertainers and gave plays and a banquet in her honor. Yangchow officialdom came forth en masse to pay their respects. Hu received them in formal attire and invited them to join in the festivities. The first play to be shown was the *Palace of Longevity*, where the Illustrious Celestial of the T'ang dynasty made his vow of eternal love. During the first scene, the actor playing the role of T'ang court musician Li Kuei-nien suddenly left the stage and charged at Hu with a bamboo rod, beating him until he was covered with blood. The actor then announced to a shocked audience that he had come to discipline his disciple and that this was none of their concern. He revealed how Hu had quit his acting profession, concealed his background, and become an official.

> As his teacher, I was forced to return home without funds. I merely asked him for a few cash in order to defray my traveling expenses, and he not only refused to see me but had me expelled. How could such a cruel disciple exist in this world!

Hu was rendered speechless, and the audience felt that they were listening to a series of lies. As if he sensed this, the teacher-actor informed them that Hu had bound feet, and invited them to investigate for themselves. A few in the crowd who were on terms of enmity with Hu ripped off his shoes and revealed the tiny lotus hooks, thus corroborating the accuser's allegations.[14]

About 1900, foot wrapping was practiced by men in Tientsin. They first wrapped a square cloth around the feet, and then wore extremely tight and unyielding socks. The object was to get the feet so formed that they were pointed at the tip, thin, narrow, flat, and balanced. There was both a capital style and later a Shanghai style of shoe, differentiated by the appearance of the tip. The capital style was so abbreviated in front that the toes were covered only up to the second joint. The shoes were made out of a colored brocade, with a black brocade trim around them.

There was a Shanghai newspaper article in 1931 about still another case of modern male footbinding. Ai Shao-ch'uan, a native of Shantung, was over fifty years old at the time the story appeared in print. His parents had bound his feet in bowed form from childhood and had dressed him like a girl. He lived peacefully in his native village and was regarded as a woman by the villagers. In 1919, he went to Tsinan to avoid local banditry. He had been living there for only ten days when he was apprehended and jailed by local police authorities. He informed reporters who interviewed him that he was fifty-one years old and that his elderly mother was still living with him. They earned a living through the rent of farmland which they owned. Mr. Ai's father had served as an official in Honan. There he lost every one of his children in infancy and finally requested advice from a temple astrologer. He was told that the chain of misfortune could be broken only if he reared his next son as if he were a girl. That is why Ai's feet were bound from infancy onwards. He had taken a wife at eighteen, only to have her die soon afterwards. At the time of the interview, he stated that wearing feminine apparel had become a natural thing with him. The Tsinan press dispatch in the Shanghai *Times*, entitled "An Old Boy With Long Hair and Bound Feet," did not mention the final disposition of the case.[15]

An unverified newspaper report was cited about a certain handsome young man who vainly searched his city for a tiny-footed bride. He also tried the villages, but was repelled by the plainness of peasant girls. He finally decided to dress as a woman, had his feet bound by an old lady, and finally took her for his wife. But the gap in ages was so great that everyone took her for his mother. A friend who had known him before marriage paid a visit, but when he got to the house he saw only a young bound-foot lady standing before him.

> Don't you recognize me? I've bound my feet; aren't they pretty? Rub them; aren't they soft? Smell them; they have no bad odor, but only a lovely fragrance.

When the friend was introduced to the wife, an old and ugly lady who looked to him like someone's grandmother, he took fright and fled.[16]

The fictional theme of a man's being subjected to footbinding was used effectively by Li Ju-chen (c.1763-c.1830), a pioneer in the move to emancipate women. Li tried to achieve his objective by couching radical ideas in story form. He is justly remembered for the novel *Ching-hua yüan*, in which events of the seventh century served as historical background. In the novel, he described a series of incidents which had supposedly taken place during the reign of Empress Wu.[17] Li wrote about a country in which the usual roles of the sexes were reversed. A woman ruled there like the Empress Wu and enjoyed the favors of male concubines. A merchant named Lin Chih-yang once visited the royal compound in order to sell a line of cosmetics to the feminine sovereign. She had him invited into the palace under the guise of wishing to discuss sales prices, but her real intent was to force him into concubinage. The author tried to show the cruelty of such practices as ear piercing and footbinding by describing the sensations of the merchant when he was forced to undergo both:

> A white-bearded [male] palace "lady" took a needle and thread in his hands and knelt before the bed [on which Lin Chih-yang was seated], saying: "Honorable wife, I am ordered to pierce your ears." Four other palace "ladies" held him fast while the bearded "lady" rubbed his right ear several times and then quickly pierced it with the needle. Lin screamed out in pain and threw himself backwards, but fortunately was supported by palace attendants who prevented [a serious fall]. The bearded one pierced his left ear in the same way; Lin again responded with a series of screams. After both ears had been pierced, ceruse was rubbed into the apertures and decorative gold earrings were inserted.

The ear piercing and footbinding which Li Ju-chen wrote about in sequence were associated practices at least as early as the Yüan dynasty.[18] Another passage in the book described how Merchant Lin's feet were bound:

> A black-bearded palace attendant, with a white roll of cloth in his hands, knelt before Lin's bed and said: "Honorable wife, I am ordered to bind your feet." Two other palace "ladies" knelt

down, grasped his golden lotuses, and removed his stockings. The black-bearded attendant sat on a footstool. He split the cloth in two, and placed Lin's right foot on his knee. Rubbing white alum between the toes, he pressed them tightly together. He forced the surface of Lin's foot into the shape of a bow, and bound it with the white cloth. Every time he wrapped the binding twice, another attendant would meticulously tie it together with needle and thread. Utmost effort was exerted in both sewing and binding. Lin was unable to move; four attendants held him tightly, while two others grasped his legs. When the binding was completed, his feet felt like burning coals, fired by a successive series of pain flashes.

Lin soon discovered that the pain of having one's feet bound was unbearable. That night, when the palace attendants in charge of watching him fell asleep, he took off the bandages to let his feet resume their normal shape. The guards discovered this on the next morning and as a punishment whipped him five times on the buttocks with a long, thick bamboo rod, causing a stream of blood. The imposition of fifteen additional strokes was suspended only after he promised under pressure to let his feet be bound once more. This was done, and from that time on he was guarded day and night. The pain was so intense that he asked for death, preferring that to a life of endless agony, but his request was denied. Within a fortnight, the flesh on his toes had begun to decay. His legs gradually withered, while his bound feet bled daily and deteriorated into two stump-like protuberances. He lost the ability to walk independently and could hobble about only with the support of attendants.

In another part of *Ching-hua yüan*, Li Ju-chen eloquently summed up the case against footbinding:

I have heard that women here observe a practice of footbinding. When the feet are first bound, the women endure every conceivable pain, rubbing their feet and crying piteously. Things reach such a state that the skin and flesh putrefy and the blood flows. They can't sleep at night or get their food to stay down, and as a consequence every sort of illness follows. I thought that these women must have been unfilial and that their mothers, who could not bear to see them receive a death penalty, punished them in this way instead. But little did I realize that this practice arose from a concept of beauty. Only such bound feet are considered beautiful! If we cut down someone's nose to make it smaller, or lopped off protruding cheeks to make them level, wouldn't such persons be considered deformed? Why is it then that the two feet are so deformed that walking on them becomes extremely difficult, and yet this is regarded as beautiful! Did Hsi Shih and Wang Chao-chün, our two ancient beauties, ever have their feet cut in half?

If you try to discover the cause of footbinding, it is none other than male lewdness. This is a practice which must be avoided by the virtuous and eradicated by the Sage.[19]

Li Ju-chen voiced his intellectual protest a century and a half ago, at a time when the craze for tiny feet must have been near its acme of popularity. While an effective critic, Li preferred to present his views in the form of fictional narrative. His contemporary Yüan Mei (1716-98), a famous poet, critic, and essayist, opposed footbinding openly and directly. In *Tu-wai yü-yen* he commented:

. . . customs change men, at first slowly, but after a long while these changes are looked upon as if they were ordained by Heaven. This is true of eating, drinking, and man-woman relationships. It is indeed strange that everyone conforms and that no individualistic view emerges. . . . What is the good of making a woman's feet so small because every generation is mad about this? I think that to maim your own daughter's limbs to make them prettier is like burning the bones of your parents in order to seek good fortune. How pitiful! [20]

Yü Cheng-hsieh (1775-1840) was another liberal scholar who defended the rights of women. Yü opposed footbinding because it so weakened women that they lost the vigor characteristic of ladies of antiquity. He also remarked that bowed shoes were formerly the humble equipment of dancing girls. Women debased themselves by wearing such shoes, remarked Yü, and so did the men who encouraged them.[21]

These voices in the wilderness, few at first but increasing with the passage of time, were forerunners of the revolutionary movement which freed Chinese women from their centuries of bondage.

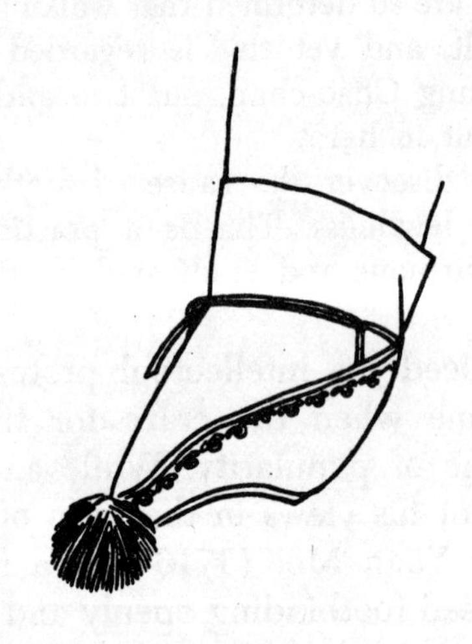

Part Three

CUSTOM

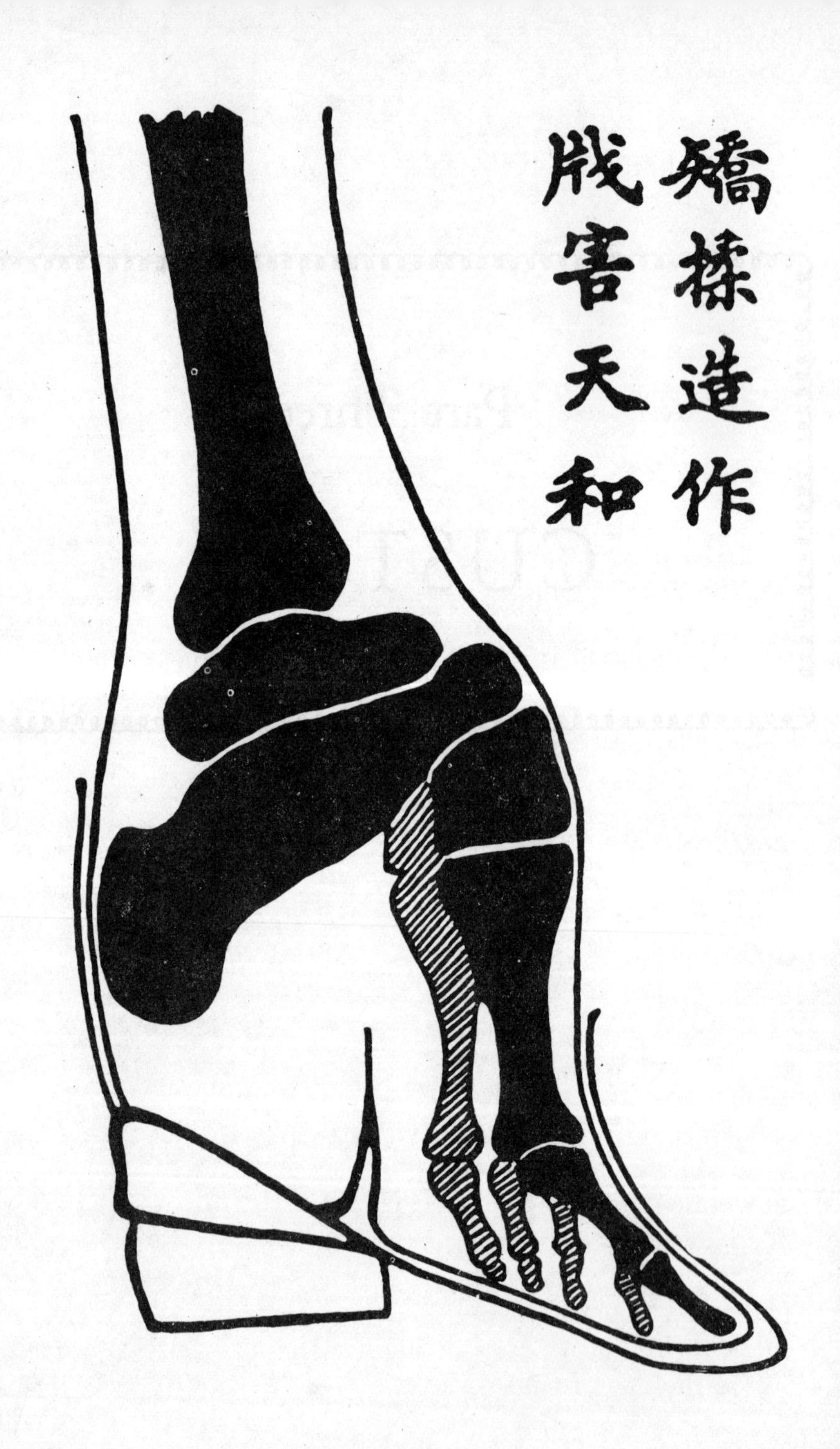
矯揉造作
戕害天和

CHAPTER NINE

Painful History of the Lotus Hooks

To the Chinese revolutionary, elimination of footbinding and emancipation of women were synonymous terms. Bringing the custom to an end was regarded as an important mission, but this was difficult because women still remained hidden and inaccessible within boudoir recesses. Foot reform enjoyed its initial successes in the larger cities and towns. Yen Hsi-shan accomplished much during his control of Shansi, but other provinces did not necessarily follow suit. While there were official orders everywhere against footbinding, enforcement depended on the ability and ingenuity of local officials.

By the late twenties footbinding was obviously on the wane. However, the conservative male view of woman as an inferior accessory and plaything remained fundamentally unchanged; in such an atmosphere, preservation of the old ways must have been regarded as natural and proper. Women stayed at home rearing children, doing household tasks, and serving their husbands. They were ignorant and cut off from the outside world. A father wanted his sons to go to school, but he ignored the intellectual development of his daughters. Conservative thinkers shied away from discussing a theme as personal as women's feet, and the peasant masses were even less inclined to talk about it. Therefore, though numerous decrees forbade footbinding, without a revolutionary change in mass outlook it was difficult to hasten the day of full effect.

The spread of public education gave educators a chance to persuade youth to break with outmoded tradition and advocate natural-footedness as a sign of modernity. Students in the late twenties and early thirties proclaimed unequivocally that they would refuse to take tiny-footed brides:

> A young boy to his mother said:
> Don't give me a bound-foot woman to wed!
> Yesterday our teacher told everyone,
> That bound-foot women are frail and dumb.
> They can't recognize words or understand books,
> And to the boudoir confine their looks.
> If with a son's wish you will abide,
> Don't arrange for me a bound-foot bride! [1]

Early revolutionary treatises facilitated the task of political propagandists by supplying them with ideological arguments. The four hundred millions of China were depicted as only half that number in actual strength because of the paralysis caused by footbinding. It resulted in "a wild disorder of flesh and blood and a violent plundering of the limbs," and it created a woman who could not "perform feminine tasks or take care of household matters; to the end of her life, she remains in an extremely weakened condition. Once the feet are bent, every illness assails the bones. Such women are inadequate as mothers and cannot produce strong children." [2] It was made clear that the feminine population had become footless because of a warped national outlook which regarded footbinding as an exalted virtue. Since parents came to expect it of their daughters and husbands of their wives, everyone wanted to perpetuate the custom of having warped extremities. Parents inflicted it on the child without considering it oppressive, and neighbors praised it as being in the normal order of human developments. China was contrasted unfavorably with Europe and the United States, where females as well as males could be fully used to serve the nation. It was further argued that binding stood in the way of feminine education, which was essential to raise intellectual levels and national prestige.

Footbinding achieved its greatest popularity towards the end of the Ch'ing dynasty, but the seeds of destruction were already evident. The frequent dynastic prohibitions against it increased awareness of its shortcomings, and an abolition movement came to be supported by liberal Chinese critics and Western missionaries. These diverse elements worked together closely as time went on; after the Revolution, the attack gathered increasing momentum and wider scope.

In August, 1928, the Ministry of Domestic Affairs announced sixteen regulations against footbinding and ordered all prefectures to carry out enforcement. The essential points were:

> Young girls under fifteen are to let out their feet if bound and not bind them if still unbound. The fine for disobedience is to be more than one but less than five silver dollars. Women over thirty are to be advised to let out their feet but not forced to do so.
>
> Three months will be allowed for persuasion, but the next three months will be devoted to enforcement.
>
> Each District Magistrate and Bureau of Public Safety Chief is to assemble the elders and seniors of his locality and ask them to work actively for abolition.
>
> The founding of foot emancipation clubs is encouraged, and free assemblage for this purpose is granted.
>
> Women investigators will be appointed to assist village and street elders in conducting periodic examinations.
>
> Primary school texts are to have a chapter added on the prohibition of footbinding so that an emancipation mood will be fostered among young students, who will then influence their families and relatives. [Popular articles intended to evoke a mass response were also inserted in the daily press.]

Propaganda, prohibition, and investigation were attempted in areas where footbinding prevailed, but the effect varied with popular attitudes and the methods used by individual administrators. One effective leader was Teng Ch'ang-yao,[3] Chief of

Civil Administration in the conservative stronghold of Shensi Province. Mr. Teng ordered foot emancipation for all women, with violators to be punished, shortly following a great fire in which most of the several-dozen killed and injured proved to be tiny footed; they had been unable to flee. Members of his Civil Affairs Office conducted private investigations and arbitrarily confiscated bindings, which soon numbered into the thousands. Mr. Teng put them in one room and invited people to attend a meeting there. Those who did had to hold their noses because of the stench.

Mr. Teng led excursions into the villages. If he saw a woman with tiny feet, he exhorted her kindly to renounce the practice and explained to her why it was injurious. If the listener got angry, Teng's co-workers sang amusing propaganda songs:

> Big sister has big feet;
> See how fast she walks the street!
> Little sister has tiny feet;
> With each step, she sways complete.
> Big sister grows vegetables, tills the fields,
> Takes cabbages to market on a carrying pole.
> Little sister, who can do none of these,
> Washes her bindings, kneeling at the river bank;
> Everyone runs away when they smell the stank!
>
> Letting out the feet is best,
> Letting out the feet is best,
> Large-footed maid walks without rest.
> But when tiny-footed maid perambulates,
> She sways twice for each step she takes.
> To go to the base of the mountain,
> It takes all day;
> Once there, hugging tiny feet,
> Mama! Mama! is all she can say.[3]

These propaganda campaigns enjoyed their swiftest success in the cities, but they encountered stubborn resistance in the interior. To reinforce the campaign of peaceful persuasion, Mr. Teng decreed in 1927 that recalcitrant footbinders would suffer these monetary fines:

> Over forty, two silver dollars; over twenty but less than forty, five silver dollars; under twenty, ten silver dollars.

This order weakened village resistance. A large Befriend the People Gathering was convened in November, 1927, at the Civil Affairs Office. Footbindings of every conceivable variety were exhibited along two corridors, like scarves in a department store. There were also several-hundred tiny red shoes on view, and foot emancipation signs were displayed inside the buildings. Mr. Teng ascended the stage and gave an amusing talk, smelling a pair of tiny shoes in his hand and pretending that this made him nauseous. When a few tiny-footed young ladies entered, he escorted them to the stage and, after friendly persuasion, removed their bindings. As a climax to the performance, he had his wife go up to the stage and show the interested crowd that her feet were natural-sized. Mr. Teng was also active in Honan, where he gave a reward of five silver dollars to anyone who brought in a hundred bindings. This produced excellent results; over 25,000 bindings were confiscated in less than a month.

A meeting at Hankow in Hupeh Province was held on April 19, 1927, open only to Kuomintang women party members whose feet were natural or had been let out.[4] A larger meeting in Chekiang that year had as a secondary motive unbinding of the breasts, which customarily were tightly bound so as not to protrude. More than a thousand women attended and were lectured to on the theme, "Not letting out the feet means that one is willing to be a man's plaything."[5] After Feng Yü-hsiang occupied Honan, he directed that family members of his armed forces lead in abolishing footbinding; this had an immediate effect.[6] A county chief in Kiangsi buried a huge collection of bindings and erected a monument inscribed with the words: "Tomb of Tiny-Foot Bindings." When school children gave a propaganda play at Lanchow in Kansu Province, a woman who had lost three toes through binding was paraded through the streets by her in-laws, with her tale of woe written out for all to see.[7] One district in Hopei issued two thousand badges to elementary school boys who would join a Society Against Marriage to Bound-Foot Women and make a written pledge to that effect. The badge was worn as a mark of distinction.[8]

There were specific instructions for letting out the feet:

1. When you make shoes to fit the foot which has been let out, the size should be one-half or one inch longer than usual. If you feel upon wearing it that the tip is too wide, stuff it with cotton. As the foot gradually gets larger, decrease the amount of cotton until eventually it is no longer needed.

2. Make a short binding cloth, one to two feet long. Bind the foot to a lesser extent, to let it gradually become more relaxed, but do not on any account suddenly eliminate use of the binding cloth. This will cause the blood to flow so violently that pain and swelling will result.

3. Wash the foot nightly in hot water, adding a little vinegar to the water.

4. Stuff cotton between the toes, allowing them gradually to expand outwards.

5. When you go to sleep, you must remove binding-cloth and stockings to allow the blood to circulate. Upon getting up in the morning, bind the foot loosely. When swelling or pain are no longer felt, remove the binding cloth completely.

6. If you follow the above method, you can let out the feet in one month's time.[9]

Women with bound feet who lived during the transitional era suffered twofold. They endured the pain and discomfort of binding in tender childhood, only to be told in maturity that their sufferings had been in vain because of the demands of the Revolution and the change in aesthetic viewpoint. The difficult position in which they found themselves is illustrated by the following incident which took place in a Shantung village. The county chief led two girls with the tiniest feet in the county to the public hall, wishing to force them to let out their feet as an example to other recalcitrants. Before the audience, each held up a dried twist of dough and explained:

> We brought these along because the county chief wants to compel us to let out our feet. Let him carefully look at these spiral shapes, already tight and dried out, sour and brittle. If he can restore them to their original prefried shape without breakage or damage, we will immediately comply with the order.

The county chief, at a loss for words, finally excused them.[10]

The tiny-footed came to be looked down upon and were made to feel ashamed. One city forbade them to appear in public places; another prohibited their walking in the streets; still another sent police to search them out and strip off the bindings. Fukienese officials at Changchow encouraged the local citizenry to whip the feet of any tiny-footed woman seen in public. In certain places, failure to exercise moderation led to such excesses that women committed suicide rather than face the shame of exposure or impoverish their parents by forcing them to pay heavy fines.[11] Some officials stressed foot emancipation because it was easily enforced against defenseless women and gave them and their subordinates a chance to increase income through levying fines, as well as to amuse themselves lewdly in the process. Many

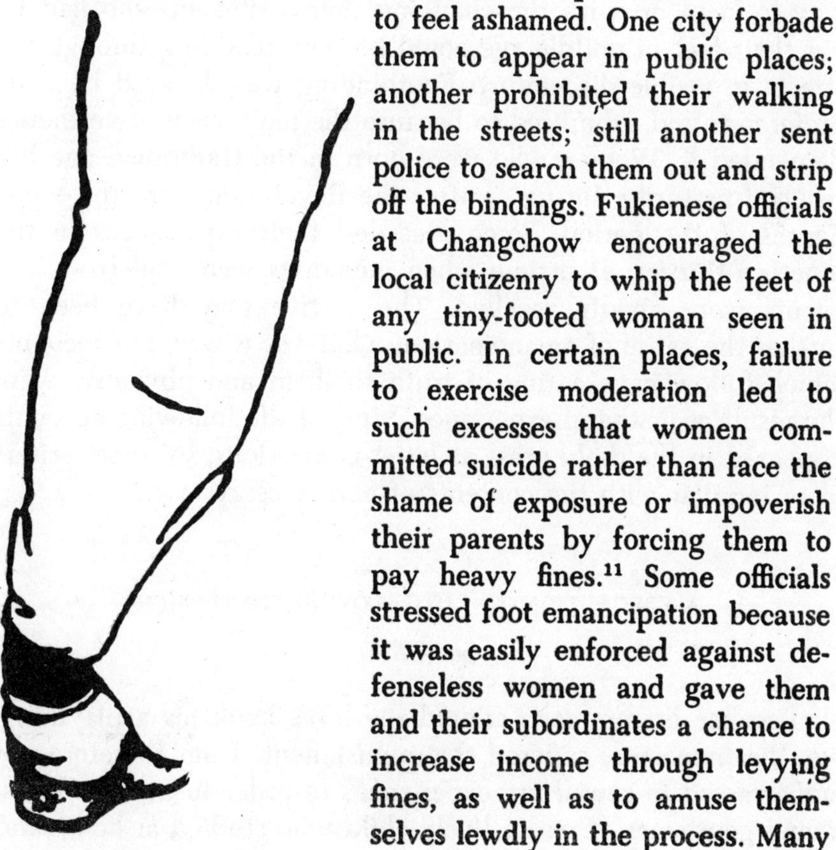

liberal thinkers of the time opposed the tendency to rely on monetary fines and punishment. "Use peaceful means to change this custom. Once the peasants understand its evils, they will change of their own accord."[12]

Wives who had formerly bound their feet now found themselves deserted or divorced. They had been forced into binding by their mothers to enhance their marital prospects, but the result was the reverse. When women heard of wives being rejected because of tiny feet, they tried everything to make the foot revert to normal size. To accelerate the process they would soak their feet in cold water nightly, suffering as much as in early childhood. No matter how hard they tried, there was really no way to keep up with the changing times. Women who had let out their feet in middle age could be seen plodding through the streets in visible discomfort. Footbinding was dictated by male preference and submitted to because the male view of aesthetics demanded it. Women who were born in the traditional age but reached maturity during or after the Revolution were the tragic figures of the period. Some recorded their experiences in the nineteen-thirties, at a time when memories were still fresh and events were vividly recalled. The motive may have been to further the cause of emancipation; whatever it was, the accounts which follow have a ring of truth to them and obviously were the result of firsthand experience. Most of the following accounts appeared in the daily press as letter-confessions, so some writers were familiar with the contents of earlier essays.

A PRECAUTION TO LOTUS-LOVING GENTLEMEN

by A-hsiu

Because literary men adored the lotus hooks as a plaything, we, the innocents, suffered this punishment. I am therefore not embarrassed to reveal my experiences in order to awaken lotus-loving gentlemen. I was a lively child who studied at home and liked to jump about and play. Toward the end of Manchu rule, when footbinding was still elevated, I was seven years old. Mother told our wet nurse to start my binding, and I informed my sisters that from the next day on my feet would be prettier than any of theirs. The wet nurse softened up my feet in a basin of water before binding them. She dressed me in new shoes and stockings and ordered me to walk, but I wept aloud from the pain in my toes. I begged mother to let out the binding, but she replied that it would have to be endured because only through it could I achieve the elegant lotus steps. She cautioned me that otherwise my feet would become foot-long lotus boats and prevent me from getting married. After school was recessed, I wanted to join my brothers and sisters in play, but my feet were immovable. From this time on, I lost my former activeness and spent restless and pain-filled nights. And the wet nurse rebound my feet when I awoke. It took a month for my toes to get tightly joined together and three to five months for them to press inwardly toward the plantar. The binding became tighter and the discomfort more acute.

I attended a birthday celebration for my grandfather in the following year. One of my cousins there had tiny feet under three inches, which prompted mother to insist that I get mine reduced to the same diminutive and lovely size. After that, the pain was increased. Mother was friendly with a tiny-footed widow named Lu and asked Mrs. Lu's mother to come to our home and bind my feet. The widow's mother was so skilled that the binding tightened with every step and lasted three or four days. I suffered severely, but under coercion from my mother dared not disobey. By the time the old woman died, more than a year later, my feet were narrow, pointed, less than a handful, and slightly over three inches. They were beautiful, but, oh, how I suffered! I began to bind them myself at thirteen; by then only tight binding made me feel comfortable and facilitated my walking.

At the start of the Republic, I went to study at a certain

girls' school. One of the courses was physical education, but my tiny feet prevented me from enrolling. My teachers told me that in keeping with the new spirit of the Republic I should let out my feet. But I declined, feeling that this would be useless since the bones were already broken. Schoolmates made fun of me, and one of them cruelly stepped on my feet, hurting me like a knife thrust. Though I wanted to fight back, I was too weak. After I married, my husband felt that everyone would laugh at me because my tiny feet were inconsonant with the times. To avoid ridicule, he wouldn't let me attend banquets or go on trips with him, so our relationship became extremely superficial. My happiness in life was entirely destroyed by having tiny feet. It is unlucky to be born a girl, but much worse to have to destroy one's limbs so that one's freedom is completely lost and even walking becomes a great problem. How incomparable and indescribable was the pain.[13]

PAINFUL WORDS ABOUT LOTUS HOOKS

by Chüeh Fei-sheng

The Record of Gathering Radishes has many poems but relatively few records of fact. But the revelations by Miss A-hsiu can be said to rouse a person from his folly. My wife also went through this experience. I wish to write of her sufferings and draw out the reader's sentiments.

My wife was born in the Ting District of Hopei Province. In keeping with custom, her feet were bound at the age of seven. Time has blurred much of her remembrance, but two incidents remain vivid to the present day. Her binding was once sewn together to make it even tighter, and she suddenly felt sharp pain along the tip of her foot, much greater than usual. She begged her mother to loosen the binding for relief, only to be told that tight binding was essential to achieve an elegant form. My wife put on her shoes as ordered, but the moment she walked on them a dart-like pain pierced her flesh. She secretly removed the binding in another room and saw that the needle used to fasten the cloth had been sewn into and through her flesh, so that the left side of her big toe was pinioned to the cloth. The binding had been so tight that bleeding was not yet visible. Her mother blamed herself for carelessness while the daughter wept.

By the age of fourteen her feet were tiny as bamboo shoots, and she had long since done the binding unaided. One day, her mother said to her: "A tiny foot should be slender, small, pointed, and proportioned. Your feet really have a major defect, because the insteps are out of proportion." My wife was determined to rectify this. She placed the soles of her feet opposite one another, sitting cross-legged, and pressed stones down on each foot. These stones ordinarily were used for beating clothing, and the pressure caused unbearable pain. After an hour, the area below her knees became completely numb. Upon completion, the swollen insteps were bound with an especially narrow cloth. Her insteps straightened out in two months, and heel and toe became much more uniform.

We married when my wife was eighteen; the shoes she wore measured 3.4 inches. Her heels were straight and even, with no puffing up of the instep. My mother and our neighbors often admired their beauty. I was from an average family, where daughters-in-law had to draw water from the well and pound the mortar. My wife, with tiny and weak feet, couldn't stand the heavy labor. Whenever foot infections caused her to have to sweep the floors on her knees, [as a type of soothing ointment] I placed bean curd peelings or vegetable leaves on her foot bindings. At such times, I couldn't help thinking of how evil and injurious this custom was; suddenly my fondness for the golden lotus came to an end.

With the success of the northern expedition, foot emancipation societies sprang up everywhere. Foot investigators came to our home several times, exhorting emancipation. My wife tried to comply, but, after thirty years of tight binding, she found that walking without bandages meant pressure with every step on the four smaller toes, curled until then inside the underpart of the foot. Severe pain was also felt along the deep crease of the sole. Two weeks of trial resulted in a puffed instep and no improvement. I saw how weak and swollen her legs were and ordered her to rebind in order to restore the previous tiny-footed normalcy.

Hereafter, I request of foot investigation personnel that they act with severity toward young girls but with leniency toward middle-aged ladies, so as to avoid a repetition of earlier suffering.[14]

AFTER READING PAINFUL WORDS

by Yü Shu-chen

Women with bound feet now must suffer the discomfort of letting them out. But few pay attention to this. I am a fairly-well educated woman who incurred a deep spiritual and physical affliction from footbinding. My desire for foot emancipation was natural, but since the bones were broken and could never be restored, I had to revert to binding because of the hindrances involved in doing otherwise. But who would have thought that a four-foot strip of binding cloth would cause me to be persecuted everywhere I went.

A few years ago, my husband and I went to live in Kaifeng. Authorities were then using foot bindings to measure the achievements of district chiefs. In other words, the responsible officials were expected to turn in binding cloths each month to prove they were getting results. A joke circulated about the district chief who, in order to comply with orders from above, bought new cloths and exchanged them for old ones with the people under his jurisdiction. Police were generally delighted to comply with these instructions, since it gave them a chance to lewdly amuse themselves. I was walking on the street one day when I suffered the great shame of having my bindings forcibly removed. The next day, I escaped to the home of my uncle in a certain city in eastern Shantung and lived there in idleness for one year. But, with the issuance of another order of prohibition there, enforced foot emancipation increased with every passing day. I was frightened, but fortunately just then my husband had to leave town on business. Again I made good my escape; this time to Shanghai, where I live peacefully to the present day. Almost every woman in Shanghai now has natural feet, and the few who do not move about unnoticed. Someone criticized me in these words: "You let out your feet but then rebound them, a sign of extreme obstinacy. It is your own fault that someone tampered with you [in forcibly removing the bindings]." I replied that there were many reasons other than preference which forced me to rebind.

The pain of foot emancipation has been described in an earlier essay. The pain after letting out the feet varies with the seasons. The blood circulates poorly in winter, making one particularly sensitive to low temperatures and causing nine out of ten to suffer from cold sores. In spring, the flesh decays, and this makes it hard to take a single step. Very quick binding alone can prevent this from happening. Emancipated feet take unsteady steps. No matter how they are let out, tiny feet have a bowed bone structure which can never be restored to what it was originally. The flesh may expand in shapeless lumps, but strengthening the foot is virtually impossible. If larger shoes and stockings are worn which, however, fail to fit, the woman stumbles about, twisting unsteadily in every conceivable direction. She is better off with feet tightly bound and relatively vigorous. Another point to mention is the swollen appearance. From antiquity to the present, woman clearly has done everything to please the opposite sex. Beautiful feminine make-up, for example, is still highly regarded by our contemporaries. The natural foot in high heels is well-suited to modern concepts of beauty. My generation, maltreated by custom, can never attain this new standard, but even a cripple doesn't forget to wear shoes. That is why we embellish these old-fashioned feet, to make them slightly more attractive. But when the tiny foot is liberated, the instep swells and the flesh becomes shapeless, like a camel's hump or a pig's foot. The poor woman stumbles about crookedly. Now while bound feet cannot achieve the natural size, they still have the qualities of being cute and petite, preserving the aesthetics of a bygone age.

Perhaps I should explain here that what I have said above pertains only to feet four-and-a-half inches or less in length, where the bones are already broken. If they have been only roughly bound to accord with former dictates of style, they can be easily let out by gradually loosening and shortening the binding. The previous essay requested that foot investigators be strict in demanding foot emancipation from the young and more tolerant toward the middle-aged. I think that such a method

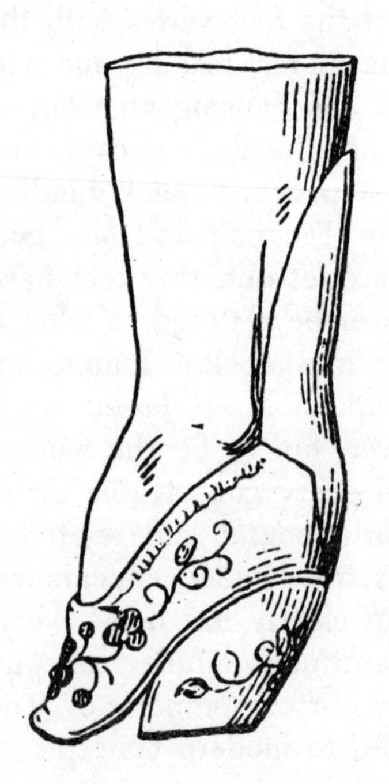

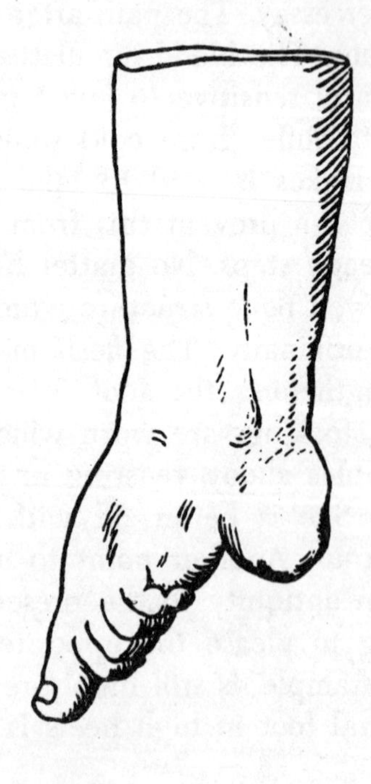

would still be unsatisfactory. If the foot is not small and the toes are unbroken, even a forty or fifty-year-old can liberate it. But for a girl of twenty who has very tiny feet, the reverse is true. It is wrong to think solely in terms of age, as wrong as it is to think of cutting the queue and liberating the feet in the same terms. The decision whether or not to liberate the foot should depend not on age, but on the way in which the foot was first bound. The best thing to do is prohibit it for the unbound, and in cases of violation severely punish the head of the household. Consider others on their individual merits; those with feet under four-and-a-half inches are few and will sooner or later die off.

The experimental Wan-tzu-fou[15] area of the Kiangsi Agricultural Improvement Society has been very effective in encouraging abolition. It reported that, "The abolition of footbinding is entirely different from the abolition of gambling or opium smoking; coercive methods should not be employed, for the

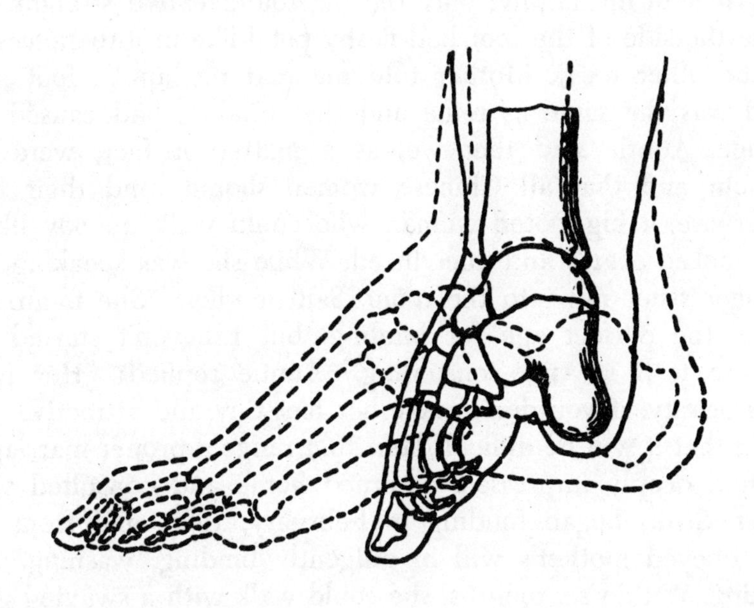

change should be made voluntarily." This is true, for with a new outlook and psychology the change will be permanent. May ladies in the women's movement take heed, to avoid making tiny-footed women like me again have to endure suffering.[16]

THE SUFFERING OF MY YOUNGER SISTER

by Chüeh Fei-shen

Having told the story of my wife, I shall now describe the suffering revealed to me by my younger sister. My family lived for generations in northern Peiping, with Manchus as our principal neighbors. That is why, in my childhood, I was never fully aware of the tiny foot. I once went with mother and younger sister to the home of my maternal aunt. There I noticed and marveled that the women all had tiny bowed feet. The next morning, I saw auntie arise and bind her feet and I stared curiously. I noticed that the shape of her foot was much different from feet in my family; only the big toe extended straight out, while the side of the foot had fleshy petal-like protuberances on it [the other toes]. Mother told me that my aunt's foot as a child was the same as mine and that binding had caused the change. Auntie said that we, as a matter of fact, were not Manchu and that all Chinese women should bind their feet. Otherwise, a big-footed woman who could walk quickly like a man looked coarse and uncivilized. While she was speaking, my younger sister ran into the room. Said mother: "She is already seven, the perfect age for binding, but I haven't started yet because it is so time-consuming." Auntie replied: "Her form lacks beauty; if you don't make her feet tiny and attractive, I'm afraid that it will be difficult later to arrange a proper marriage." Mother, deeply impressed, returned home and consulted with father. Sister began binding in February, 1908, and from the start obeyed mother's will in diligently binding, washing, and walking. Within six months, she could walk with a swaying gait. But the two smallest toes on both feet suddenly developed corns, hurt intensely from the slightest touch, and caused her to cry incessantly. Poor sister was sunk in despair. When auntie visited, and mother asked for her expert advice, she advised that, "When a girl first has her feet bound, one must exert pressure to make her oblivious to pain. Then success is relatively easy." She opened sister's binding cloth, looked over the foot, and said:

> Because she places her body weight on the heel when she walks, the fourth toe is not yet deeply bent. With every step she takes, her little toes rub against the sides or soles of the shoe, causing the corns. The way to alleviate this is to clear away the corns and very tightly rebind the four toes so that they bend under. This will make them coil deeply toward the plantar. Try to force them to become narrow and thin, and then force them toward the heel of the foot, curving the arch downward. The foot will naturally become smaller.

She requested a pan of boiling water and personally washed sister's feet in it. She cautiously rubbed where the flesh protruded, vigorously pressed on the ankle, and lanced the corns. This took her more than ten minutes, with mother pinioning sister's arms so that auntie could work undisturbed. She then used a cloth five feet long and two inches wide to force the heel and four toes to arch downward. She bound the arch and toes twice for each time she wrapped the binding around the heel. With each complete turn, she added a little sputum to make sure that the binding wouldn't work loose. The shoes which had to be worn were hard to get into because of the increased amount of binding cloth, and sister had to be supported before she could stand on her feet. Auntie dragged her hobbling along, to keep the blood circulating. Sister wept throughout but mother and auntie didn't pity her in the slightest, saying that if one loved a daughter, one could not love her feet. Mother gradually also became adept at binding, cajoling sister with sweet-sounding words. As she got older, sister became deeply aware of mother's fondness for it and became more cooperative. The ugly, coarse cloth shoes which had first been worn were replaced by elegant looking ones with wooden soles. [This replaced the older netted tip style.] By fourteen, her feet had already become models. Her soft toenails were sunk into the shriveled flesh; her thighs were very thin; and the plantar was as smooth as a flat board. At eighteen, she married a Mr. Chen and had to wait on her mother-in-law daily. She was always on her feet and could rest only noon and night. Her complaints because of ailing feet annoyed her husband, and he ordered her to let them out. However, her mother-in-law not only opposed this, but ordered sister to make new shoes just slightly smaller than her actual foot size. And she would revile her for not binding tightly enough. When sister gave birth, before the one-month period of prescribed rest had ended her mother-in-law personally bound both feet tightly for her. [There was a common belief that the bones opened up at childbirth and that, since the feet were somewhat relaxed, vigorous binding might make them even smaller.]

This happened more than ten years ago, but younger sister sighs grievously every time she thinks of it. Mother and my other two sisters had natural feet, so only she suffered this poison. It must have been her fate. Looking at it this way, footbinding was a product of the social environment; it is a distortion of fact to say that women did this to please their husbands.[17]

HALF-FOOT-LONG LOTUS

by Chüeh Fei-sheng

I now write about a mature woman who was insulted by her husband and mother-in-law because her feet were irregular. A certain family had three sons. The eldest son's wife had perfectly proportioned tiny feet. When the next son was ready to wed, emphasis was placed on the golden lotuses of the prospective bride. By 1915, maidens in Peking with tiny feet were becoming scarcer with each passing day. This scarcity delayed the marriage. The second son finally took a bound-foot bride from an outside district. On the wedding day, everyone scrutinized her as she walked with her buttocks swaying back and forth, and in general agreed that she must have false articles beneath her skirts.

Her husband heard this rumor and on the wedding night discovered that her feet were actually larger than her shoes. Moreover, they were plump and too large to be grasped in the hand. Dismayed by the deception, the groom retired. The bride realized how he felt and wept by the side of the bed as she confessed:

> I was orphaned in childhood, and my stepmother falsely consented to continue the old customs. But by the time I was promised in matrimony only this half-foot-long lotus had been produced. How could I bear to renounce your marriage proposal because of my lower extremities?

The groom was moved by her candidness and accepted the situation, advising her only to exercise the utmost care in concealing the truth. She made the heel higher than usual, to give the illusion of smallness, and used an iron heel instead of the usual bamboo one to give her firmer support. She stood and walked with apparent difficulty, clinging to walls for assistance. But once, when walking on a rough road, her foot came out of the shoe. Bystanders saw this and made a laughing matter of it. Her mother-in-law felt that she had disgraced the family name and asked her why her feet seemed as large as a maid servant's. "What face do you have? Take off your shoes and let me see how you bind." She did as she was told, removing the bindings. The old lady saw that her ankle was crooked, and that the five-inch sole was flat. The second toe bent under the big toe and the other three under the sole, towards the plantar. Her foot was completely off standard. The more she looked, the more she frowned. The chagrined bride, daily ridiculed by everyone, determinedly said to her mother-in-law: "I'm willing to endure any suffering if only you can force my foot to become smaller." This remark pleased the old lady, and she ordered her to wear cotton cloth shoes with firm and unyielding sides and soles. The sole was gradually transformed into a bowed shape. Then the cotton cloth was discarded in favor of a stronger and less flexible type of Peking cloth. Her mother-in-law supervised the binding day and night. She beat on the crooked heel with a pipe bowl to straighten it out. She forbade the girl to wear padded cotton shoes, even in the dead of winter, and only let her wrap the tip of the foot with cotton [as protection against the cold]. To curve the plantar, only bowed wooden soles were selected. In a few months, there was progress towards better proportion, with heels level and the plantar curved. She once caught a feverish cold and removed the bindings, but her mother-in-law so scolded her for doing this that she cried all night and almost killed herself by drinking kerosene from a table lamp. The suicide attempt made the old lady more understanding. After her death the daughter-in-law refused to let the feet out, because she had already suffered twice to achieve the tiny model. Unlike everyone else, her second toe is not bent under but extends under the big toe. If it could be photographed, it would make a rare view.[18]

LOST FREEDOM TEARFULLY ENDURED

by Mrs. Hsiu-chen

I was born in the south, at the end of the Manchu dynasty. My mother started the binding when I was just seven years old. I was used to freedom and wept, but mother did not pity me in the slightest. On the contrary, she said: "No matter how it hurts, I forbid you to loosen the binding." I was formerly very active, but became as dull as a wooden chicken and tearfully endured my suffering. Every few days the binding was redone, tighter than before. Sometimes I covertly loosened it, but if mother found out she reviled me and made it even tighter. After a few months, the toes bent inwards. In hot weather I suffered from intermittent fevers and stomach pains. There was a putrid odor everytime the binding was unraveled. To cure this, before binding, my feet were washed in a water mixed with pungent wild peppers; alum was also placed on the foot surface and between the toes. Alum reduced perspiration and killed the odor; after that, I always used it. My feet achieved the model shape in three years, a little over four inches long. Only the big toe protruded; the others were bent in towards the plantar and were tightly bunched together like so many superfluous warts. The surface was slightly humped and had several corns on it from the peeling of the flesh. My feet were so weak that I had to lean on walls for support in walking, tottering as if I were about to fall. I married at fifteen, and from then on bound by myself. I was most ashamed to let others see me do this, because of the weird and most unaesthetic appearance of the bare feet. Ten years ago, when the emancipation movement arose, I entered school to study. Family members encouraged me to let my feet out. This I did gradually, feeling that the bones were soft and the veins loose. Every night I washed the feet in warm water; gradually I cut the cloth shorter. After three years, while my feet had become somewhat plumper, the toes were still bent under and had failed to stretch out. So when I entered school, fearing that classmates would laugh at me, I stuffed cotton in my socks [in the place where the toes should be] and pretended that I had natural feet. Though I walked rather slowly, no one realized why.[19]

THE TWIN-HOOKED MAID

by Lotus-Loving Scholar

Two years ago, my wife hired a maid servant named Chang. She had twin hooks under her skirt, slender and not enough to grasp in one's hand. This is what *Tun-fang yu-chi*[20] meant in saying that they could be placed in a glass; such words were true. Though the maid was middle-aged, she still had an air of elegance about her. But she walked in a rather forlorn manner and could barely fulfill household tasks. My wife encouraged her to let her feet out, but this so increased her pain that she decided against it. She was of a gentle nature, and our family greatly enjoyed conversing with her. My wife was especially fond of her and always rendered a helping hand. One day, the maid unexpectedly spoke in great detail about footbinding experiences:

> I was born in a certain district in western Honan Province, at the end of the Manchu dynasty. In accordance with custom, at the age of seven I began binding. I had witnessed the pain of my cousins, and in the year it was to begin was very much frightened. That autumn distress befell me. One day prior my mother told me: "You are now seven, just at the right age for binding. If we wait, your foot will harden, increasing the pain. You should have started in the spring, but because you were weak we waited till now. Girls in other families have already completed the process. We start tomorrow. I will do this for you lightly and so that it won't hurt; what daughter doesn't go through this difficulty?" She then gave me fruit to eat, showed me a new pair of phoenix-tip shoes, and beguiled me with these words: "Only with bound feet can you wear such beautiful shoes. Otherwise, you'll become a large-footed barbarian and everyone will laugh at and feel ashamed of you." I felt moved by a desire to be beautiful and became steadfast in determination, staying awake all night.
>
> I got up early the next morning. Everything had already been prepared. Mother had me sit on a stool by the bed. She threaded a needle and placed it in my hair, cut off a piece of alum and put it alongside the binding cloth and the flowered shoes. She then turned and closed the bedroom door. She first soaked my feet in a pan of hot water, then wiped them, and cut the toenails with a small scissors. She then took my right foot in her hands and repeatedly massaged it in the direction of the plantar. She also sprinkled alum between my toes. She gave me

a pen point to hold in my hands because of the belief that my feet might then become as pointed as it was. Later she took a cloth three feet long and two inches wide, grasped my right foot, and pressed down the four smaller toes in the direction of the plantar. She joined them together, bound them once, and passed the binding from the heel to the foot surface and then to the plantar. She did this five times and then sewed the binding together with thread. To prevent it from getting loosened, she tied a slender cotton thread from the tip of the foot to its center.

She did the same thing with the left foot and forced my feet into flowered shoes which were slightly smaller than the feet were. The tips of the shoes were adorned with threads in the shape of grain. There was a ribbon affixed to the mouth of the shoe and fastened on the heel. She ordered me to get down from the bed and walk, saying that if I didn't the crooked-shaped foot would be seriously injured. When I first touched the ground, I felt complete loss of movement; after a few trials, only the toes hurt greatly. Both feet became feverish at night and hurt from the swelling. Except for walking, I sat by the *k'ang*. Mother rebound my feet weekly, each time more tightly than the last. I became more and more afraid. I tried to avoid the binding by hiding in a neighbor's house. If I loosened the bandage, mother would scold me for not wanting to look nice. After half a year, the tightly bound toes began to uniformly face the plantar. The foot became more pointed daily; after a year, the toes began to putrefy. Corns began to appear and thicken, and for a long time no improvement was visible. Mother would remove the bindings and lance the corns with a needle to get rid of the hard core. I feared this, but mother grasped my legs so that I couldn't move. Father betrothed me at the age of nine to a neighbor named Chao, and I went to their house to serve as a daughter-in-law in the home of my future husband. My mother-in-law bound my feet much more tightly than mother ever had, saying that I still hadn't achieved the standard. She beat me severely if I cried; if I unloosened the binding, I was beaten until my body was covered with bruises. Also, because my feet were somewhat fleshy, my mother-in-law insisted that the foot must become inflamed to get the proper results. Day and night, my feet were washed in a medicinal water; within a few washings I felt special pain. Looking down, I saw that every toe but the big one was inflamed and deteriorated. Mother-in-law said that this was all to the good. I had to be beaten with fists before I could bear to remove the bindings, which were congealed with pus and blood. To get them loose, such force had to be used that the skin often peeled off, causing further bleeding. The stench was hard to bear, while I felt the pain in my very insides. My body trembled with agitation. Mother-in-law was not only unmoved but she placed tiles inside the binding in order to hasten the inflammation process. She was deaf to my childish cries. Every other day, the binding was made tighter and sewn up, and each time slightly smaller shoes had to be worn. The sides of the shoes were hard, and I could only get into them by using force. I was compelled to walk on them in the courtyard; they were called distance-walking shoes. I strove to cling to life, suffering indescribable pain. Being in an average family, I had to go to the well and pound the mortar unaided. Faulty blood circulation caused my feet to become insensible in winter. At night, I tried to warm them by the *k'ang*, but this caused extreme pain. The alternation between frost and thawing caused me to lose one toe on my right foot. Deterioration of the flesh was such that within a year my feet had become as pointed as new bamboo shoots, pointing upwards like a red chestnut. The foot surface was slightly convex, while the four bean-sized toes were deeply imbedded in the plantar like a string of cowry shells. They were only a slight distance from the heel of the foot. The plantar was so deep that several coins could be placed in it without difficulty.[21] The large toes faced upwards, while the place on the right foot where the little toe had deteriorated away pained at irregular intervals. It left an ineffacable scar.

My feet were only three inches long, at the most. Relatives and friends praised them, little realizing the cisterns of tears and blood which they had caused. My husband was delighted with them, but two years ago he departed this world. The family wealth was dissipated, and I had to wander about, looking for work. That was how I came down to my present circumstances. I envy the modern woman. If I too had been born just a decade or so later, all of this pain could have been avoided. The lot of the natural-footed woman and mine is like that of heaven and hell.

Love of the lotus disappeared when I heard her words; my wife was also similarly affected. I have recorded this in order to warn the young girls of today against binding their feet.[22]

The use of medicinal waters to hasten the footbinding process, mentioned in the maid's account, was known throughout China. There were many prescriptions designed to soften the bones and make binding painless. Washing the feet in a broth of boiled monkey bones was cautioned against, as this made the feet so soft that one could never walk again. An approved prescription was to take a half ounce each of tannin, balsam seeds, and pomegranate skin, and boil these in water with three-tenths of an ounce of wormwood. Another method was to boil one-tenth of an ounce of almonds and four-tenths of an ounce of the bark of mulberry roots in five cups of water, until only three cups of the liquid remained. Then a half ounce of tannin and one-tenth of an ounce of frankincense were added and melted through further boiling. The feet were washed in this mixture once every three days; softening was guaranteed after more than ten applications. Still another way to "shrink the golden lotus" was to boil together white balsam, including blossoms, branches, leaves and roots, pound it into a powder, and add a little alum. The feet were bound while they were still warm from having been washed in this mixture. Another bone softener was an ash mixture made by burning together a similar amount of borax, China Root paste, and buckwheat sticks. Boiling water was added, and the feet were washed in it while the water was still hot. If the feet became so soft that walking on them proved impossible, the antidote was to wash them in water made by boiling together an ounce of raw alum, an ounce of purple copper powder, and a large bowl of *Yin-yang* water. This restored their original hardness. Soaking the feet in the blood of a newly-killed sheep was described as a special technique practiced only in Shansi. Special mountain herbs were also said to be especially efficacious and to produce wondrously quick results.

Corns were removed by directly applying to them a mixture of salt, vinegar, and overly ripe black plums. There was a special concoction designed to eliminate sores, and a way to make the bones extremely soft at the time of footbinding by applying a poultice. Another healing application consisted of a mixture of buckwheat and water chestnuts. An application of live centipedes and a fragrant hemp oil is also mentioned. Scars were removed by applying an astringent nut which had been ground into a medicinal powder. This was also efficacious for the relief of sore insteps. There were at least several dozen home remedies designed either to soften the feet or to cure different kinds of foot afflictions.[23]

HARASSED AND PERSECUTED

by Mrs. Meng

A woman of slight education, I now tell of my sufferings, to cause golden lotus lovers never again to regard women as playthings and to encourage pro-natural foot advocates to be unrelenting in their efforts.

I was born at T'ung District [near Peking] and at the age of two was betrothed to an old friend of the family named Meng. In 1901, I reached the age for footbinding. But just then the Manchu court sent down an order forbidding it. My family had suffered from the Boxer Rebellion and, knowing the inconvenience of tiny feet [in being unable to flee in a time of chaos], they did not intend to have my feet bound. But my fiancé's family informed my parents through the matchmaker that they disapproved. Mother decided to accommodate them and told me:

> Binding a child's foot creates a lifetime of difficulties. But since this custom is established, I fear that everyone will criticize me if I go against it. You'll want to be praised and revered, so you must endure the pain of severe binding. A daughter's pretty legs are achieved through the shedding of tears.

Having finished speaking, she started binding. I was a naturally active child, but with feet bowed my freedom was suddenly lost. Every day I sat immovable by the *k'ang;* when I heard the call for binding I tried to hide and had to be forcibly detected. Fortunately, my feet were small and achieved the model without requiring a full exertion of force. I also thought that tiny shoes were pretty, but mother told me that I couldn't wear them yet because my feet were not completely bowed. She reminded me of the saying: "Try for pointedness and slenderness before eleven; after twelve, try for a bowed appearance."

> We shall now force the heel towards the arch, so that the foot is bowed both front and back. After two months of your feeling discomfort in the plantar your foot will be bowed, and you can wear the tiny shoes whose tips touch the ground but have an empty arch in the center.

She later taught me how to balance myself while wearing them.

The binding was so tight that my left arch swelled, while the flesh deteriorated and was filled with pus. Scabs opened from each binding, and an ugly goose-head bump developed. When I was fourteen, father feared that my feet would become so tiny that walking would be seriously hampered and forbade mother to bind them for me any longer. From then on, I bound them myself. When I inspected them under a lamp, they were like two hooks. The flesh was scarred, only the main toe protruded, and the little toes sloped under. How could anyone ignorant of this custom have recognized that it was a human foot?

I married in the spring of 1912, and prior to the wedding

made ten pairs of bowed shoes and twenty pairs of flat shoes. [On the wedding day, village mothers-in-law opened the box of the bride's shoes and let everyone criticize them for craftsmanship or measure them for size.] The wedding guests praised my feet for being tiny and regular, greatly pleasing me. Mother-in-law was so fond of my feet that she ordered servants to do the manual labor. She let me sit with guests and, in order to impress the neighbors, had me change into new bright-colored shoes about once every three weeks. Then I realized that I had not suffered in vain. Even after years of marriage, it is strange to admit but I was ashamed to have my husband witness the daily binding.

After the military uprising of July, 1912, our resources dwindled and our servants scattered. I had to wait on my in-laws and take care of household matters. My legs swelled, and from midnight on I would become feverish. When my husband ordered me to let my feet out, I refused: "My mother never intended to bind my feet and did so only because your family insisted. Now you want me to let them out so that you can use me. I went through this torture once and can't bear a repetition of it." But later, I loosened the binding somewhat.

In 1930, a natural-foot society was convened. I was once standing outside my door when a woman foot investigator passed by and encouraged me to let out my feet. I tried to do as directed but, after tottering about for a few steps, discovered that my feet were bleeding. The investigator noticed my difficulty, inspected my feet, and compassionately rubbed the places where the veins had been injured and broken. "My mother forced me to do this when I was an ignorant child. Today I realize that the custom is unsanitary but, with such tiny feet, how can I change?" The investigator taught me another way to let them out which, unfortunately, had no effect. She later revisited, and we became like sisters to one another. This was another strange consequence of the foot emancipation movement.[24]

古式晉鞋

圖二十七

北式纖履

圖二十八

十餘年前山西式之棉鞋

圖二十九

A SELECTION OF TINY SHOES

Top: old Shansi style. Center: Northern style. Bottom: Shansi-style silk shoes worn in the 1920's.

THE TINY-FOOTED MISS

In the autumn of my sixth year, mother bought me embossed pointed shoes. She selected the 24th day of the eighth lunar month, which was the birthday of the Tiny-Footed Miss, to start my footbinding. That morning, she gave me water chestnuts and rice dumplings to eat, pleasing me very much. [This was done in the hope that the foot would assume these shapes.] The cloth was eight feet long and three inches wide. It was unusually long because of the above average length of my foot. The first three times, binding was not so tight as to be painful. On the fourth day, mother said that the real binding was to start. Then such pain was felt that I wept, asking that she relent. My toes were bent under and hurt like fire. The pain was unendurable, and that night I opened the bindings, only to be beaten by mother. It hurt all day, but everyone ignored my cries; I didn't feel like eating during the day and couldn't sleep at night. In less than a month, the binding cloth had stretched by a foot. The toes from the second to the smallest one were bent in one month's time.

The most feared and painful thing was the washing of the feet, done once every six or seven days. Opening the binding was comforting at first, but it became discomforting after the toes were bent under. Taking off the binding caused the whole foot to feel numb. Corns were removed, and the old skin was cut away, after which the foot was tightly rebound. I would sit around all day, immovable. A needle-like pain was felt with every step I took, but mother forced me to walk so that the bones could be more easily broken. After three months, every toe but the big one was completely bent under. Shoes worn when binding had first begun now seemed too large. Mother was a northerner, and she inserted bamboo slips in the binding, making it so tight that it had to be rebound only every other day. This added to the pain. Mother was going to place a copper coin on the foot surface, to prevent it from arching too much, but changed her mind.

Footbinding was usually considered completed when the bones were broken and the four toes were bent in a neat row towards the plantar. But mother kept binding for three more months, until the surface and the big toe looked like one bone. The foot was about three inches long, with the front about as wide as one's finger and the heel less than an inch wide. It was impossible to get it more slender. Pressure was always applied near the little toes, and I wept throughout. The "breaking" process took place from the age of six years and eight months to seven years and five or six months. The northern custom was to start when the child could walk, at about four years of age.

A neighbor's child started at five. Father opposed early binding, but mother took advantage of his having gone to another province to start the binding when I was six years old. Mother bound my feet for the next five or six years, but never again as tightly as she had that autumn. My feet recovered from their ailments, and binding became an accustomed thing. I couldn't walk distances, but I could get about freely and slept well at night. My feet were still bound tightly, however, after each washing. Father returned when I was nine and, when he saw that I had tiny feet and did not cry, remarked to mother that binding was after all not very difficult to accomplish. At thirteen or fourteen, mother ordered me to bind by myself, not letting me use a shorter binding or eliminate the use of the bamboo splints. I would have liked to have let my feet out after starting to study, but discovered that I couldn't walk a steo if the bindings were loosened.[25]

A PERFECTLY-WITHERED LOTUS

by Jen-shan

My wife, a native of western Peiping, once revealed to me her childhood experience of footbinding. Women in her family bound their feet; otherwise, they could not get married. Her elder sister started at four and achieved four-inch lotuses after two years of suffering. Her second and third sisters had similarly tiny feet. But by the age of eight my wife still hadn't begun, because her mother was bothered by a coughing illness which kept her in poor spirits. One day grandmother came to visit. She lived in a part of south Peiping where everyone bound and knew such a perfect technique that even someone slightly grown could achieve three-inch lotuses. Grandmother began the process a few days later.

Grandmother first washed the child's feet in warm water for about an hour to soften them. Then she used a five-foot cloth, pressing the toes towards the plantar but leaving the large toe exposed. She forced the large toe upwards with a smaller binding. My wife had to wear a hard-soled shoe and felt such fire-like pain that she couldn't walk. A few days later the binding was tightened, using an inflexible eight-foot cloth made of western horsehide. Each toe was bound tightly with white cloth; the other cloth bound the entire foot and was sewn into place. Shoes with very hard sides and a thin sole were worn; bone piercing pain was felt with the slightest step. Grandmother ordered her to walk, saying that otherwise the toes couldn't be forced under to reduce the foot and achieve a beautiful effect. Deterioration of the flesh occurred a few days later. The feet were washed nightly, with the peeling flesh removed and alum sprinkled on. Grandmother told her: "Because you're so big, this is the only way to reduce your feet. We can get them to a little over four inches in about

forty days." The forty days of pain were indescribable. Shoes were changed every ten days, each smaller than the last. Three-inch lotus hooks, in a bowed and new moon shape, resulted after about half a year. At fourteen, she wore wooden-soled bowed shoes and usually felt no pain in walking. She was of robust physique, enjoyed perfect health, and was stronger than her three sisters [who had bound at a much earlier age]. Though she had suffered, the result was attractive.[26]

PAINLESS BINDING

Because I was not the eldest, mother did not start binding my feet until I was thirteen. Even at that age I was about the size of an eight or nine year old, with small hands and feet. My feet were first washed in hot water and then rubbed for one hour. A six-foot cloth was slowly and rather loosely wrapped around them. Mother then placed my feet by the *k'ang* and slowly but firmly pressed down on them with both hands, gradually bending under the toes. The binding felt loose and in no way painful. This was followed by daily binding and washing; the feet were massaged by hand until pain was no longer felt. The feet, bound more tightly daily, gradually became smaller.

The toes were inspected daily, to see that they were bending under towards the heart of the foot. Even when they were tightly bound, I felt no pain. Because mother was sympathetic, she would tightly bind, put silk stockings on my feet, and then massage them vigorously both inside and out. [The foot was stretched out flat on the *k'ang*, with the girl in a reclining position.] This brought me relief in about half an hour. The vigorous massage restored blood circulation, and the cloth seemed to impinge only lightly on the bone structure.

In less than a year, the feet had become pointed and less than four inches long. The method was painless; massaging accounted for sixty to seventy per cent of the results, the binding only thirty to forty per cent. The foot never swelled or suffered any malfunction; I was able to walk slowly but comfortably. It was only at night, sleeping footbound near the hot *k'ang*, that I felt distressed. If it was too hot my feet swelled and hurt, but the only way to avoid this pain was by frequently changing positions. Mother's massage had great effect. Women who still bind their feet would diminish discomfort considerably by following this method.[27]

A SPECIAL WASHING FORMULA

by Lin Chang-liu

I am a southerner, born at the end of Manchu rule, at a time when women still revered bound feet. Mother started to bind mine when I was four. She first went to a pharmacy to buy three-tenths of an ounce of grease[28] and half an ounce of almonds. She boiled these in water and soaked my feet in the solution until the water got cold. Alum powder was sprinkled between the toes as a perspiration preventative. Mother used a pen to trace the shape of my natural feet, as a remembrance. She bent my toes towards the plantar and bound the foot, leaving the large toe outside of the binding. She wrapped a second cloth around my heel and big toe, getting the toe to point upwards like a new moon. The end of the cloth was sewn in place. She told me to walk, saying that if I didn't the foot would be badly shaped and would suffer from a multitude of ailments. The pain was severe, but I dared not disobey her for fear of otherwise becoming ill and requiring medication. The next day mother washed my feet in a medicinal mixture and bound them tightly. This became a daily habit, and I did nothing but walk around. After five or six days, I discovered upon removal of the binding that all the toes except the big ones were bruised. Mother wiped off the blood and changed the binding cloths. After four years, my feet were properly formed. They were three inches long and an inch wide at the heels, with big toes pointing upwards like a new moon. I disliked the morning binding intensely, because it was time-consuming and very smelly besides. Later, mother bought three-tenths of an ounce of borax and mixed it in with the foot-washing water. This prevented the smell for five days. I washed my feet and changed the binding cloth daily. The cloth was three feet long and an inch and a half wide. Mother made all my shoes but the sleeping shoes; these I made myself. Women at that time knew how to sew. The toes were already fixed towards the plantar, with the small toes close to the heels. There was a deep, ugly-looking crease in the plantar. When my feet were placed flat on the ground, the big toes were the only ones visible, pointing upwards. Mother praised me for my tiny feet, and I felt very proud of myself.

When I reached the age of nine, natural feet began to prevail. Father was made school principal in Pin-chiang[29] and took mother and me there. Father thought that since as principal he was advocating foot emancipation, it was only proper that he order me to let my feet out. I was unwilling, because I thought that tiny feet were the most beautiful. But I changed my mind as I learned about the harmfulness of footbinding. To let out my feet, I washed them three times in a special medicinally prepared water which made the bones very soft. I then pulled the four toes flat and massaged them. The letting out process was completed in less than half a year. My feet were natural again, but quite thin and narrow and only a little over five inches long. Now they have grown an additional inch. The formula which I used to wash my feet startled everyone with its effectiveness.[30]

THREE-INCH LOTUS DREAMS

by Chin So-hsing

I lived in Men-t'ou Village[31] as a child; it was a village where girls considered tiny feet beautiful. When I was just six years old, mother started my footbinding. She first bound the right foot, then the left, and had me wear red cloth shoes.

After a long time, I no longer felt pain, and by the age of eight or nine could do the binding myself. By eleven, my feet were 4.5 inches long, and bowed. On grandmother's birthday, I went with mother to visit her. My cousins had tiny feet, and my uncle laughed at me for having such big and fat feet by comparison, saying: "Who would be willing to be your matchmaker?" Everyone who heard this remark laughed, making me feel so ashamed that I determined to bind my feet to the utmost in order to wipe out the disgrace. That night, when everyone was asleep, I rebound so tightly that I had to clench my teeth because of the pain.

My sleep that night was filled with dreams of tiny three-inch feet. The next morning, though the pain had lessened, I had to cling to the walls for walking support. After ten days of treatment my feet measured only 3.8 inches, which was seven-tenths of an inch less than before. Three or five days later, my toes became swollen and filled with pus. After one month, they had become nine-tenths of an inch smaller, or 2.9 inches. My feet had become the best of the surrounding villages![32]

The pain involved initially in footbinding must have been extreme and at times excruciating for the women who recorded their experiences to have remembered these details of early childhood so vividly. The intensity of suffering must have depended somewhat, however, on the nature of the daughter-mother relationship and on the amount of maternal care devoted to the binding process. In one case, frequent massage alleviated discomfort; in others, the maternal reminder that only in this way could beauty be achieved afforded some solace to the young girl who was approaching womanhood. The greatest cruelties must have been inflicted by either stepmothers or those in a prospective mother-in-law status. The element of motherly love was missing in either instance, and the absence of words of comfort must have intensified the terror and dread felt by the unprotected child. Our recorded biographies reflect the modesty of the writers, women of respectable backgrounds, and no reference is made to the sexual attraction for the male which the tiny foot possessed.

CHAPTER TEN

Ladies of the Bound-Foot Era

This chapter includes the translated statements of elderly Chinese ladies as they recall a central event in childhood--the binding of feet to stunt growth and conform with the aesthetic and social standards of a bygone era.[1] Their testimony has been supplemented by other records in narrative form.[2] Eleven women were interviewed in Taiwan between October, 1960, and May, 1961. While general areas of agreement emerged, there was occasional divergence on specific points. For example, all informants agreed that binding was painful, except for one, a seventy-one-year-old Taiwanese. When Mrs. Ch'en Cheng Chien was asked how she felt at the start, she stated:

> It didn't hurt. Mother liked her daughters very much and when the process started was very comforting, telling me that when I married small feet would be considered the most beautiful and would impress everyone. I never stealthily removed the bandages, as I wanted to be beautiful. I liked making the shoes very much. Because my family was relatively well-off, I often competed with my sisters to see whose foot was the prettiest and who made the most elegantly embroidered shoes. Every day we were very happy together.

When asked about her mother's reactions, Mrs. Chen replied: "I was unaware of pain and never told Mother that my feet hurt, so I don't know."

Mrs. Ch'en must have enjoyed a happy childhood and the kind of loving maternal care which minimized the discomfort involved. But her reactions contrasted sharply with those of other informants. There was a seventy-two-year-old mainlander from Kiangsi named Madam Hsiung who, when asked, "Was footbinding painful?" remarked: "It was very painful at the start. I cried and cried everytime. But the pain left after several months." "How did your mother feel when she first began binding your feet?" "She surely felt bad, but with unbound feet a girl could not easily find a husband." Mrs. Yang Mien, an eighty-one-year-old Taiwanese, had this to say:

> My foot felt very painful at the start, and the heels became odoriferous and deteriorated. Cotton and wine were used to cure it. My whole body became emaciated, my face color changed, and I couldn't sleep at night, frightening my mother.

"How did mother feel when she first began binding your feet?" "I cried out because of the pain in my foot, and Mother and Grandmother could not bear to see me cry, so we cried together. . . ." "Did someone have to support you when you walked?"

> A person's support wasn't needed, for I was able to walk by holding on to the wall for support. But when I first started footbinding, I couldn't even do that, for when I stood up it hurt. I had to sit down, and sat most of the day. My family were very good to me and would take food in for me to eat. . . . Five days after the foot was bound, it could be washed, but it hurt painfully. Very young children probably didn't know severe pain.

(The photographs indicate that Mrs. Yang Mien, who still binds, was subjected to a more severe foot compression than Mrs. Ch'en, who gave up the practice at the age of twenty.)

The statement that one out of ten girls died from footbinding was undoubtedly an exaggeration, perpetrated by missionaries and others who were unalterably opposed to the practice. An objective historian remarked that as a custom it was more inconvenient than dangerous. He noted that "among the many thousands of patients who have received aid in the missionary hospitals, few or none have presented themselves with ailments chargeable to this source." [3] One Chinese doctor, in speaking of the indirect adverse effects, stated that it caused the menstrual flow to become irregular. Tight binding brought this about by constricting veins and slowing circulation. Disease symptoms were constipation, a sore back, dizziness, and vomiting.

> These finally become chronic complaints. The irregular flow of blood causes such worry and is so uncontrollable that finally a doctor is sought. A good doctor can alleviate the condition, but one ignorant of its causes can imperil the patient's life.[4]

It is apparent, however, that women who completed the binding process without medical complications enjoyed a normal life expectancy; nine of our eleven elderly informants had outlived their husbands.[5] They lived quietly and simply, confined to the home but amply looked after by children and grandchildren. Some had given up the practice; others bound to the present day. Varying in age from sixty-six to eighty-nine, they answered the following questions:

When did you bind your feet? (and, if the feet had been let out) When did you let them out?

How did your mother feel when she first began binding your feet?

What shape of bound foot was considered most beautiful?

What was the relationship between footbinding and age?

Was it painful to walk with bound feet?

How far could one walk on bound feet?

How was the foot bound?

What did you do when you went to sleep?

How often were your feet rebound?

What were the shape and color of the shoes?

MRS. YANG, WHO HAS LET HER FEET OUT

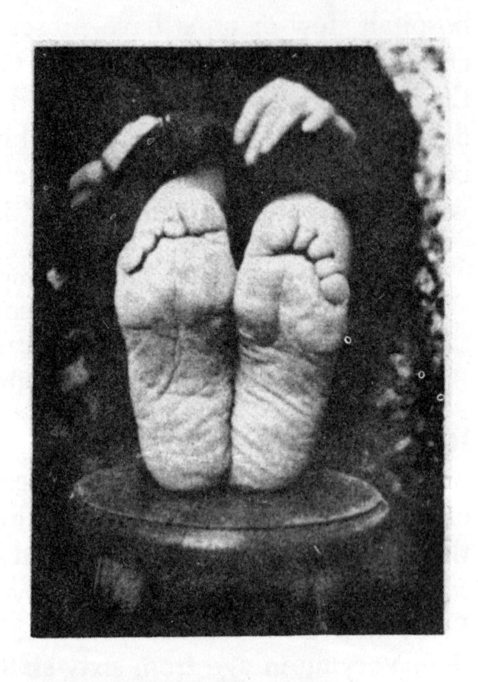

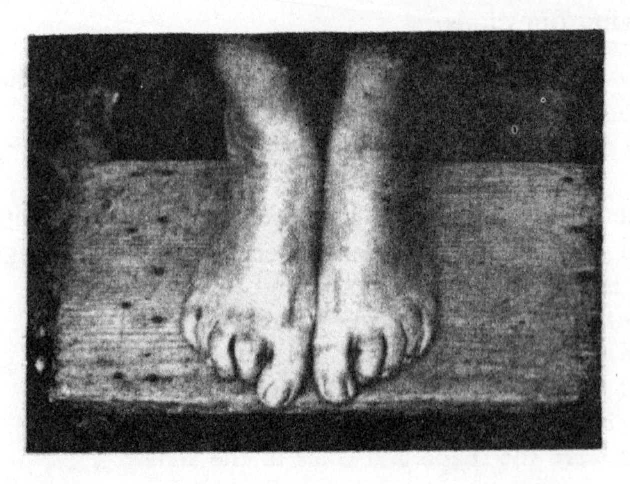

MRS. CH'EN, WHO STILL BINDS

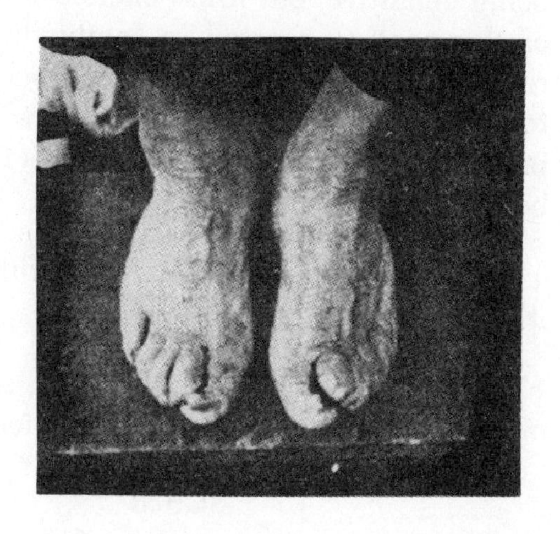

Were shoes and cloth part of the dowry?
How prevalent was this practice?
(If the feet were let out) Why were your feet let out?
When did this practice originate? [6]

This study is of limited scope and makes no pretense of being definitive, but it has elicited information as to how women of this century reacted to footbinding. Our questions and the replies of informants are recorded below; informants are referred to by a number in parentheses, which is the order of their presentation in the sixth footnote. (Regular footnotes are numbered without parentheses.)

A. When did you start footbinding and when did you give it up?

(The Chinese add a year at birth, so one year should be subtracted to determine the chronological age.)

	Started	Gave it up
1. Feng	3	26
2. Hsiung	11	over 30
3. Kuo	8	still binds
4. T'ung	7 or 8	23 or 24
5. Ch'en	9	still binds
6. Wu Han	4	still binds
7. Yang	9	about 36; later rebound
8. Ch'en Chien	4	20
9. Liang	3	still binds
10. Ting	5	30
11. Shih	4 or 5	still binds
12. Nan-t'un (for most Taiwanese)	6	—
13. Liu	12	15

There was a wide variation in the starting age, ranging from three to twelve. Some informants volunteered details:

I started to bind my feet when seven or eight years old and let them out in about 1918 or 1919. The revolutionary army was then fighting with the military warlords; to flee from the calamities of war, many women let their feet out for convenience, and thus started a trend. (4)

I began footbinding at the age of nine, but before nine I wore small shoes to prevent my feet from getting any larger. I let them out during the Japanese occupation but later rebound them again. (7)

I started when four or five. At first my foot was merely wrapped around with a cloth to keep it from growing larger. I started to bind tightly when about fifteen years old. (11)

The usual age for starting [in South China among the upper class] was between three and four. The child was carried and didn't walk about for three to four years afterwards. The shoe was smaller than the foot, with the rear part of the foot extending beyond the shoes. (13)

Most Taiwanese girls were six when they began to have their feet bound. However, some said that it was easier to have this done at an earlier age. (12)

According to one writer, it was customary in the villages to begin between five and seven years of age. The bones were still fragile, and the foot could easily be bound small. If one waited longer, the hardening of the bones impeded the process, and the sufferings of the child increased immeasurably. Another generalized that, "Most begin from five to eight years of age. Parents inflict this process when the child is barely able to travel about on its own. Upper-class families begin it when their children are four years old."[7] In Peking at the turn of the century, feet were generally bound at seven, with the earliest and latest ages for starting being four and eight, respectively. It took five or six years to complete the compression.[8]

B. Who taught you how to bind your feet?

The replies indicate that a mother almost always personally taught her daughters, with grandmother occasionally assisting. At least in one instance, the wife did not start binding until she had first secured the husband's consent. (11) Somewhere between the ages of eight and thirteen, girls began binding their feet themselves and unaided. One woman stated that ". . . after about the age of thirteen, I began to bind them myself as tightly as I could, so they would look pretty." (5) To another lady, this became a portent of her mother's death:

> The footbinding was started when the coming of the new lunar year was being celebrated. Mother told me that she wanted to make me a pair of red shoes to wear, but I replied that I wanted white shoes and didn't like red shoes. This was an ill portent, as Mother died soon afterwards. [To the Chinese, the color white symbolizes death.] I was eight years old when I started footbinding by myself, and was taught to do so by my foster mother. (6)

Yang Mien (7) was seized by conflicting emotions, the desire to be beautiful and the fear of intense pain:

> Grandmother helped me bind my feet, but she died when I was ten, and from then on Mother helped me. Mother was very strict. My foot felt very painful at the start. The heel of my foot became odoriferous and deteriorated. Cotton and wine were used to cure it. Because of the pain in my foot, my whole body became emaciated. My face color changed and I couldn't sleep at night, frightening my mother. I did not dare stealthily remove the binding cloth because of the pain, for I would have been beaten. When I saw how pretty the tiny feet of others were, I liked that very much. My cousin told me that no one wanted to marry a woman with big feet, while a woman with tiny feet was considered most beautiful.

Ch'eng Cheng Chien (8) remembered the early days of

binding as a sort of pleasant family get-together. Mrs. Ting (10) said:

> I thought it interesting and amusing to have a white cloth wrapped around my feet. . . . Mother taught me [how to bind]. Grandmother was still alive and in good spirits, so sometimes she helped with the instruction.

Mrs. Liu had her feet bound rather late, after the Revolution:

> I was born in Shanghai and spent the years from three to eight in Canton. In 1915, at the age of twelve, while in Fuchow, Fukien, I started footbinding. Mother didn't want my feet to get too large, so she had me wear linen shoes. I didn't oppose this, as I also wanted a sleek, slim foot. The method was to use a square white binding, bound very tightly. It was covered with a tissue paper [a type of writing paper] so that I could get my feet into linen socks and then shoes. This was rebound every night. A ribbon was placed on the top of the binding, about four to six inches above the ankle. The foot would become larger if washed, so it was usually kept bound, and alum was used. I kept the binding on when asleep, but sometimes opened it at night against my mother's orders, which had to be obeyed. I would bind it again in the morning. I bound my feet for three years, but gave up the practice in 1918 when I started middle school.

Our Nan-t'un informant from Taiwan (12) stated that:

> As a rule, the girl's feet were bound by her mother. The mother, in order to persuade a daughter to let the feet be bound, told her how important it was and also how nice it was to do this. During the footbinding era, the daughters of wealthy families were supposed to have their feet bound. In this way, they could show others that they were neither the daughters of poor families nor maid servants; because at that time poor women and maid servants usually did not have their feet bound.
>
> The majority of girls had their feet bound whether they liked it or not. However, when the mother started the binding, the girl would cry out with pain and wish to discontinue. If the girls had

a chance, they would secretly undo the bindings. Sometimes, because of the tightness of the binding, the girl's feet became swollen and the skin turned a bluish color.

Mothers did not let their daughters untie the bindings, because they wanted them to look like members of rich families. In order to prevent unbinding, they therefore tied their hands to a pole. In this way, they could not undo the binding. Mothers felt that this was not serious, for once the girls got used to the binding they would like it.

A mother was willing to go to any lengths to ensure that her daughter's foot became tiny enough to win social admiration. The tiny foot, at first considered as a form of beauty, in the course of time became a mark of distinction as well. Families which claimed an aristocratic ancestry therefore felt duty-bound to stamp their own flesh with this sign of gentility. It was the mother's first task on arising, and the daughter was powerless either to resist or to stop the pain. She could only weep and beg for permission to unloosen the binding. At this stage even the most indulgent mother proved unresponsive and deaf to entreaties. The request to desist might so anger her that she bound even more tightly. Sounds commonly heard were those of the child crying and being reviled at the same time. "One pair of tiny feet, but two cisterns of tears." The mother first tried to soften the flesh of the foot and bend under the bones of all toes but the big toe. This part of the task did not yet involve great suffering. But after about half a year the bones of the toes gradually curved inwards, and increasing pressure was applied. The more the flesh deteriorated, the tighter the foot was bound, to accelerate the process. The deep bending of the bones so that they could fit into a bowed shoe signified fulfillment of the mother's task. These bowed feet were called Golden Lotuses, but the as-yet-unbound feet of a young girl were called Foot Sprouts. The large, stout leg, considered hard to bind, was regarded disdainfully. But girls with small slender legs were comforted, for these could be made to conform most closely to the feminine ideal. Old ladies in the village praised or criticized foot sprouts for either having or lacking the essential qualities. Binding of long and plump legs began earlier, shortly before or after the fifth birthday, out of fear that they might later become increasingly difficult to bind.[9]

C. How did your mother feel when she first began binding your foot?

The replies show that, in most instances, maternal feelings of compassion were more than offset by social considerations. A daughter whose feet were well bound found it easier to get a husband, and her family might be more highly esteemed in society. There was also the aesthetic factor, for only tiny feet were considered beautiful.

Mother did not feel bad about the pain suffered when my feet were bound, for the following reasons. Small feet were then thought to be beautiful. If a person were plain-looking but had small bound feet, she might still be considered a beauty. If she had naturally large feet, however, no matter how good-looking she might be, she was not thought pretty, and no one wanted to marry her. (1)

Mother surely felt bad, but with unbound feet a girl could not easily find a husband. (2)

At that time, noble ladies all had their feet bound. Bound feet, therefore, were not only beautiful but represented family background and social standing. Due to these factors, Mother did not feel bad about it. (3)

For the sake of the future, Mother did not feel bad at seeing her daughter suffering from physical pain. The neighbors criticized her if the foot were not bound properly. Mother would find fault with my sisters if their feet were not bound well. (5)

Mother died soon afterwards, so I was extremely upset. From the age of five, I was reared by another family. My feet felt extremely painful, but I dared not cry in the presence of my stepmother. Sometimes I stealthily removed the binding when my stepmother was not around. She once discovered this and beat me for it, which made me think longingly of my deceased mother. My stepmother was very strict about footbinding. She would take me walking to let the many passers-by see my bound feet. I became aware of the reason for our strolls and therefore dared not let out the binding any longer. My stepmother said that girls all liked to be considered beautiful and that feet had to be bound small. Otherwise, everyone would laugh at a girl who had natural, unbound feet. (6)

Mother enjoyed doing this [footbinding] very much, because the customs of the time required that women bind their feet in order to achieve the tiny foot which symbolized beauty. (9)

When I first started, my foot didn't hurt too much. This was because the first step was to use a white cloth to wrap around the foot and merely prevent it from getting larger. So there was no pain involved. The real tightening of the bandage started when I was about ten, and that was painful. Mother felt bad, of course, but she was willing to go through with it in order to see that her daughter grew up to be beautiful. I never loosened the bandages, since I didn't feel extreme pain. Some girls tried to do this, but their mothers prevented it and reminded them that by loosening the binding they would fail to grow up attractive. And girls ten years of age were generally willing to suffer pain for the sake of beauty. (10)

I remember that, when the binding first began, I did not feel pain and, in fact, thought it very interesting. Mother told me that only through footbinding could a woman become more beautiful. Therefore I gladly endured the process. Mother did not feel bad when she saw me in pain because she was doing this to enhance my attractiveness. My feet, even after ten years of age, did not feel pained but only restricted. Perhaps other girls secretly removed the bandages, but if their mothers found out, they were either beaten or the binding was sewn to prevent its being loosened. (11).

There was also a practical factor involved in the degree to which feet were reduced, for while a mother wished that her daughter's feet be as small as possible, she had to consider the economic situation of the family. If the family expected the girl to work in the future, her feet could not be too small. So many country women did not bind their feet. (4)

The informants sometimes volunteered statements about how they had reacted; and here reactions differed from "I was unaware of pain. . . ." (8) to ". . . I cried out because of the pain in my foot. My mother and grandmother could not bear to see me cry, so we all cried together." (7) Mrs. Yang also stated:

> Grandmother fooled me by telling me that I could let my foot out. I was very happy. But then she took a piece of bamboo, formed it into a "u" shape, and pressed two of these very tightly around the heels of my feet so as to inhibit their growth. This kept the heel rigidly in place and prevented it from turning inwards; it was very painful.

The young child might rationalize the suffering because of her feminine vanity:

> At first, I suffered very much, and often spent sleepless nights because of the pain. But I did it to be beautiful. [Did you ever stealthily loosen the bandages?] The women of my family all bound their feet. I, in the hope of being beautiful, never loosened the bandage because of the pain and gradually got used to it. Other girls loosened the bindings, but if caught they were beaten and forced to bind them tightly again. I didn't dare do this, and suffered from beginning to end. (5)

D. What shape of bound foot was considered the most beautiful?

Our informants agreed that the smaller the foot, the more delicate and beautiful it was thought to be. This was because "the small foot symbolized aristocracy and beauty." (11) There were other secondary attributes: "The surface of the foot had to be as high as possible, for if the surface were low the foot would be too long." (3) "A swollen appearance or an arched shape of the instep were regarded as the ugliest." (4) "The most beautiful foot was high, straight, and erect. This meant that the instep should be high and erect, while the area from the instep to the toes should be straight." (5) "The smallest foot . . . was considered the most elegant and upper class. The front of the foot was supposed to be somewhat pointed." (6) Mrs. Yang (7) was the only informant to offer the striking statement that ". . . some children started the footbinding process as early as one month and four months of age. They were such tiny infants that they were unaware of the pain. These bound feet were the most beautiful." Mrs. Yang's allegation that footbinding started in infancy was also found in studies of China made by late-eighteenth-century Western authors, but these appear to have been based on hearsay and misinformation.[10]

> Before a marriage was arranged, questions were asked about the size of the prospective bride's foot. Women seldom went beyond the confines of home and were rarely seen by outsiders. The foot and not the face was used by a prospective suitor as the determinant of a woman's beauty. (10)

Mrs. Liu (13), the informant who started footbinding last, in 1915, presented a different sequence:

> On the wedding day, the groom first looked at the bride's face, then at her hands to see if they were rough or smooth, and finally at her feet, both front and back.

> On Taiwan, . . . in the olden days before the Japanese period [prior to 1895], men and women appreciated small feet. It was more important than the face, for it represented wealth, beauty, and nobility. Big feet indicated that the girl was humble, ugly, and poor. (12)

To the male connoisseur, beauty was not merely related to the size of the foot, but to its being properly proportioned in relation to the feminine figure. A five-inch foot was considered more attractive than a smaller one which puffed out and resembled a horse's hoof or pig's foot. The tiny, well-bound foot was a rarity, but weird shapes were commonplace. The praiseworthy foot was small, slender, bowed, soft, fragrant, and proportioned, free of swelling and disfiguration.[11]

The concept behind this custom extended beyond the confines of China proper, to be adopted by the Koreans in modified form. A Chinese envoy to Korea in about 1875 allegedly saw women there with bound feet. The toes, however, were not bent under, but were kept uniformly close together.[12] On September 15, 1962, I interviewed a sixty-seven-year-old lady in Seoul concerning foot compression and got the following information. The Korean *yangban,* or upper-class lady, wore linen socks (called *poson*) from infancy on, in contrast to wives and daughters of commoners, who often wore rubber shoes and no socks. A somewhat wider *poson* was also worn by the upper-class male, for his feet were expected to be smaller than those of common laborers. A boy with big feet might be criticized for having "feet as large as a cow thief's."

Yangban ladies washed their feet daily, but in a basin different from that used when washing the rest of the body. Servants helped the child until about the age of eight. From then on, as in China, the feet were washed in strictest privacy. Linen socks were worn during the day; before marriage the girl slept barefooted, but married women always wore unlined socks in bed. They were instructed never to expose the feet, even to their husbands. The feet were usually concealed under long skirts.

Koreans pitied bound-foot Chinese, feeling that they were out of balance. The ideal Korean foot was shaped "like a cucumber seed," narrow, neither short nor long, and without bones protruding from either side. Girls over ten years old might try to make their feet smaller by forcing the second and fourth toes under the middle toe. Our informant, who had done this, also wore extremely tight linen socks in order to produce a smaller effect. Our interview indicates that twentieth-century Korean ladies, while not binding their feet, did compress them in unyielding linen socks. Two toes might be forced under the middle toe but, unlike the Chinese, the toes were never bent under the foot surface and towards the plantar.[13]

E. What was the length, shape, and color of the cloth used in footbinding?

The length of the cloth varied from five to twelve feet, with most informants estimating it at six feet. It was usually about two to three inches wide. (The old Chinese foot measurement was longer than the current one by about two inches.) As for the cloth itself, which might be woven on small hand looms: "the material was a hand-woven white cotton cloth." (1) "There was no limit as to color and quality." (4) "The woman might choose any kind of material, though the delicate and soft were best." (2) "There were two kinds of colored cloth, black and white, with rules as to quality." (3)

> There was one kind of very finely woven and relatively expensive cotton cloth. Most people used ordinary cloth, five feet long. There were people who specialized in selling things needed by women with bound feet, and they knew the regulations for these things. (6)

The reason for also having black cloth was given by Mrs. Ting (10), who explained that the cloth ". . . was usually white, but some village girls and old ladies used black instead. This was because village women were afraid that a white cloth might easily become dirty." (10) "Women either wove the cloths themselves or purchased them in the market." (11) "Even the poorest women had two pairs of binding cloths, but well-to-do people had many more than that. During the rainy season, two pairs were insufficient." (5)

This custom so influenced the Manchus that they too came to prize it, though having tiny feet was officially forbidden. Towards the turn of the century, attempted foot reduction by Manchu women had become commonplace. Manchu girls in their teens did this voluntarily and by themselves, without parental coercion, and tried to achieve a sleek and trim, knife-like effect. The feet were first washed and then bound with a white cloth about three feet long and two inches wide. But, like the Koreans, the toes were not at all bent or broken, for the object was only to make the foot slender and thin, with the toe's drawn closely together. After binding, unyielding cloth socks were worn. Great pressure had to be applied to get them on, and so much time was required that one often had to rest midway through. The ladies who submitted to this were able to walk without swaying from side to side like the Chinese.[14]

F. What was the relationship between footbinding and age?

Informants agreed that early binding meant less pain and a smaller foot. What was the youngest age? Madam Feng (1) placed it at three, but was contradicted by Madam T'ung, who said that ". . . usually footbinding started at about five or six years of age. Children below five knew nothing and could not endure a little pain." The age of five was selected because ". . . the child had soft bones and would suffer less pain." (2) If begun earlier than seven or eight, according to Mrs. Ch'en Shih-ch'ou (5), a person later could not walk without great effort. Mrs. Ch'en Cheng Chien (8) supported her contention that the process must start when one was still a young child by saying:

> My sister-in-law was an adopted child. She began the process when she was grown up, so her feet could not be bound small.

MRS. WU HAN

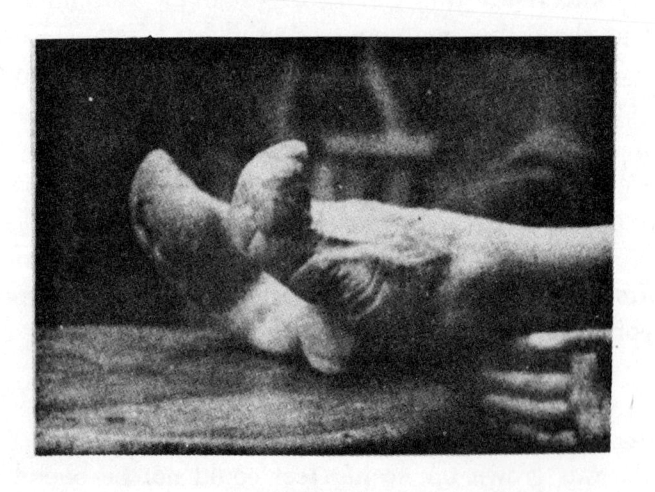

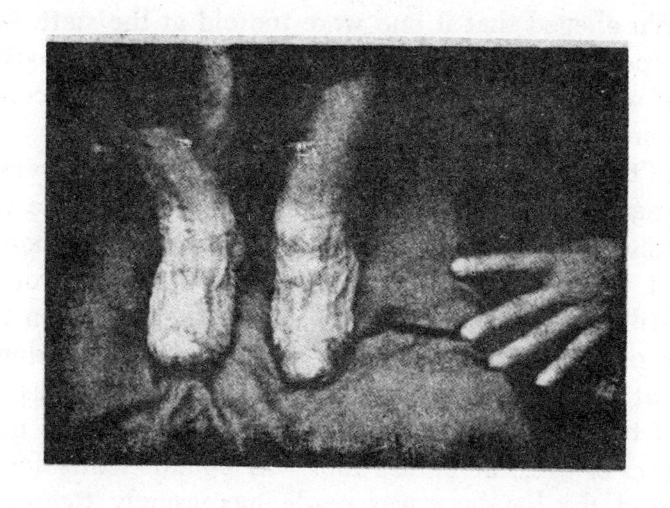

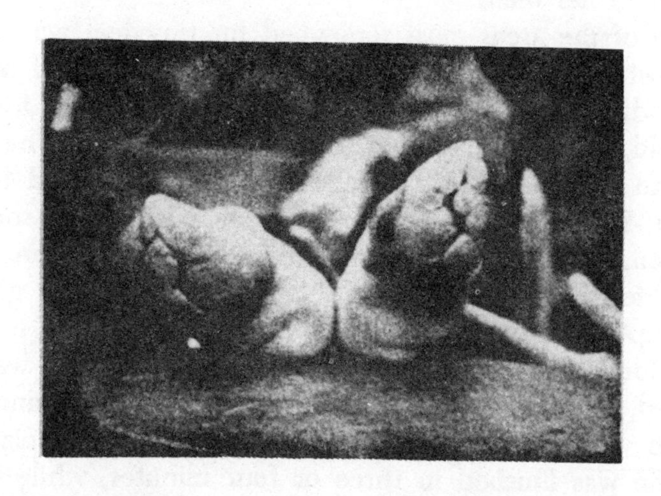

> Her stepmother, not understanding this, beat her over the head so severely with a stick that blood poured from the wound.

Mrs. Wu alleged that if one were too old at the start, the bones of the feet hardened and the foot was not attractive looking. (6) "There was no way to bind a foot small if the process started after one was ten years old." (9)

The two ladies (10, 11) from Lukang, Taiwan, were in such fundamental agreement that it is possible to get the following composite picture from their testimony. It was generally best to start when the child was five or six years old, for the feet were still small and soft. This was also the age when the child was beginning to think of being pretty. Pain was endured more easily at a later age. At first, only a white cloth was wrapped around the foot to prevent its growth. When a little more than ten years of age, the child's foot was bound tightly for the first time, and the bandage was made increasingly tighter. By the age of about fifteen, pain was frequently felt. If the foot was not constantly bound, it could easily get larger, even when the girl was in her teens.

One of the areas most renowned for tiny feet was Ta-t'ung in Shansi Province, a stronghold of conservatism and tradition. Footbinding there started when the child was about five or six years old, with bones neither too soft nor too hard. The parents chose an auspicious day, burned incense, and prayed for good fortune. Before beginning, the belly of a lamb was sometimes cut open, and both of the girl's feet were forced into it. The lamb cried out piteously and soon expired, but the girl's feet were kept in its belly for about two hours. The child invariably cried aloud because of the fright and pain. The feet were then removed, with the fresh blood dripping from them, and bound at once with white silk by an old woman who specialized in this. She was finished in three or four minutes, while the feet still felt the softening effect of the hot blood. Neighbors then came by to offer congratulatory toasts. The girl lay down and didn't get up for a week, by which time the feet, minus one layer of skin which had peeled away, had to be rebound.[15]

G. Could you walk unaided with bound feet; was it painful?

The ability to walk was directly influenced by the tightness of the binding. "If the binding was let out a little when you started, you could walk." (6) "If bound tightly, you couldn't walk." (9) Mrs. Feng (1) stated that one could walk without undue difficulty if the feet were bound well. "I started at three to have my feet bound and for the next five years rarely walked on them. The process was completed when I was eight years old, and from that time on they never hurt me."

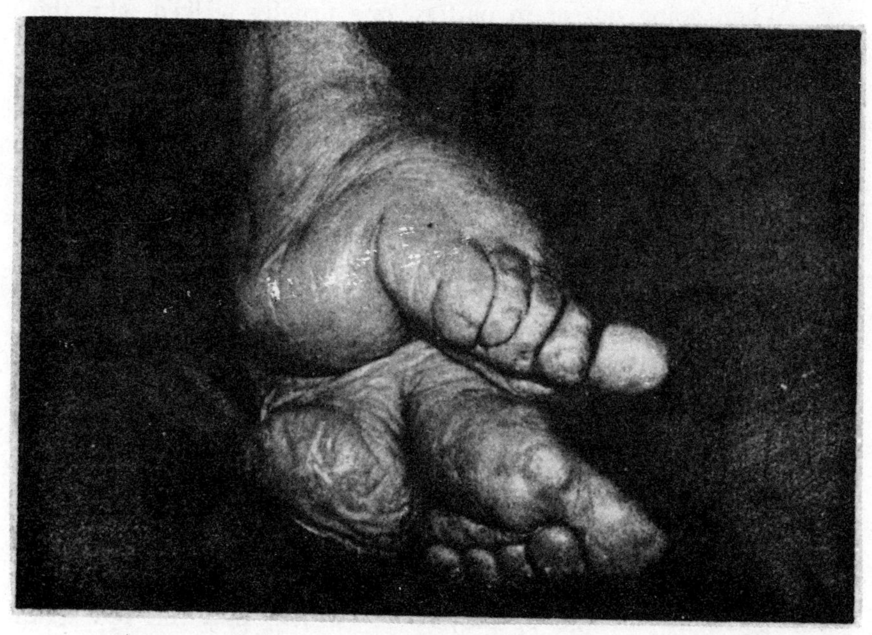

The first steps must have been the hardest. At the beginning I couldn't walk. But I had to practice walking in my room, so that I could get used to it and it would not feel painful. (3)

When I started footbinding, I couldn't walk, for when I stood up it hurt. I had to sit down. A person's support wasn't needed, for I was later able to walk by holding on to the wall. I sat most of the day. My family were very good to me, and would take food in for me to eat. (7)

Walking was an absolute necessity for the girl reared in poorer circumstances: I had many household tasks to do, so I had to walk with my bound feet from the very start. I could walk by myself unaided, but at first not too far at any one time. I had to rest every once in a while and rub my feet. By the age of sixteen, I was completely used to walking. Women in the wealthy families, however, never did manual labor but only learned to sew and embroider. (5)

When going out or to parties, one usually walked with the support of maid servants, to show one's nobility. (3)

At that time, a woman rarely left the gates of her home. If she did go out, she went in a sedan chair and rarely walked. (1)

Where was the pain felt? When I walked, I felt pain on the bottom of my toes. I walked on the heel of my foot because of the pain in my toes. (13)

Our two ladies from Lukang (10, 11), in central Taiwan, presented a detailed picture of how walking was influenced by the practice of footbinding. There was no hindrance to walking at first, because at the age of five or six a white cloth was merely wrapped around the foot to inhibit its growth. But after ten the binding was more tightly applied, causing pain to be felt. This pain could be alleviated by exposing one's feet to the breeze. Some girls, at the age of eleven or twelve, had the feet compressed with bamboo tubing to prevent their getting larger; even though hampered by these contrivances, they were able to walk.

. . . at about fifteen, walking became a problem [to me] because of the tight binding. If I wanted to go out, someone had to help me get into a sedan chair. Because of this, women rarely went out. . . . One could walk, but not very steadily. . . . Most of a woman's activities took place in either the home or garden; formerly women rarely walked on the streets, except for amahs or servants. (11)

But old ladies, or young ones whose feet were just then feeling the pain of tight binding, were supported by servants when they walked. I think footbinding was a painful and immoral thing. (10)

Matignon, the French doctor in China in the late nineteenth century, stated that footbinding produced a forced flection of the foot and caused the weight of the body to rest completely on the heel-bone. And because this point of support was inadequate, women had to use walking sticks as they became slightly advanced in age. They walked with their arms held lightly apart as if for balance, with their chests thrust forward and their pelvic region pushed backwards, as if they were pursuing their centers of gravity. Matignon said that they maintained an unstable equilibrium and, with heels together, might easily lose their balance. He was working in a Peking hospital one day when a woman about forty came to see him about her teeth. "At a given moment, wishing to make her incline her head slightly to the rear, I exercised pressure with my thumb vertically against her upper dental arch. The pressure was slight but sufficient to make my client fall over backwards." [16]

Our Nan-t'ung informant revealed that one cure for badly swollen feet was to immerse them in urine. This was supposed to bring quick relief. Another Taiwanese stated that when the foot was let out, it was immersed in urine, for in that way the foot did not feel too painful. (11) "When the Japanese sent down their order [outlawing footbinding in Taiwan], I began to let my feet out. I immersed them [for one week] in a jar of clear urine to soften the bones." (7) This technique of soaking the feet in urine may have been fairly common in the Taiwanese countryside, as two other ladies corroborated this in discussions with our assistant in Lukang. There were also women in Hunan Province who soaked their feet daily in urine and then bound them tightly, believing this to be most efficacious.[17]

Urine was also used medicinally, both on the mainland and in Taiwan. A Taiwanese once told me that her mother was revived during a fainting spell in the 1930's by being made to drink the urine of a young boy. A thirty-year-old friend from Peking said that when he was about seven and enrolled in a private school, someone asked him for a specimen of his urine in order to cure an illness. He added that only the urine of boys was used. I interviewed sociologist Nagao Ryūzo on August 19, 1961, and questioned him briefly on this point. Mr. Nagao stated that the drinking of urine represented a very old tradition in China, and that, while living in Fengtien, Manchuria, he had never seen this done but had heard about it. A child's urine was used, but he did not know which sex it was. He had never heard of soaking the feet in urine, but it was a general custom among the uneducated to wash cuts with it. A Chinese pharmaceutical treatise of the Ming dynasty indicated that urine was used in the following ways: it was efficacious in curing headaches, chills, blood spitting, various blood diseases, dog, snake, spider, and bee bites, cuts from wounds, and obstructions of the bowels. It also served as a demulcent medicine in alleviating cases of fatigue. The urine of boys under the age of twelve was best, and it was made more palatable by mixing with either cooked vegetables or soups. It sometimes cured supposedly incurable illnesses. Its quality was coolness, and therefore it was particularly effective in the treatment of fevers. An old lady of eighty was once seen who looked only half her age. When asked the reason, she replied that she had drunk urine daily for more than forty years. Its multiplicity of uses included that of being an underarm deodorant. The person with underarm odor was advised to wash his armpits several times daily with his own urine, heating it prior to application.[18]

H. How was the foot bound?

The foot was bound in a variety of ways, but with one objective in mind: to bind the cloth tightly and effectively. There was no definite way, but the general principle was to bind it so tightly that it couldn't be let out. (9) "The binding of well-bound feet did not get loosened and have a swollen look; such women did not feel pain when walking." (3) One common method was to place one end of the cloth on the surface of the foot below the ankle, pressing it down by hand. The other end of the cloth was then wound around the heel and returned to the original position. All the toes were forced under the foot surface, and great pressure was applied in binding. (2, 3, 4) "Usually the front part of the foot was wrapped around two times and the rear part three times." (5) The front part of the bottom of the foot was pressed down so as to connect with the heel. The shape of the foot was like a figure 9 and the toes were in an upside down position towards the underside of the foot. (12)

> Later one took the big toe and tried to have it touch the heel of the foot. Therefore the shape of the foot encased in white cotton cloth resembled a fist. After a long time, the foot became so much insensitive dead flesh. (11)

> Women sewed the binding into place with needle and thread. White cloth was used, and the foot was bound tightly both front and back. One had to use needle and thread when the foot was first bound, for in that way you prevented the binding from being opened. Later, my foot became terribly painful, and when Mother opened the bandage and looked at my foot it was already slightly odoriferous and rotted. (6)

"I inserted the end of the cloth into my own bandage, and never had to use needle and thread to tighten it." (5) "I did not sew the binding fast." (8) "Some women wore socks on top of the binding. Linen socks and then shoes were worn. (2; cf.4)

Whether or not one wore socks was one's own choice." (3) "After binding, one did not have to wear socks." (9) "Feet well-bound needed no socks, and the binding would not get loose. But there were large small feet, and it was hard to bind them tightly, so in those cases socks had to be worn." (5) "Two multi-colored ribbons were sometimes placed on the shoes to help tie the bound feet to them."

Strength was applied not only in binding, but in tightly sewing the binding. By preventing loosening, success was ensured. The foot did not become smaller because of the binding, but because this caused the flesh to rot away. A mother who wished to accelerate this might break open the flesh with porcelain tiles in order to speed the process of decay. Bone softening medicines were also used. Besides the lamb's blood technique popular in Ta-t'ung, there was a formula which consisted of a broth made from monkey bones. The legs were bathed in this broth daily, and as a result the bones naturally softened and became easy to bend and bind.[19]

I. What did you do when you went to sleep?

The binding was not to be loosened during the sleeping hours, for otherwise the feet would grow larger. (11) Some women, who sought comfort, always loosened the bandage but later discovered that their feet could not be bound as small as before. (5) When going to bed, almost all ladies ". . . wore sleeping shoes over the bandage. I could not sleep if these were not worn." (7) Mrs. Liang (9), our oldest informant, told us that she expected her corpse to be dressed in bedroom shoes prior to burial. In order to keep these shoes from getting soiled, she always swept the bedroom clean. (8) Sleeping shoes were worn because ". . . it was unaesthetic looking [to see the bare foot]; therefore everyone had in readiness sleeping shoes, put on only when one went to bed. When I got up in the morning, I changed them for ordinary shoes." (10) One of the mainlanders wore soft bedroom sandals over her regular shoes instead of changing as the others did. (1)

Sleeping shoes were kept in a special drawer in the bedroom and were only worn when preparing for bed. They were usually red, elegantly styled, fragrantly perfumed, and of a satin or silk texture. These shoes were greatly prized and sought after as love tokens. A woman might secretly give them to her enamored as proof of love sentiments, preferring them to shoes she had worn on the outside which might soil his hands. Sleeping shoes under the bedcovers excited the male because of their fragrance and softness, and because the deep red of the shoes effectively contrasted with the white of the thighs. One type of sleeping shoe had detailed pictures of amorous play embroidered on it. These varied greatly in price, depending on the skill of the artist, and cost as much as five ounces of silver per pair. Perfumed sachets were placed in the sides of sleeping shoes to offset foot odors and emit a pleasant fragrance.[20]

J. How often did you rebind?

Mrs. Yang (7) rebound her feet every day, although:

> . . . when my feet were first bound, I was distressed. To distract myself from this, I tapped my feet on the wooden bed to help me forget the pain. The toenails could not be cut during the first lunar month of the year, for we were told that the foot would smell if they were cut at this time.

A few informants may have exaggerated about how often they washed after the binding was removed. Mrs. Ch'en (8) claimed that she washed her feet once every two days, while Mrs. Liang (9) stated that she washed them about this often only during hot weather. To prevent unpleasant odors, alum was rubbed between the toes. While Mrs. Ch'en (5) rebound daily, she only washed her feet once every three or four days out of fear that they might grow larger.

> In my youth, I would wash my feet once every two days. Now I wash once every three or four days. In the winter, it's all right if I take a few more days between washings. I also used to change the bandage daily, but now that I'm old I change it once every three days. If you wash the foot when it is first bound, it can be painful. If later you wash it slowly, it feels very comforting. (6)

The two ladies from Lukang (10, 11) admitted that they only washed their feet once every six or seven days. This statement was corroborated by our Nan-t'un informant's (12) remark that women "... usually washed their feet and bathed once a week." Mrs. Liu (13) alleged that some women didn't wash their feet more than two or three times a year. Foot washing was done infrequently. (4) There were villagers who didn't wash all year and only bound the foot roughly so that it resembled a pig's foot or a rice dumpling.[21] Swatow ladies of the eighteen-eighties washed their feet once a month, or oftener, with the bandages still on them. They were put into a bucket of hot water and soaked. The bandages were then removed, the dead skin rubbed away, and the foot kneaded more fully into the desired shape. Pulverized alum was laid on, after which clean bandages were quickly applied. A failure to rebind quickly led to renewed blood circulation in the feet and multiplied the pain, which was felt the least when the feet were benumbed by the firmness and pressure of the bandages.[22]

It was common to leave the feet unwashed during bathing, placing them outside of the bathtub. (4, 5) There was a widespread superstition that the woman who removed bindings and washed her feet in the same basin as the rest of her body would be changed into a pig in the next life.[23] Like the Korean upper class, mothers or servants might do the washing for the girl in childhood, but this ceased with adolescence. "When I got bigger [over ten years of age], I washed them myself in a private room out of shame that someone might see my bare foot." (10) "When

I got older, . . . I had a servant bring water into a private room, where I did the washing myself." (11) Did a husband ever help with the washing? "Women washed their own feet, and never asked servants or husbands to do this. It would have been unthinkable!" (5) "Rich or poor, before or after marriage, one washed her own feet." (3) "A husband cannot wash his wife's feet." (6) This was the testimony of women reared in conventional circumstances, but our earlier discussions of the sexual implications of footbinding show that washing the foot or covertly seeing it being washed was an erotic attraction to the foot fetishist.

K. What were the shape and color of the shoes?

There was no limit to the style, color, or embroidery, and individual preference determined selection. The colors red and green were preferred. (2) Mrs. Feng (1) stated that black shoes with embroidered flowers were worn before marriage, and similarly embroidered red shoes were worn after marriage. The bride wore red shoes at her wedding, but there was no color limitation on other occasions. (3, 5) Elderly ladies wore black shoes as a rule and red embroidered shoes on birthdays or holidays. (10) "A woman who becomes advanced in years shouldn't wear red shoes." (6) According to Mrs. Feng (1), there were both flat and high-heeled shoes, the former often worn during adolescence. However, Mrs. Kuo (3) stated that only high-heeled shoes were worn. She must have been referring to the exception rather than the rule. Mrs. Ting (4) usually wore flat-heeled shoes, reserving high heels for going out or attending parties.

> High heels were for the sake of beauty and were allowed to be worn before or after marriage. Flat heels were also worn whether one was married or single. I started to wear high heels at about seventeen or eighteen years of age. (5)

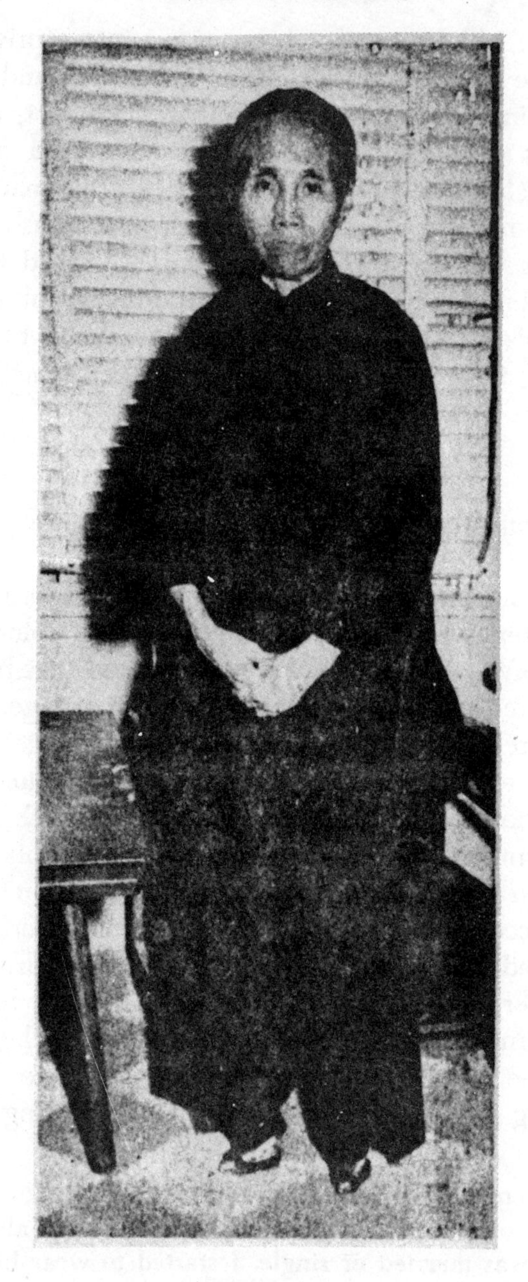

MRS. KUO

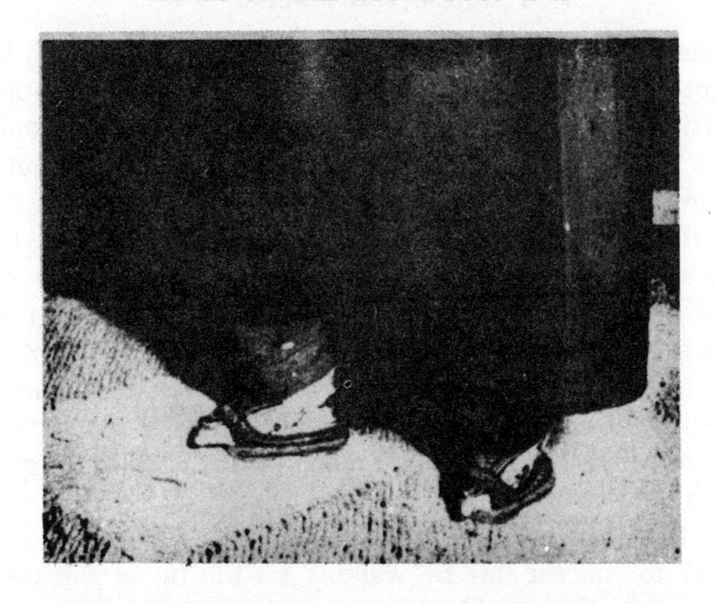

Mrs. Liang (9) started when she was ten years old. "High heels were not only easier to walk on, but were prettier in appearance." (6) "I didn't wear flat-heeled shoes, because you couldn't walk on them. . . . A woman with bound feet had to put her weight on the heel when walking." (8) For rain wear, the entire sole of the shoes was augmented by a wooden surface. There were false "three-inch lotuses," one technique being to place the high heel of the shoe under the sole of the foot and use an additional piece of wood to support the heel of the foot. (3) There were ladies, who were either too old to start footbinding or had given it up because of the pain, who wore special shoes. They had a high heel, so they walked with the swaying gait of one with real bound feet. But they feared that others would discover that their feet were not bound. (10) The natural-footed might try to conceal this by walking on the tip of the toes in specially made shoes, with the rest of the foot being concealed under their long trousers. (11)

Green as well as red shoes were worn on congratulatory occasions, with white shoes worn when attending the funerals of one's closest relations. The color yellow was considered unsuitable. Young people wore red and green laces, the middle-aged either black laces or black with white intertwined. Poems in praise of tiny feet invariably referred to the red shoes:

> Wearing red shoes, standing by the gate;
> And, oh, how he becomes emotionally agitated!
>
> Seeing him entering,
> She hastens to the *k'ang*,
> Changes into red shoes.

Women whose heels were so wide that they protrude beyond the shoe were ridiculed with this folk saying:

> Rowing a lotus boat in front,
> Selling duck eggs in the rear.[24]

L. Were shoes part of the dowry?

Shoes and binding cloths were essential parts of the dowry, with the amount varying according to one's resources. The woman's family supplied the dowry in most cases, but among the wealthy it was provided for by the husband's family. (7. Yang: Interviewer's note to reply 13.) The shoes might be placed inside the man's shoes and with the binding cloth alongside. (1)

> There were usually four, eight, twelve, or sixteen pairs of shoes. Clothes were divided the same as shoes, for use in the four seasons. . . . The formal ceremonial dress was made by the bridegroom's family, while the shoes were made by the bride herself. (4)

Mrs. Ch'en (5) stated that, while most brides had at least six pairs of shoes, she had twelve pairs. (cf. 8)

> The dress and hair ornaments were prepared by the bridegroom's family, but shoes and other things were prepared by the bride herself. After the wedding, the bride gave her husband's sister, mother, and grandmother one pair of new shoes each. This was called "dividing the shoes." (5)

Mrs. Shih (11) also made twelve pairs of shoes as part of her dowry, eight pairs less than Mrs. Ting (10). The bride sometimes had to send each woman in her husband's family a pair of shoes, making them as attractive as possible. (6; cf.9) By giving her mother-in-law a pair of beautiful tiny shoes, the bride indicated her skill as a shoemaker. (11) However, if the husband's family were considerate, they might say that other things could be sent in place of the shoes. (8)

These shoes were displayed during the wedding, and people who came to see the bride's dowry would comment on how small and beautiful the shoes indicated that her feet must be. (12) On the wedding day, the bride with an especially small foot might place her foot on the table for everyone to see, putting it on top of a spoon to prove how small it was. (13) (A Chinese spoon is about two inches long, and arched.)

> When I married, I did not see my husband, because of my parents' wishes, until the wedding night. Because of the darkness of the room, some brides didn't see their husbands clearly enough to recognize them until several days after the wedding night. (11)

In keeping with custom, the newlyweds visited the bride's maiden home. This was called "return to the gate." The day they came back from the visit, the bride had to present a pair of shoes to each in-law. These shoes, made before marriage, were called "return to the gate shoes." (3)

The size and shape of the bride's feet were considered vitally important. When she alighted from the sedan chair to enter her husband's home, she was surrounded by friends and neighbors who inspected her foot size. Everyone praised the tiny-footed bride, pleasing the parents and delighting the groom who saw her for the first time. If, however, her feet exceeded the norm, everyone laughed at her, and the father-in-law felt mortified. There was and still is a Chinese custom called Disturbing the Bedroom on the wedding night, whereby tricks are played on bride and groom by the wedding party. At Ningpo, any guest could hold the bride's hand or foot without being refused. Some would even measure the foot with a ruler and make sarcastic remarks if it were large or poorly shaped.[25] So there was a constant social pressure on the bride-to-be to bind effectively and avoid being publicly shamed.

M. How prevalent was this practice?

Regardless of class or relative wealth or poverty, all women bound their feet. The only exceptions were nuns, Manchu women, and maids, though maids who bound their feet were considered much more valuable. (1) Most women bound their feet. Exceptions were few, for those who did not bind their feet in fear of pain would soon be in fear that they would be old maids to their dying days. (2) The only ones who did not bind their feet were either servants or women who did not have a mother to look after them. (6, 8) Only aboriginal women did not bind their feet. (7) Two ladies admitted that poor women did not bind their feet, one saying this was because they had to perform arduous labor. (5, 3) Mrs. Ting (10) said that the average family had maid servants and that with bound feet one couldn't wash clothes or do any work which required kneeling. She said that women with bound feet were called "Wives" or "Fine Footed," while those with natural feet were called "Coarse Footed." The only exceptions to binding were women who specialized in types of heavy work. (11)

> Today there are many women over sixty years old who still bind their feet. Those over fifty often seem to have had their feet bound in earlier days but to have unbound them later. It is seldom that a woman under fifty has had her feet bound. It seems that more mainlanders than Taiwanese had their feet bound. (12)

Footbinding generally prevailed, but it differed in intensity from province to province. Sometimes within a single province, natural and bound-foot areas existed side by side. The natural foot predominated in such southern provinces as Fukien, Kwangtung and Kwangsi. After the Revolution, the last strongholds for this custom were the areas around the Yellow River, followed by the Yangtze and Pearl River regions in that order. Northern cities in Hopei, Honan, and Shantung followed the trend towards modernization, but the majority of villagers retained their footbinding habit in the face of change. The direction of the abolition movement was generally from south to north, dependent on the facility of communications, with inaccessible northern villages being the most conservative.[26] The upper classes bound the feet carefully and to a diminutive degree, but the attention devoted to tight and rigorous binding tended to decline as one moved down the social scale.

Adele Fielde, a missionary observer in Swatow who spoke the local dialect and lived there from 1877 to 1887, mentioned that the rich bound their daughters' feet at six or eight years, but that the poor did not start until the girl was thirteen or fourteen. She noted that only the very rich could afford to have their feet bound so tiny as to completely incapacitate themselves for labor of any kind, and that even middle-class bound-foot women sometimes had to walk four or five miles daily. There were some village girls who had their feet slightly bound just before marriage and unbound them soon after the wedding festivities ended. There were also natural-footed women who, on approaching a town or on a festival day, would make an effort to simulate the tiny-footed style. In Miss Fielde's time, before the anti-footbinding movement gathered momentum, the women were as insistent as the men on the preservation of this custom.

> For a Chinese woman the greatest sorrow is that of having no sons; the next to the greatest is that of being unlike her neighbors. The smallest feet are made by those who determine to be elegant at any cost, and these draw their own foot-ligatures tighter than anyone else would draw them.[27]

John F. Davis, writing a half-century earlier, penetratingly observed that the idea behind footbinding seemed to be exemption from labor, and that "as small feet make cripples of the women, it is fair to conclude that the idea of gentility which they convey is from a similar association."[28]

The fact that total incapacitation through binding was a luxury enjoyed only by the wealthy class would seem to substantiate Veblen's theory that one rationale behind footbinding was to demonstrate the pecuniary reputability of the male owner by showing that his woman was useless, expensive, and had to be supported in idleness. In a footbound state, she was consequently valuable as evidence of the owner's pecuniary strength. Veblen went on to say that the constricted waist and bound foot were repulsive to the untrained sense, but unquestionably attractive to men "into whose scheme of life they fit as honorific items sanctioned by the requirements of pecuniary reputability." Women willingly altered their persons to conform as nearly as possible to the instructed taste of their time, and the mutilation served its purpose by proving physical disability and by decreasing the visible efficiency of the individual.[29]

N. How did this practice end?

The question referred to the situation either on the mainland or on Taiwan, depending on where the woman was at the time. First, citing the testimony of the mainlanders: "After the Republic began, people didn't bind their feet, and those who had done so began to let them out to develop naturally." (2)

> Everybody was letting their feet out, so I did the same. City people were the first to respond to this reform. Country people were comparatively bigoted, but they too gradually followed the example set in the cities. (4)
>
> In the thirty-second year of Kuang-hsu [1906], the Manchu government sent down an order that the feet were to be unbound. Those who refused would have both legs cut off. I therefore let them out, but later there was further foot growth. If I had kept binding them, I could today wear three-inch embroidered shoes without difficulty. (1)[30]

When Mrs. T'ung (4) was asked how her feet were let out, she replied that

> . . . by untying the bandage, the process was completed once and for all. After that, thick socks made of a doubly folded material were worn, instead of the binding cloth. At first my feet did not feel accustomed to walking, but this feeling was overcome after

two or three years. After letting my feet out, they grew much longer.

The way in which the Japanese abolished footbinding was described in detail:

> After the Japanese occupied Taiwan, they forced the women to untie their bindings and forbade young girls to start to have their feet bound. Women with bound feet did not like to remove the bindings, however, for if they did they could not walk. There was also the belief current that if a woman unbound her feet, it was because she was being punished for having done some terrible thing like having had intercourse with someone other than her husband. (12)

The Japanese felt that both footbinding and pigtails were unsanitary and that the foot's freedom of movement was restricted. Therefore, soon after they occupied Taiwan, though I forget which year it was, they sent down a strict order that feet be let out and pigtails cut off. The Japanese had a spirit for accomplishing anything they wanted. If someone didn't let her feet out, they would force her to and say that they would immerse her feet in a liquid medicine. [Perhaps a reference to a concoction for causing the bones to stretch out.] Therefore, though people felt it a pity to give up bound feet, they had to let them out. When the foot was let out, it was immersed in urine, for in this way the foot did not feel too painful. [But she referred to feet in general and not to her own feet in this way.] After the foot was let out, a white cloth was still wrapped around it, for otherwise the sole of the foot would feel painful and even bleed when one walked on it. (11)

The Japanese said that if they found someone who hadn't let her feet out, she would have to do this in front of everyone. . . . Some women did not obey, however, so even today there are a few left with bound feet. Letting out the feet was more painful than having bound feet. It had to be done very slowly, for otherwise the foot felt so painful that one couldn't walk. When the foot was let out, the area between the toes and the heel of the foot bled easily. Walking was about the same for me before and after I let out my feet. (10)

The Japanese strongly called on all women to let out their feet and also made it definite that men had to cut off their pigtails. I didn't want to let out my feet. The Japanese beat me so severely with a stick that finally I had no other recourse. That is why my feet now are much larger than they used to be. I didn't want to let my feet out, for no one regarded such feet as good-looking. But the Japanese beat me very painfully, so I had to. . . . They finally saw that I had let my feet out and didn't come around anymore. I was very happy about this and therefore secretly bound them again. But I did not dare to go outside for fear that the Japanese would discover this. (6)

Forty years ago the Japanese ordered bound feet to be let out and strictly carried the order into effect. I was then in my thirties and was glad to let them out, because bound feet were very inconvenient. For example, I could not walk in the street in the rain. Besides, since my husband was an important local official, I had to form a model. But my feet were too small, and bled between the toes when being let out. I could not walk because of the pain. Local officials reported this to the police chief and the mayor. After examination, they permitted me not to let my feet out; that is why I still have bound feet today. (3)

The Japanese came when I was eight years old. My sisters then all had tiny feet. Gradually the Japanese decreed the end of footbinding, and they were very strict about it. My sisters wanted to let out their feet, while I had already done so, so we were not punished. I was nineteen when I married and let out my feet the following year because my husband wanted me to. He said that it was easier to walk without bound feet. I was stout, and he saw how awkward it was for me to walk. He was from Taichung city and understood women. . . . I have now had "big" feet for more than fifty years, and am really embarrassed by this. (8)

When the Japanese sent down their order, I began to let out my feet. I immersed them in a jar of clear urine to soften the bones and was able to start letting them out by soaking them this way for one week. After that the bones opened, but the pain was so intense that I was unable to walk. I then became ill.

The Japanese burned faeces pots which they discovered [in the bedrooms, for being unsanitary]. Since women could not urinate and defecate on the outside [as men could in large earthen pots], they were very unhappy about this. [The Japanese may have done this to prevent women from spending most of their time, tiny-footed, concealed in their bedrooms.]

When I married, my foot was three inches. My husband, his mother, and his whole family were very happy about this. When the Japanese issued their decree, I was very pleased. I thought that it would be convenient to let them out and that I would no longer have to make shoes. My husband was head of the village and, as such, considered a model. Everyone therefore let out their feet [after I did]. But I found that I was unable to walk and therefore later had to rebind. (7)

My husband was then working for a Japanese organization. . . . My feet had been bound too long and were too small. They were not easily let out, so I did not unbind them. Even if I could have done so, I would not have, for I spent many years in getting my feet bound small. Feet let out were ugly! It was also very hard to walk on them. Once let out, they could not grow like natural feet nor remain like small feet. And that would be repulsive. (5)

When the Japanese prohibited footbinding, Mrs. Liang (9) also let her feet out but discovered that she couldn't walk, so she had to bind them again. She was in her forties at the time. She replied to a question as to whether bound feet were beautiful by saying that it depended on the era. "If everyone binds their feet, the only thing to do is to bind them also. It is very fine that no one binds feet any longer." (9)

Chinese revolutionaries strove to end footbinding by fiat, feeling that it was a corrupt and reactionary practice which kept women in ignorance and apathy. In March, 1911, Sun Yat-sen issued an order of prohibition, decrying it as an evil custom which hurt the family and wrought havoc on the nation. Sun portrayed the footbound as unbalanced and listless, rarely leaving the confines of home, and ignorant as a consequence. To ensure a sound national foundation, he demanded that the Ministry of Civil Affairs carry out the order in every province and heavily fine continued offenders.[31] The reform movement enjoyed its greatest success in the large cities, but the countryside remained adamant. The northward march of the revolutionary armies in 1928 was attended by a series of provincial decrees which not only forbade footbinding but outlined ways to effect the task. In general, reliance was on inspection and dissuasion rather than on legal penalties, with foot emancipation meetings frequently convened. The gradual extension of educational opportunity also militated against the practice, and by the early thirties it was obvious that the aesthetic outlook of the Chinese male was changing. Many men who had formerly felt that a woman's tiny foot was more important than her facial beauty were influenced by the influx of Western standards and became natural-foot advocates. "Everything new is beautiful, everything old is ugly."[32] Women with bound feet found themselves deserted or divorced. This psychological change in male viewpoint made it obvious that the custom would eventually vanish, even without recourse to propaganda or coercion.

Footbinding flourished in Taiwan until 1915. Japanese authorities deplored the practice, but at first were afraid that positive commands against it might increase the state of unrest and further hamper their efforts to secure the island militarily. However, by April 15, 1915, the twentieth anniversary of Taiwan's occupation by Japan, the Governor-General felt that the time for action had arrived. Footbinding was prohibited by official decree and the effect was immediate; more than 700,000 women complied. This figure increased yearly, owing to both government prohibition and a gradual shift in public sentiment. Statements of our informants make it clear that the Japanese were not above resorting to brutality when necessary to force compliance from stubborn conservatives.

O. When did this practice originate?

Not every lady was asked this question. Two replied (1, 9) that it originated with the Chou dynasty (ca. 11th century B.C.). A sixty-one-year-old Taiwanese named Lai Jan, father of one interviewer, furnished us with a popular account of its origin:[33]

> Chou-wang, the last ruler of the Shang dynasty, was extremely cruel and merciless. He especially hated T'ang Wu, one of the feudal princes under his command, and plotted his death incessantly. He once killed one of T'ang Wu's sons, made a meat stew of the corpse, and ordered T'ang Wu to either eat the meat or be killed for disobeying a royal decree. T'ang Wu did as told, but vomited each bite; each morsel of flesh he spit out became a rabbit. This is how rabbits originated. The act was indicative of T'ang Wu's supernatural powers.
>
> T'ang Wu had a beautiful daughter named Ta-chi, whom Chou-wang coveted and was about to summon. Ta-chi was so grieved at this that she became ill. A fox spirit over a thousand years old then entered Ta-chi's body; it was in the external form of Ta-chi that the spirit joined Chou-wang's harem. Chou-wang was delighted and spent days and nights in its company, oblivious to affairs of state. The fox spirit could change into human form in every detail but the feet, which remained its own. To conceal this fact, it bound its paws in white cloth. When the emperor asked why, it said this had been done to prevent the foot from growing and to preserve its beauty. The fox then danced to music beside a lotus pond in such a lovely way that its feet were praised as three-inch lotuses. Chou-wang was so delighted that he ordered every woman in the empire to bind her feet, and from this time on the practice of footbinding in China became universal. The dissolute sovereign was finally overthrown in a revolution led by T'ang Wu.

MASCULINE IMPRESSIONS

Mrs. Shih's (11) husband, born in 1890, was questioned briefly on the same day as his wife. He said that when he was a child men liked to smoke opium. But, in the late Meiji period, the Japanese forced those who had not started the habit to stay away from it and limited opium consumption by addicts. In this way, the opium habit was gradually eliminated. In his youth, Mr. Shih grew a long pigtail, but cut it off when the Japanese prohibited both it and footbinding. He was then about thirty years of age, living in an age when only a woman with bound feet was considered beautiful.

Nagao Ryūzo, the Japanese sociologist in China for about forty years, knew of no special footbinding festival. However, at the start parents might place the picture of a god of footbinding on the wall, after which a ceremony was held. Nagao first saw bound feet in Shanghai about 1900 and remarked on their extreme smallness. The woman sometimes could not walk unaided, but either had to ask for assistance or cling to furniture or walls. These were usually the women of the rich. Women of workers and farmers had bound feet, but they were large enough to permit walking. Rich children might start binding at three, farmers' children at four or five years of age. Nagao believed that the so-called "three-inch golden lotus" did not refer to the actual foot size, but rather to the shoe size. The shoe covered the toe area, while the heel was concealed by the trousers.

According to Nagao, the way in which the foot was rubbed as a prelude to sexual intercourse was determined by one's social rank. High-class ladies wore special silk socks in the bedroom, and these were rubbed by the man. However, lower-class men were so fond of this practice that they might force the ladies to remove the socks as well so that the bare foot could be rubbed.

Japanese visitors to China felt strange when they first saw

bound feet, but as they got used to the idea thought them attractive and more seductive than natural feet. Nagao personally was not interested in such Chinese women, but liked their feminine weakness in appearance and walk. This view was formerly widely held by his Chinese contemporaries and influenced even the Manchus. Manchu women wore shoes in which only a white contrivance in the center showed beneath the trouser, in order to give the illusion that they were tiny-footed.

Nagao concluded that the Chinese relinquished the practice not because of foreign ridicule, but because of the changed mental outlook caused by the inroads of Western civilization.

The traditional male attitude was given in two interviews, first involving a mainlander and then a Taiwanese. T'ung Hui ch'uan, the husband of Mrs. T'ung (4), was born in 1894 in I-ts'ang, Hupei, the same city as his wife. He was two years her senior. Here is our recorded interview:

1. Did your wife have bound feet?

Yes, but not too small. They are now a little more than five inches.

2. What was your wedding ceremony like?

My wife and I were engaged in childhood but did not see one another until marriage. The wedding feast lasted three days, and we were afraid that the guests would indulge in the sort of rough horse-play which was permitted at the wedding. So both of us were very shy and dared not cast a look at one another. I did not look at her until three days after our marriage. This was not like modern couples, who do exactly as they please.

3. At that time did you think that bound feet were beautiful?

Of course bound feet are more elegant and graceful. This was especially so when wearing the ancient skirt and sash, swaying with every step.

4. Which do you now think more beautiful, small or natural feet?

Women now all have large feet. They jump and run when walking and fail to give the onlooker a gracious feeling. I think that small feet are more beautiful, but for those who have them work is not as convenient as if they had natural feet.

5. Was another person's support needed when walking?

The "three-inch lotus" was extremely rare. Ordinary women had to work at home, so they usually had feet of about five inches. They could not only walk fast, but could also carry water. To indicate some aesthetic feeling, they were, however, supported when getting in and out of sedan chairs. The wealthy had maid servants to support them when they went out walking, but the poor did not.

6. When were the feet let out?

In 1913, the [Kuomintang] revolutionary forces issued a command against footbinding. When it was issued, women felt happy because they would be relieved from the pain of bound feet. Men made no objection; for beautiful as bound feet were, they were inconvenient for work. Many women were afraid to let their feet out, through fear that the revolutionary army might not succeed. If it failed bound feet might still be fashionable, but once the bandage was loosened small feet could never be as small as before.[34]

7. What was the good point of bound feet?

They were beautiful, and, besides, bound feet could limit a woman's movements.

8. Was this custom widespread?

The custom of bound feet has been handed down from ancient times. Whether rich or poor, women all had their feet bound, for otherwise they would be laughed at and could not get married easily. But women of poor families, for the sake of working convenience, usually did not bind their feet to as small a degree as did the rich.

We were also able to discuss footbinding with Madam Liang's (9) son, born in Taiwan in 1896, the father of four children:

1. When did your wife bind her feet and when did she let them out?

She must have been ten when she started and sixteen when she gave it up, because the Japanese sent down an order forbidding it. She is now sixty-three years old.

2. Did your mother bind her feet?

Yes, and they are tiny, about three inches long. She is now eighty-nine and very healthy, living in Chang-hua County [Taiwan].

3. Did your mother have to be supported in her youth when she walked?

No, and neither did women in general, except those who were too fat.

4. Did women still bind their feet when you married?

I married at twenty-five [1921], and by that time no one did any more.

5. Did your mother work in the fields in her youth?

No woman with tiny feet worked in the fields, because of the inconvenience caused by the water there. But they could do household tasks such as cooking, washing clothes, and drawing water. Mother did all of those things in her youth.

6. What kind of shoes does your mother wear?

They are all high-heeled shoes, because she can't walk on shoes with a flat heel.

7. Were tiny-footed women often seen in the streets?

Women with three-inch feet could not walk long distances. When they left their homes, most of them rode in sedan chairs. But poor women had to go out to the streets to work. Their feet were often five to six inches long, the so-called semi-large tiny foot.

8. What kind of women had the tiniest feet?

Women of wealthy families or prostitutes; in other words, those who did no manual labor.

9. When and how did the Japanese prohibit footbinding?

They did this more than forty years ago. There were ten families in each *chia* grouping. The *chia* leader was held responsible for seeing to it that each woman in the ten families let out her feet. Those who disobeyed were fined two yen, with which one could then buy six piculs of rice. But no one disobeyed the order. Most of the women so affected cried, feeling that it was a pity to have to let out their feet.

10. Why didn't your mother let out her feet when the anti-binding Japanese order was issued?

The objects of the Japanese decree were the children who were just starting to bind their feet and young ladies. But Mother was then over forty and had bound her feet for tens of years. If she suddenly let them out, she wouldn't have been able to walk. So her petition to retain this practice was approved by the local Japanese police office.

11. What are the good points about footbinding?

This is a social custom, transmitted from the time in antiquity that a prince of Shu took Su-ta-chi as his wife. She was a wolf in disguise, with a very tiny foot. Everyone imitated her, and that is how the practice was transmitted until the present day.

APPENDIX ONE

*Form of the Golden Lilies**

The form of these "golden lilies," or kin lien, *as the Chinese call them, is accurately described in the following paper, taken from the* Transactions of the Royal Society of London. *It was written by Bransby Blake Cooper, esq., surgeon to Guy's Hospital; and was communicated to the Society by the secretary, P. M. Roget, M.D., March 5th, 1829.*

A specimen of a Chinese foot, the account of which I have the honor to lay before the Royal Society, was removed from the dead body of a female found floating in the river at Canton. On its arrival in England, it was presented to Sir Ashley Cooper, to whose kindness I am indebted for the opportunity of making this curious dissection. Without entering into an inquiry whether this curious dissection and, as we should esteem it, hideous deformity, of the Chinese female foot, had its origin in oriental jealousy, or was the result of an unnatural taste in beauty; I shall content myself with describing the remarkable deviations from original structure, which it almost everywhere presents. It may be proper, however, to remark, that as this conformation is the result of art, commenced at the earliest age, and exercised

* **Taken from *The Chinese Repository*, v.3, 538-42, April, 1835—No. 12. Dr. Cooper's findings are summarized in Werner, *Descriptive Sociology of The Chinese*, 143.**

on the persons of females only, we should naturally expect to find the most perfect specimens among those of the highest rank. Now as this body was found under circumstances which lead me to suppose that it was one of the lower orders, the measured proportions of the foot are therefore to be considered somewhat above the more successful results of this cruel art, when completed on the feet of those in more exalted stations of life.

To an unpracticed eye, the Chinese foot has more the appearance of a congenital malformation than the effect of art, however long continued; and although no real luxation has taken place, yet at first sight we should either consider it as that species of deformity, vulgarly called club-foot, or the result of some accidental dislocation, which from ignorance and want of surgical skill, had been left unreduced.

From the diminutive size of the foot, the height of the instep, the want of breadth, and above all, the extremely dense nature of the cellular tissue of the foot, it is evident that progression must at all times be difficult, and even the poising of the body when in the erect position, must require unusual exertion of muscular power, which, considering the disadvantages with which these muscles have to contend, is a matter of no small astonishment.

From the heel to the great toe, the foot is unusually short, not exceeding five inches, and is said in some instances to measure even less than this; and the great toe itself, which, in its natural and free state, projects forward in a straight position, is bent, with a peculiar abruptness, upwards and backwards, whilst the remaining toes, with the exception of the first phalanx of the second and third, are doubled in beneath the sole of the foot, so as to leave scarcely any breadth at this part of the foot, which in the unconstrained limb is commonly the broadest; and the striking shortness of the heel, scarcely projecting beyond the line of the leg, which itself descends upon the foot at a considerable obliquity from behind forwards, imparts an appearance to the foot, as if it were kept in a state of permament extension. The upper surface of the foot is very convex; but its convexity is irregular and unnatural, presenting a sudden and prominent projection just anterior to the external malleolus, and above the outer extremity of a deep cleft which traverses the sole of the foot. But as it is in the sole, that the most remarkable alterations are produced, I shall give a particular description of it first.

Sole of the foot. In describing the sole, we will suppose the foot to rest upon the heel, as it would do were the individual placed horizontally upon the back. In this view, we observe the great toe bent backwards towards the leg, and immediately beneath the articulation of its two phalanges, the second toe is so twisted under it that its extremity reaches to the inner edge of the foot; its nail occupies the centre of this position, having a considerable projection of integument beyond it. Next, but still anterior to the ball of the great toe, are the two extreme phalanges of the third toe; they are placed more obliquely than the phalanges of the second toe, and consequently do not reach so far inwards across the foot. The nail of this toe is somewhat nearer its extremity, but more completely on its anterior surface, so as nearly to touch the edge of the preceding one. A corn which appears on the space external and posterior to the nail of this toe seems to indicate that as the point of the fore part of the foot which is first subjected to pressure. We now come to the ball of the great toe, which separates the toes already described from the two outer ones; it does not present its usual full, convex appearance, but is flattened on its under surface, and compressed from before backwards by the position of the third and fourth toes. The position of the two remaining toes is very remarkable, and differs essentially from that of the others; for while in them only two phalanges are bent under the plantar region of the foot, in these all the phalanges are bent underneath it in such a manner as to produce a visible depression in the external edge of the foot. The fourth toe is placed more obliquely than the third, with its nail very much contracted, and is situated on its anterior edge; a large corn presents itself more external to the nail than in the third toe. The last or fifth toe stretches in the transverse direction across the under surface of the foot, and forms the anterior boundary to a deep cleft which occupies the center of the sole. This toe is so much expanded as to appear the largest; externally and posterior to its nail, it has two corns, placed much in the same manner as that in the fourth toe. But the strangest feature in this deformity, is the cleft or hollow just mentioned; it is very deep, with a slight obliquity from without inwards, and extends transversely across the whole breadth of the foot between the toes and the heel. To judge from its appearance, one might suppose that the heel and toes had been forcibly brought together, so as considerably to diminish the whole length of the foot, and to convert its natural longitudinal hollow into that deep concavity. The heel, which forms the other boundary of the cleft, presents a large square surface, if not entirely flattened, yet with a striking diminution of convexity, so as to suggest the probability that it affords the principal point of support in progression; a surmise which is further corroborated by the great density of the skin in this part.

Dorsum of the foot. The external character of the foot is completely altered here also; the direction of the leg downward and forward, forming before an obtuse angle with the foot, so as to give it an appearance of permanent extension, is the first circumstance worthy of notice. The dorsum rises with an unusual convexity, not only from behind forwards, but also from side to side; it affords a distinct protuberance situated just before the external malleolus, and above the outer extremity of the cleft in the sole, which is here very conspicuous; anterior to this eminence, the dorsum presents a plane surface facing outwards, till it slopes off rapidly beneath where the toes are turned under the sole. There is but a trifling alteration in the aspect of the inner surface of the dorsum, this side of the foot having undergone but little distortion: but the manner in which the dorsum is united with the great toe, deserves yet to be particularly noticed. A considerable angle distinguishes their point of junction, resulting from the dent or hollow, which the abrupt direction of the great toe upwards and forwards produces upon that surface. In this view we have the dorsum of the great toe with its aspect directly upwards; whilst the inner surface of the first phalanx of the second toe, has its dorsum turned outwards. Only a small portion of the inner surface of the third toe can be perceived in this view, whilst the remaining toes are buried beneath the foot. Posteriorly, there is little to remark, beyond the extreme shortness of the heel, which is not flatter, but wider than in the natural condition.

The integuments covering the heel are unusually dense, hard, and resisting, and the cuticle is of a remarkable thickness. The subcutaneous structure resembles rather the fatty sole of a horse's foot, than any human tissue. The skin which covers the rest of the sole, presents a corrugated appearance, and is somewhat thicker than in an ordinary foot; but in those places where it had been defended from external pressure by the intervention of the toes, which passed under it, it does not deviate from the natural construction. On the dorsum, the integuments offer nothing unusual; unless it be the nail of the great toe, which, as might be anticipated from constant compression, is rendered particularly convex from side to side. The other nails are not visible in this aspect of the foot. The tendons do not appear to have undergone any change, further than as their direction depended upon the altered position of the bones. It is, however, in the skeleton of the foot, that we observe the greatest changes produced by art. The powerful effect of long continued pressure over the direction even of the bones is here very striking.

The position of the os calcis is very remarkably altered; instead of the posterior projection which usually forms the heel, a straight line is preserved in this direction, not deviating from the line of the tibia; and the projecting point, which forms in an ordinary foot the most posterior process, and into which the tendo Achillis is inserted, touches the ground, and becomes the point d'appui for sustaining the whole weight of the body. The articular surface of the calcis, in connection with the cuboid bone, is about half an inch anterior to, and two inches above this point; while the astragalar joint is behind, and somewhat below the calco-cuboidal articulation; consequently, the direction of the os calcis (in its long axis), instead of being from behind forwards, is from below upwards, with the slightest possible inclination forwards. The most prominent parts of the instep are the round head of the astragalus, and the cuboidal articulation of the os calcis. From this, the remaining tarsal bones slope downwards at nearly a right angular inclination to join the metatarsal bones whose obliquity is still downwards, until they rest on their phalangeal extremities.

The length between the os calcis where it touches the ground, and the most anterior part of the metatarsal bone of the great toe, is four inches. The length of the foot, including the toes, 5¼ inches. The height of the instep, 3½ inches. Thus the arch of the foot has a span of two inches and a quarter, with the height of two inches, which space is fitted up with the condensed cellular substance before described. The cleft of the sole traverses the foot at this place, and is three inches in depth. The width of the foot at its broadest part is barely two inches. The points of support are the os calcis, the anterior extremity of the metatarsal bone of the great toe, and the dorsal surface of the fourth and fifth toes, which are bent under the foot so as to press the ground at this part.

Such are the anatomical particulars of this singular deformity; and although Nature has, by providing an accumulation of fat, thickening the skin and cuticle, and widening the surface of the heel, done her utmost to rectify the evil consequences of an unnatural custom, yet the awkward gait of a person attempting to walk on such deformed members may be easily imagined. Under such circumstances, in order to preserve equilibrium in an attempt to walk, it must be necessary to bend the body forwards in an uneasy position, and at the expense of a muscular exertion, which in ordinary progression is not put forth. To what extent the general health of the unfortunate individual thus deprived of the natural means of exertion may be affected, is a curious subject of inquiry, and remains, I believe, to be ascertained. I may be permitted to add, that the existence of this extraordinary custom, though familiar to our ears, is presented in a forcible light to our imagination by such a specimen as I have the honor to present to the Royal Society.

In offering to the Royal Society this brief sketch of the dissected foot, I do not pretend to attach to the subject any more importance than it deserves; nevertheless I have thought it would be considered as curious, and calculated to interest scientific men. And further, as its description has hitherto formed a desideratum in our accounts of anatomical curiosities, I have thought that my endeavor to supply it would not be unacceptable.

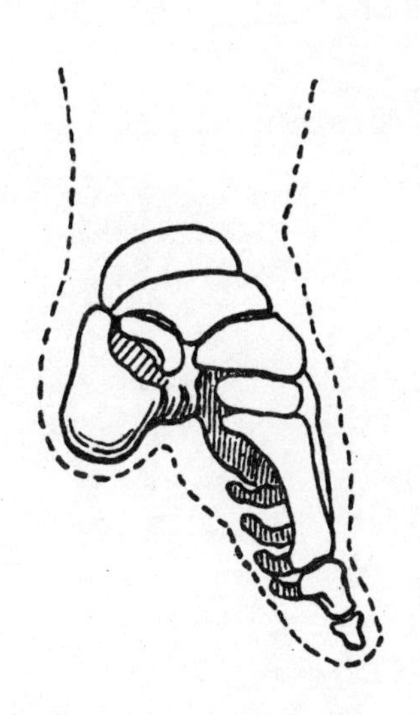

APPENDIX TWO

*The Physiological Effect Produced by Footbinding**

The result of footbinding, which injured a normal part of the human body, had a certain physiological effect over and above its hampering the freedom to walk erectly. The most accurate and profitable study concerning its effect was that done by Dr. Hideo Tsunoda, formerly a physician at the Taihoku (Taipei) Hospital. The essential points concerning his first topic, an explanation of the changes which had to take place in bound-foot Taiwanese women, as well as their external appearance, are as follows:

When walking erect, the conspicuous changes which take place in the external appearance of the abdomen or the pelvis are: 1) the outside swelling of the abdomen; 2) the conspicuous vertical groove along the line running down the center of the back, caused by tension especially of the back muscles and the muscles along the backbone; 3) the special conspicuousness of the forward curve of the lumbar vertebrae. The first two phenomena have appeared as the result of the third one, the cause of which cannot always be seen as a peculiarity of Chinese women. However, I believe that at least in Taiwan this is caused by footbinding. The weight of the body is transferred to the lower extremities, with the pelvis serving as a go-between. When the

* Taken from *Taiwan Igakkai zasshi* No. 29, January, 1905, 179-210.

lower extremities are unable to completely support this body weight, they must devise a way in which to cause this [body] gravity to be lessened.

There are two ways to do this. One is to reduce the body's weight when it is transferred to the pelvis, while the other is to use the pelvis itself to reduce the weight [supported by the lower extremities].

A). Reducing the Gravity When the Weight Is Transferred to the Pelvis

According to Meyer, the important point of the torso is from the first nodule of the first cervical vertebrae, passing through the sixth cervical vertebrae, the ninth thoracic vertebrae, and the third sacrum. Therefore, from the make-up of the frame of the body, what we call the curving of the lumbar vertebrae expresses in a broad sense the area from the ninth thoracic vertebrae to the third sacrum. Now when the body's weight is transferred to the pelvis, in order to reduce this weight why must the lumbar vertebrae become so strongly curved?

The curve of the lumbar vertebrae is probably caused by the slanting of the body weight on the sacrum. Here the great weight of the body (like the women of the Ryukyus who place objects on their head) or the lesser support (like the footbound Taiwanese women) develops this curvature [of the lumbar vertebrae]. This fact must become exceedingly clear and, though it is not clear whether this curvature is caused by frequent running forward of the lumbar vertebrae or by the severe sloping forward of the sacrum, or if it is first formed through an interdependence of the two factors, probably the larger part [of the curvature] is caused by the change in the direction of the lumbar vertebrae.

B). By Means of the Pelvis (Itself), Causing a Reduction of the Body's Weight Which Must Be Transferred to the Lower Extremities

1). The pelvis is required to expand towards the transverse

diameter, because to support ordinary body weight with a lesser support of the lower extremities, the transverse diameter of the pelvis must be much wider than the transverse diameter of the spinal column. For example, when the transverse of the pelvis is three times larger than the transverse of the spinal column, the lower extremities can support the body's weight with a supporting strength of only one-third of the ordinary body weight. (In other words, if the transverse of the pelvis is three times larger than the transverse of the spinal column, two-thirds of the body's weight is supported by the pelvis and the rest by the legs.)

2). The height of the pelvis requires that it be low. When a [flat] dimension which supports a body's weight becomes larger, the pressure received by its parts becomes less. Because of this, the venter of the ilium does not assume an almost vertical position, but rather one which is almost horizontal. Consequently the height of the pelvis must be reduced.

An Abstract of Dr. Tsunoda's Discussion Concerning the Direct Influence Which Footbinding Exerts on the Pelvis

1). As a result of footbinding, when the woman stands erect there is a noticeable curve of her waist. My conjecture is that this [curvature] is principally caused by the [slanting of] the lumbar vertebrae, and that the jutting out of the tip of the sacrum is relatively moderate. Mr. Habeler, while doing a measurement of pelves in Peking, proved that the entrance to the pelvis is not heart shaped but almost round, and that its vertical and transverse diameters are almost identical in length. This [the round shape of the entrance to the pelvis of the foot-bound woman] can also be presumed by comparing the lengths of the outer symphysis lines between the natural-footed and footbound Taiwanese women whom I measured. The comparison of the measurement of outer symphysis lines is as follows:

Footbound Women	18.9 cm
Natural-Footed Women	19.3 cm

2). The Enlargement of the Transverse Diameter

There are two ways in which to enlarge the transverse diameter of the pelvis. One is to elongate the front half of the pelvis's transverse diameter; the other is to elongate the width diameter of the sacrum. Now do the pelves of footbound women really form an enlargement of the transverse diameter? When these are inspected one hv one, the elongation of the front [upper] half of the pel [illegible] the transverse diameter can be imagined to have been produced through a large angle of the pubic arch. According to Habeler, the angle of the pubic arch among the Chinese is much greater than that of the Japanese and the Ainu.

Next, concerning the sacrum bone, Habeler states that a comparison of the width and length of the Chinese sacrum shows that it is larger than its counterpart among the Japanese and Ainu. Has the pelvis formed like this really been elongated along its transversal? Habeler has also stated that the pelvis of the Chinese, as compared with the Japanese and Ainu, is the smallest, while the length of the outer symphysis line is not much different from the other two races. The distance between the [left and right] front side iliac spines is a little short. However, the distance between the [left and right] back side iliac spines is remarkably large, while the distance between the [left and right] acetabulums is not much different [as compared with the Japanese and Ainu].

I further present my comparative estimates as follows:

	Bound-Foot Taiwanese	Natural-Foot Taiwanese	Japanese
Outer Symphysis Line	18.9 cm	19.3 cm	19.6 cm
Interval of the Iliac Crests	26.3 cm	27.3 cm	26.4 cm
Percentage	13.9	14.3	13.5

Therefore the transverse diameter of the pelvis, concerning both actual number as well as comparative examples, offers not the slightest proof that the pelvis of the bound-foot woman becomes especially enlarged. One becomes aware instead that the transverse of the pelvis of a woman with bound feet becomes reduced as compared with that of her natural-foot counterpart. I assume that these matters should subsequently be solved by securing a still larger amount of material.

3). The Height of the Pelvis

According to Habeler, the height of the [pelvis] of the Chinese woman is only slightly more than the Japanese and the Ainu at the pubic symphysis [union of the two pubic bones at the lower interior part of the abdomen], but the heights of other parts [of the pelvis], especially the overall heights, are noticeably lower than those of the Japanese and Ainu.

Notes and References

NOTES TO CHAPTER ONE *Introductory Remarks*

1. The quotation and general description of the footbinding process are taken from the writings of Adele M. Fielde, a missionary of discerning observation who lived in Swatow in the eighteen-eighties. (See *Pagoda Shadows*, 27–28.)

2. Translated from Matignon, *La Chine Hermétique*, 227–28.

3. *Ts'ai-fei lu* 采菲錄, hereafter abbreviated as *TFL*, 3.19–23. The footbinding record is preserved in these four monographs; for a description of editions, see Chapter Ten, Note 2. "... the oppressor always strives to dwarf the oppressed; man intentionally deprives women of their opportunities. We leave idle in women qualities of great brilliance that could be rich in benefit for themselves and for us. At ten the little girl is quicker and more clever than her brother; at twenty the young fellow is a man of wit and the young girl a great awkward idiot, shy and afraid of a spider; the blame is to be laid on her training...." (Stendhal's views as cited in *A History of Sex*, 263.)

4. "When you walk, don't turn your head; when you speak, don't open your mouth too wide; when you sit, don't move your knees; when you stand, don't shake your dress; when you are happy, don't laugh aloud; when you are angry, don't shout aloud." (A ninth-century manual, partially translated in my article, "T'ang Courtesans, Ladies and Concubines," *Orient/West*, vol. 7, no. 3, March, 1962, 63.)

5. *Nü-erh ching* 女兒經.

6. Chia Shen 賈伸 states that this ditty originated in Ch'ing-yüan County 清苑 and cites it as evidence that footbinding was a restrictive device. (Cf. *Chung-hua fu-nü ch'an-tsu k'ao* 中華婦女纏足考, 2a–b.)

7. This remark was made by the Sung philosopher Ch'eng I 程頤 (1033–1107) and was later cited favorably by Chu Hsi 朱熹 (1130–1200).

The Sung was a transition period; women were urged not to take a second husband if the first one died, but remarriages were still commonplace. (See *Chung-kuo fu-nü sheng-huo shih* 中國婦女生活史, 137–39.)

8. *Lang-huan chi* 瑯環記, ch. 2.

9. Matignon, *La Chine Hermétique*, 236. Dr. Matignon, who spent several years in China, served in a Peking hospital in about 1895. Anti-Chinese prejudice is apparent throughout his book, first published at Lyon in 1899, but in the chapter on footbinding he gives his information fairly objectively. His remarks are repeated almost verbatim by Vincent, *La Médecine en Chine au XXe Siecle*, 107–18; Vincent presents additional photographs and X-ray pictures of interest. (Cf. Davis, *The Chinese*, vol. 1, 269–70: "Quite as absurd, and still more mischievous, is the infatuation which among some Europeans attaches beauty to that modification of the human figure which resembles the wasp, and compresses the waist until the very ribs have been distorted, and the functions of the vital organs irreparably disordered.")

10. 瞿思九; the quotation is given by Chia Shen, op. cit., 2a.

11. Taiwanese Doctor Chang Hui-sheng, interviewed by Gerald L. T. Lai on April 6, 1961. (The original interview, translated from the Chinese, is in the writer's possession.)

12. Mr. Nagao Ryūzo 永尾竜造, interviewed in Tokyo in August, 1961. Mr. Nagao, a Japanese sociologist who lived in China for about forty years, wrote a three-volume detailed work on Chinese customs with the title *Shina minzokushi* 支那民俗誌. These volumes were numbered 1, 2, and 6. Volume 1 contained 673 pages, volume 2 numbered 883 pages, and information on footbinding was included in vol. 6, pp. 822–57. All of these books have been out of print for more than twenty years.

Mr. Nagao made available to me his unpublished, handwritten notes on footbinding, part of a more general sociological study. He originally planned to produce 30 volumes, but over 70,000 pages of manuscript were destroyed in 1942 by a fire at the Japanese Foreign Ministry. Since then, he has reassembled over 100,000 notes on year-round festivals, birth, wedding, and funeral customs.

13. See Chapter 4 ("Lotus Lovers") for details. Okuno Shintarō 奥野信太郎 remarked on the sexual attractions of footbinding in the October, 1962, issue of *(Bungei shunjū) Manga Tokuhon*, 68–73. This was a part of his study entitled, "Shinsen ni kawaigarareta onna" 神仙にかわいがられた女 (see Bibliography).

NOTES TO CHAPTER TWO *Origin and Presence*

1. *Chinese Repository*, April, 1835, v. 3;537. This story may have been copied in part from an Indian tale about a woman with the feet of a deer.

2. For a detailed account, see Chapter Ten, 280, and for Chinese references see *Ku-chin shih-wu k'ao* 古今事物考 and *Chien-hu-chi* 堅瓠集. The "club-foot" version is in Matignon, *La Chine Hermétique*, 232.

3. Many works give theories regarding the origins of footbinding; these place it anywhere from the Chou to the Six Dynasties period. Clear and fairly comprehensive listings are given by Chia Shen, loc. cit.; cf. *TFL* 2.13–15.

4. *Ta T'ang hsin-yü* 大唐新語. The *ch'e-fu chih* 車服志 section of *Hsin T'ang-shu* similarly remarks that women who lived during the reign of Chung-tsung 中宗 (ca. 684) wore the same kind of shoes as men. T'ang poetic allusions to women who had natural feet are listed in many references, including *Tzu-yu pao* 自由報, July 23, 1960, 4 (Taipei).

5. See Mahler, *The Westerners Among the Figurines of the T'ang Dynasty of China*, 107, various plates. This shoe style is the dominant one to be seen on T'ang figurines.

6. Sung and Yüan allegations that Yang Kuei-fei had bound feet are to be found respectively in *Shih-hua tsung-kuei* 詩話總龜 and *Lang-huan chi*. Cf. *Chung-kuo fu-nü sheng-huo shih*, 126.

7. Lin Yutang, *My Country and My People*, 166; Levy, H., *Harem Favorites of an Illustrious Celestial; Lament Everlasting (The Death of Yang Kuei-fei)*.

8. Levy, H., "T'ang Courtesans, Ladies and Concubines," *Orient/West*, Tokyo, March, 1962, 62–64.

9. 張邦基, cited in the *Cho-keng-lu*, a Yüan source of the highest value. (See Herbert Franke's comments on this source in *Historians of China and Japan*, 128–29.)

10. Li Yü 李煜, famed for his poetry, and his favored consort Yao-niang 窅娘. For citation and further discussion, see Naka Michiyo, "Shina fujin tensoku no kigen," 33–35. R. H. van Gulik, *Sexual Life in Ancient China*, 216, states that "all literary evidence points to the custom having begun in or about her time, that is in the interval of ca. 50 years between the T'ang and Sung dynasties."

11. *Nan-shih* 南史 5.21a (Taipei: *I-wen yin-shu kuan* photolithograph edition). The emperor was Hsiao Pao-chüan 蕭寶卷 (r. 498–501), who was killed by Liang Wu-ti 梁武帝 and given a reduced posthumous title as Marquis of Tung-hun 東昏侯.

12. Beal, *Buddhist Records of the Western World*, XXVIII.

13. Beal, op. cit., vol. 2, 71–72.

14. See Levy, *Ladies, Consorts and Concubines in Chinese Literature*, ch. 6, 25; *T'ang yü-lin* 唐語林 5.24b.

15. See N. C. Kuan, *Quarterly Review of Social Science* (Peiping: Academia Sinica), January, 1937. (As cited by Gamble)

16. There was a poetic reference to this empress, Hsiao-chou Hou 小周后, holding her shoes and walking in her stockinged feet, indicating that women of eminence still did not bind their feet at that time. (*TFL* 1.40)

17. van Gulik, *Sexual Life in Ancient China*, 222.

18. *TFL* 1.30 cites an event recorded in *Sung-shih* 宋史, but I have been unable to locate it. The citation is as follows: 治平元年韓維為潁王記室侍王坐, 有以弓鞋進者, 維日王安用舞靴. *TFL* 1.39 and 4.16–17 present a slightly modified version of this incident, taken from the Sung reference *Wen-chien chin-lu* 聞見近錄, in which Han Wei refers instead to military

shoes. (王安用武靴) A commentary follows, explaining that such shoes, used in hunting, were pointed and bowed in an upwards direction.

19. L. C. Goodrich, *A Short History of the Chinese People,* 140.

20. Quotation from a presumably Yüan dynasty source to prove the author's contention that footbinding became a means of teaching chastity and preventing women from becoming lewd. (*TFL* 3.120)

21. Levy, *Harem Favorites of an Illustrious Celestial,* 45.

22. Levy, "T'ang Courtesans, Ladies and Concubines," *Orient/West,* March, 1962, 49.

23. Cf. Wang, *La Femme dans la Société Chinoise,* 15; *Chung-kuo fu-nü sheng-huo-shih,* 133–34.

24. Levy, op. cit., 63–64.

25. Lin Yutang, op. cit., 165; for relevant passages in Chinese, see Chia Shen, op. cit., f. 8b.

26. Cf. Nagao Ryūzo's handwritten notes; discussion in *TFL* 2.351, in which the possibility is raised that these remarks were attributed to Chu Hsi by later generations.

27. The play, called *Golden Lotus Oppression* 金蓮刧, was published about 1907 and appeared partially in the 晶報 press. (See *TFL* 2.351.)

28. Fielding, *Strange Customs of Courtship and Marriage,* 87. It was feared that the vindictive spirit of the first husband would hover about, presumably because of his wife's failure to preserve her chastity.

29. Palace ladies in the harem of Emperor Li-tsung 理宗 (reigned 1225–64) bound their feet tiny and straight in a style called "Quickly Mounting A Horse" 快上馬. (*Sung-shih* 宋史, *Wu-hsing chih* 五行志, cited in *TFL* 2.15.)

30. Philosopher Ch'eng I 程頤 (1033–1107) made stringent statements; these were later repeated by Chu Hsi 朱熹 (1130–1200) in support of

similar arguments. Though these Sung thinkers urged women to remain widows after the death of the first husband, second marriages by Sung ladies were still commonplace. (*Chung-kuo fu-nü sheng-huo-shih*, 137–39.)

31. *Lang-huan chi*, ch. 2.

32. *Nü-erh ching* 女兒經.

33. *TFL* 1.42.

34. Chia Shen, op. cit., f. 6b.

35. Ibid, loc. cit.

36. *Chan-yüan ching-yü* 湛淵静語 1.1b–2a. The official was Ch'eng Huai 程淮, a sixth generation descendant of Ch'eng I 程頤. The latter's biography is in *Sung-shih*, 427.9b–14b.

37. These possibilities are raised in *TFL* 3.121.

38. 薩都刺 (Chia Shen, loc. cit.)

39. Gamble, "The Disappearance of Footbinding in Tinghsien," 181. Mr. Gamble observed that the custom of footbinding was not commented on by other early European or Western Asiatic travelers. Toriyama, *Shina. Shinajin*, 140, mentions that Odoric came to the Mongol capital, or what is now Peking. Sir John Mandeville (1322–55) also mentioned footbinding, but he was believed to have taken his account from Odoric. (Werner, *Descriptive Sociology of the Chinese*, 143.)

40. Cf. "Shina fujin tensoku no kigen," 54.

41. *TFL* 3.52; *Sung-shih* 宋史, *Yü-fu chih* 輿服志.

42. *TFL* 1.263; Chia Shen, op. cit., f. 7a.

43. See *Yeh-huo p'ien* 野獲篇; *TFL* 3.120; 160.

44. 張獻忠; 玉臂峰; 玉蓮峰; *TFL* 3.160; Chia Shen, op. cit., f. 7b. A Chinese friend informed me that a temple and monument were later erected in memory of those martyred. (Interview in Taipei, March 6, 1961.)

45. "Fu-jen chi" 婦人集 (in *Hsiang-yen ts'ung-shu,* vol. 1, ch. 2, f. 15b).

46. Tu Fu-weng 杜負翁, "T'ien Kuei-fei" 田貴妃 (in *Chung-yang jih-pao* 中央日報, April 22, 1961).

47. The incident was said to have occurred in the Ch'ung-chen 崇禎 era (1628–43) and to have involved official Chou Yen-ju 周延儒 (see *Ming-shih* 明史 308, 22b–27a, biography listed under traitorous ministers).

48. Clement Egerton: *The Golden Lotus,* 4 vols., London, Routledge and Kegan Paul Ltd., 1955. Certain of the episodes which Egerton rendered in Latin are translated into English by Lawrence E. Gichner in *Erotic Aspects of Chinese Culture* (1957), 86–115. *Kin Hei Bai* 金瓶梅, vol. 3, 367–69, discusses problems of dating and authorship and dates publication of *Chin P'ing Mei* towards the end of the sixteenth century; cf. Ch'en Shou-yi, *Chinese Literature,* 489–92.

49. Egerton, op. cit., I, 93: "Hsi-men took off one of her embroidered shoes, poured a cup of wine into it, and drank." The original passage in Chinese (*Chin P'ing Mei* 金瓶梅, edition with preface dated 1695, ch. 6, f. 8b–9a) 西門慶又脱下他一隻綉花鞋兒擎在手內放一小盃酒在內吃鞋盃耍子 is translated by me as follows: "Hsi-men lifted up one of her embroidered shoes which he had removed, placed a small full wine-cup in it, and teasingly drank a cupful from the shoe."

50. *Chinese Repository,* vol. 3, 537–42 (April, 1835).

51. Ibid., 538.

52. Doctor Cooper's medical description of this bound foot has been placed in an Appendix; q.v. Matignon, *La Chine Hermétique,* 222–27, gives the medical results of his examination of the tiny foot belonging to a twenty-year-old girl who had died of tuberculosis.

53. Hsu, *Americans and Chinese,* 255.

54. *TFL* 1.133; 4.349.

55. *TFL* 2.98–99.

56. *Li-weng ou-chi* 笠翁偶集 (*TFL* 2.16).

57. Yüan Mei, *Ta-jen ch'iu-ch'ieh shu* 答人求妾書.

58. *TFL* 1.139.

59. 王大娘的纏足布又臭又長, still used in referring to a long and dull lecture.

60. *TFL* 3.251–52; the area was known as Ho-t'ao 河套, comprising a series of counties.

61. Inoue Kōbai 井上紅梅, *Shina fūzoku* 支那風俗, vol. 1 (上), preface. The three-volume work was published at Shanghai in 1919–20. For his remarks on footbinding, written as part of a general study of Chinese women, see v. 3 (下), 414–25.

62. Ibid., loc. cit., 422–23.

63. 捂 (*TFL* 3.75).

64. 小脚姑娘 (*Sekai dai hyakka jiten* 世界大百科辭典, 349).

65. Nagao Ryūzo's handwritten notes; also see *TFL* 1.119; 3.156; Nagao, op. cit., VI. 857.

66. 四隻; 四至. (*TFL* 3.75)

67. *TFL* 3.75, 192–95. It would seem more logical to conclude that this signified subservience to her husband.

68. 鬧房.

69. See *TFL* 1.282–83; 3.90, 227.

70. 晾甲, 晾脚. (*TFL* 2.317–19)

71. "Ta-t'ung liang-chiao hui" 大同晾脚會, in *Central Daily News*, Taipei, November 20, 1961.

72. *TFL* 2.16–17.

NOTES TO CHAPTER THREE *Emancipation Movements*

1. Ch'e Jo-shui 車若水; *Chiao-ch'i chi* 脚氣集.

2. Nagao Ryūzo, op. cit., VI, 822–23.

3. Cf. *Ch'ih-pei ou-t'an* 池北偶談; *Shu-yüan chui-t'an* 菽園贅談; Nagao, op. cit., VI, 827–29.

4. See *Chung-kuo fu-nü sheng-huo-shih,* 232–33.

5. Cited by Chia Shen 賈伸, *Chung-hua fu-nü ch'an-tsu k'ao,* f. 11a.

6. Quoted by Chia Shen, op. cit., f. 11a, and a writer in the Chinese press (*Tzu-yu jen* 自由人, Taipei, July 23, 1960, 4).

7. Yüan Mei's letter is cited by Chia Shen, op. cit., f. 11a.

8. Chia Shen, op. cit., 11b. Kung's biography is in Hummel, *Eminent Chinese of the Ch'ing Period*, I, 431–34.

9. Chia Shen, op. cit., 11b.

10. *TFL* 3.128.

11. *Cheng Kuan-ying* 鄭觀應, *Sheng-shih wei-yen* 盛世危言, section called *Nü-chiao p'ien* 女教篇.

12. Ch'u Jen-hu 褚人穫, *Chien-hu chi* 堅瓠集.

13. Gamble, "The Disappearance of Footbinding in Tinghsien," 182; Nagao, op. cit., VI, 822.

14. The full text of this memorial is in Chia Shen, op. cit., Appendix, f. 17a–18b.

15. *TFL* 2. 171. The terms were 添足董事 *(t'iēn-tsŭ tŭng-shih)* and 天足董事 *(t'iēn-tsŭ tŭng-shih)*.

16. *TFL* 1.45.

17. *TFL* 3.1–7.

18. *TFL* 3.71.

19. Remarks attributed to Hsü Chien 徐建 in the course of a lecture before the Shanghai Natural Foot Society. (*TFL* 3.55–6)

20. The quotation is from *Pagoda Shadows* by Adele M. Fielde, 28.

21. See *TFL* 3.307–25, for accounts of footbinding by foreigners, as well as our appended bibliography.

22. This quotation and description of the Ladies Society are contained in an anonymous letter, written to *The Spectator,* March 19, 1898, issue, 406–7. The letter was from Shanghai, dated December 20, 1897.

23. *Spectator,* loc. cit.

24. Little, *Intimate China,* 134–63, has details on the early anti-footbinding movement, written primarily from a propagandist view. For Gladys Aylward's experiences, see *The Small Woman,* 71–75.

25. See *Encyclopaedia Sinica,* 1917, 29–30 and 186–87.

26. "Lun Tung-fu Ch'ing shih ch'an-tsu chin-ling shih" 論東撫請設纏足禁令事.

27. Kiangsi press editorial in about 1929, cited in *TFL* 2.279. Preceding pages (275–78) record press criticisms of official excesses committed during anti-footbinding campaigns. For provincial enforcement in the post-revolutionary era, see Chapter Nine.

28. *Encyclopaedia Sinica,* loc. cit.

29. "Footbinding, although still widely practised, has received its deathblow among intelligent Chinese. Too much credit for this reform cannot be given to the noble band of women missionaries who fought the stubborn battle for a hundred years and are fighting it today. Praise is also due Mrs. Archibald Little, who did much to enlist officials and gentry in the movement." (Bashford, *China. An Interpretation,* 139; cf. *Intimate China,* 145–63.)

30. Liang Ch'i-ch'ao published this essay in 1896 in the *Hsin-min ts'ung-pao* 新民叢報, when he was a member of the Society for Outlawing Bound Feet. (Cited by Chia Shen, op. cit., f. 13a–b.) Lin Yutang described one father so moved by Liang's essays that he decided against having his daughter's feet bound. (*Shun-shi ching-hua* 瞬息京華, 11.)

31. Poems by Lin Ch'in-nan 林琴南, cited by Chia Shen, op. cit., f. 14a–b. Lin's liberal views on eliminating footbinding were diametrically opposed to those of Ku Hung-ming. However, both men resisted moves to reform the written Chinese language and adopt a vernacular style.

32. Chia Shen, op. cit., f. 15a.

33. Matignon, *La Chine Hermétique*, 233.

34. Chia Shen, op. cit., f. 15b.

35. *The New Republic*, Dec. 18, 1915, 170–72, by a Chinese writer who signed himself Suh-ho. Bashford, writing in 1916, remarked that the wives of very few officials had then unbound their feet, and that "...the cruel custom has thus far disappeared among only a small section of the people." (*China. An Interpretation*, 139)

36. See Chapter Nine.

37. Sidney D. Gamble, "The Disappearance of Footbinding in Tinghsien," *American Journal of Sociology*, September, 1943, 181–83.

38. *TFL* 4.251.

39. For references to the above statements, see Nagao, op. cit., VI, 823–27, part of a 35 page essay on footbinding.

40. *Dai Hyakka Jiten* 大百科事典, Tokyo, 1932, vol. 18, 264–65.

41. Gotō Asatarō 後藤朝太郎, *Shina no otoko to onna* 支那の男と女, Tokyo, 1939, 27–29.

42. The information which follows has mostly been taken from a comprehensive Chinese monograph on efforts by the Japanese to change customs in Taiwan during the early period of their occupation. (*Taipei wen-wu* 台北文物, vol. 9, no's 2–3, 13–22.)

43. Naka Michiyo 那珂通世, "Shina fujin tensoku no kigen" 支那婦人纏足の起源, *Shigaku zasshi*, 1898, vol. 9, no. 6, 32–33.

44. The speaker was 黃玉階. (*Taipei wen-wu*, loc. cit., 20.)

45. Ibid., op. cit., 21.

46. 天然足會.

47. *Taipei wen-wu*, loc. cit.

48. The ditty originated in Fukien's T'ung-an 同安 District. (Chia Shen, op. cit., f. 1a.)

49. 臺華章.

50. 不敢毀傷孝之始也.

NOTES TO CHAPTER FOUR *Lotus Lovers*

1. This custom was observed as long as footbinding in Peking flourished and was still noted at the start of the twentieth century. (Nagao Ryūzo's handwritten notes.)

2. For this and the monographs on footbinding by Fang Hsün 方絢 which follow, see *Hsiang-yen ts'ung-shu* 香艷叢書 vol. 8, ch. 1.

3. *TFL* 3.83–84, included in a section on jokes about the lotus.

4. The ditties are recorded in *TFL* 2.229, 307; other information is in *TFL* 2.272, *Ling-nan tsa-chi* 嶺南雜記, *Nan-Yüeh pi-chi* 南越筆記, and Nagao Ryūzo's handwritten notes.

5. *TFL* 2.18–19. The first two ditties are from Honan, the third from Kiangsi, and the last quoted by Ku Chi-kang 顧頡剛 in *Wu-ko chia-chi*

吳歌甲集 (a selection of Kiangsu odes). The Buddha's Hand 佛手 is a fragrant tropical fruit, so called because of its resemblance to a hand.

6. *TFL* 2.296; the quotation is from the writings of a twentieth-century imitator of Fang Hsün's *Golden Garden Miscellany* named Hsü Hsiao-t'ien.

7. *TFL* 2.295.

8. *TFL* 2.230, 295, 302. To be ugly but have tiny feet was called "The Good Fortune of the Fragrant Lotus."

9. 金園雜纂, in *Hsiang-yen ts'ung-shu*, vol. 8, ch. 1.

10. According to Hsü Hsiao-t'ien, to have elegant stockings but worn-out shoes indicated a lack of planning by the wearer. (*TFL* 2.296)

11. 蘇州頭揚州脚. Hsü Hsiao-t'ien remarked that the beauty of Suchow women was questionable, but that even the poorest of Yangchow women had tiny and regular feet. (*TFL* 2.296)

12. The tiny shoe was sometimes given to the lover; at other times he purloined it. (*TFL* 2.304–6)

13. See monograph by the anonymous contributor who used the pseudonym, Hunanese Fool. The doctor who used these remedies was Dr. I Sung-yu 易松友 from Changsha. (*TFL* 4.124–25)

14. Cf. *Pi-tsou-chai yü-t'an chieh-lu* 敝帚齋餘談節錄, in *HYTS*, vol. 3, ch. 1, f. 5a; *TFL* 1.83–84; 3.264.

15. *TFL* 3.176.

16. The historical references were to: 1) the beautiful Hsi Shih 西施; 2) the Prince of Wu 吳王, who took in Hsi Shih as his beloved consort and let her monopolize his time to the ruin of his state; 3) Minister P'i 嚭 of Ch'u 楚, who fled to Wu, became Prime Minister to the Prince of Wu, and misled him politically.

17. See the complete essay in *TFL* 1.7–22.

18. *TFL* 1.215–16 has a Chinese translation of Professor H. Laderland's remarks about footbinding which appeared in the January, 1928, issue of *Sexualwissenschaft* XIV. Ku Yen 顧寅 was the translator. The comment about tiny-footed women giving one the same feeling as a virgin was made by Nagao Ryūzo when interviewed in August, 1961.

19. See Matignon, *La Chine Hermétique*, 234–35; Chung Cheng, "Feet," 7–8. "I was careful to wipe her thoroughly between her toes.... At last I fulfilled my desire to lavish caresses with my tongue, as freely as I liked, on those beautiful feet...then I bent over to kiss and caress her feet." (Tanizaki, *The Key*, 20, 25, 56, et al.)

20. *TFL* 2.234. The American, described as a fluent speaker in Chinese, had his name transcribed as *Fei-erh* 斐爾.

21. 諦明, meaning Truth and Enlightenment.

22. *TFL* 3.143–45.

23. *TFL* 4.78. The notice was by Yao Ling-hsi; the book was called *Chin-yün-ch'iao* 金雲翹.

24. *TFL* 4.207–9. This essay, by "One Who Knows Pity," also described these variant lotus grips:

Ring and little fingers are wrapped around the toes. The toe area is encircled by the thumb and middle finger; the index finger presses on the instep.

The shoe is pointed towards the wrist, with the thumb pressing on the outside of the heel. The heel is hooked from behind by the forefinger, while the remaining fingers hold the inside of the heel.

The heel is placed in the palm, with the big toe resting on the middle finger. The other four fingers are wrapped around the front and instep.

25. Cf. *TFL* 2.336–37; 4.261–62.

26. Cf. *TFL* 2.127, 225; 3.100–104. The woman in Peking reacted to her feet being grasped by vigorously responding with her tongue against the man's. Her eyes were almost completely closed; her throat made a sound like a child ready to suck its mother's breasts. She wound her legs around the man's waist, used her ankle to pull him in towards her and save his strength, and moved with him in rhythmical unison.

27. *TFL* 2.144–54.

28. *TFL* 4.359. There were one to three prostitutes mentioned for each location. Other names were Moon Tower, Multicolored Lute, and Cassia Red.

29. *TFL* 1.271–72; 3.84, 91–93. To commemorate the stage incident, the writer composed a series of stanzas in T'ang poetic style. (*TFL* 1.271–72)

30. Ku Hung-ming 辜鴻銘 (1857–1928), as quoted by Lin Yutang in *Shun-hsi ching-hua,* 75–76. For Ku's opinions on women, see his *Spirit of the Chinese People,* 74–100. Western writers shared his criticism of tight-lacing of the waist. "To Western eyes, bound feet are as great a deformity as is the tight-lacing of European ladies to the Chinese; but physically the former is much less injurious than the latter, which not only deforms the skeleton, but displaces almost every one of the internal organs." (Blake, *China,* 12)

31. 孫慕韓. (*TFL* 1.278)

32. *TFL* 2.333. My translation has corrected one obvious error in the text, the use of the character 大 where 小 was intended. (Also see *TFL* 3.252)

33. *TFL* 2.333. Doctor Chang Ching-sheng 張競生 later retracted these statements, said that footbinding destroyed sexual desire, and came out publicly in favor of natural feet. His change of view was attributed to his having gone abroad for post-graduate study.

34. *TFL* 1.282.

35. *TFL* 2.232–33.

36. Se comments by Yao Ling-hsi in *TFL* 3.181.

37. *TFL* 2.215. The official was Chang Ch'iu-fang 章萩舫, his concubine 金小白.

38. *TFL* 2.215, 223, 226.

39. *TFL* 4.219; 1.286.

40. *TFL* 2.238.

41. *TFL* 1.124; Matignon, *La Chine Hermétique,* 235.

42. *TFL* 3.79–80. The Pei-ning 北寧 Railroad went through an area of rich agricultural villages. For corroboration of other statements, see *TFL* 2.191–93, 213–14; 3.87, 133, 304–5.

43. 重門疊戶.

44. Cf. van Gulik, *Sexual Life in Ancient China,* 216–22.

NOTES TO CHAPTER FIVE *Wondrousness of The Lotus*

1. "And there is still no end to dreaming and debating on the feminine mystery. It is indeed to preserve this mystery that men have long begged women not to give up long skirts, petticoats, veils, long gloves, high heeled shoes; everything that accentuates difference in the other makes her more desirable." *(A History of Sex,* 217)

2. *TFL* 4.44–54.

NOTES TO CHAPTER SIX *Secret Chronicle of the Lotus Interest*

1. See Chapter Ten, Note 2.

2. "The fashionable size is about four inches, but many reach to five and seven inches. The size depends upon the time when it was begun and the regularity and tightness with which it is maintained." ("Report of the Peking Hospital in 1868," as cited in Werner, *Descriptive Sociology of the Chinese,* 143.)

3. *TFL* 4.225–236.

NOTES TO CHAPTER SEVEN
Reckless and Cruel Treatment of the Drunken Lotus

1. This was literally a reference to cultivating the technique of *t'u-na* 吐納, practiced by Taoists who expelled the bad air from the stomach and

inhaled the clean fresh air. Reference to this type of deep breathing exercise was made in *Chuang-tzu.*

2. The French writer Denis de Rougemont refers to the war-like language of love, which could be traced back to the third century cf the Christian era. "All this confirms the natural—that is to say, the psychological—connexion between the sexual and fighting instincts. The language of love (in the twelfth and thirteenth centuries) was then enriched with phrases and expressions which had unmistakably been borrowed from the art of giving battle and from contemporary military tactics." (*Love in the Western World,* 252–58)

3. ". . .virginity is one of the secrets that men find most exciting the more so as they are greater libertines; the young girl's purity allows hope for every kind of license, and no one knows what perversities are concealed in her ignorance." (*A History of Sex,* 218)

4. See the account in *TFL* 4.360–64. The pen-name of the author (五四老人) probably referred to his age.

NOTES TO CHAPTER EIGHT *The Tiny Foot in Truth and Fiction*

1. *Sha-jen pi-chi* 傻人筆記, 81.

2. A reply by Lotus Craver on the merits of footbinding, in the December 9, 1922, issue of *Hsiao-hsiao Press* 小小報 (cited in *TFL* 2.299–300).

3. *Sha-jen pi-chi,* 83.

4. Inoue Kobai 井上紅梅: *Shina fūzoku* 支那風俗, vol. 3 (下), 414–16. A Chinese friend, whose grandmother had bound feet, remembered as a child how her foot odor annoyed him. They lived in the country and she rarely washed, he explained.

5. *Sha-jen pi-chi,* 84–85.

6. Nan-kung Po 南宮搏, *An-kuo fu-jen* 安國夫人. The passages which have been translated are scattered throughout the book.

7. See *Meng Li-chün* 孟麗君, by Ch'i Lü-ho 戚綠荷(Ta-ta t'u-shu-chü 大達圖書局, 1936).

8. 梁山伯 and 祝英臺. The modern version of the story as given above is told by Nagao, "Tensoku ni kansuru shizoku," 849–51. The butterflies are described in *Shih-wu i-ming lu* 事物異名録.

9. Nagao Ryūzo's handwritten notes.

10. An account written in stylistic imitation of *Liao-chai chih-i* 聊齋誌異, called *Lien-chai chih-i* 蓮齋誌異, (in *TFL* 3.140–42). The author used the pen-name of Hsiang-fu 薌腐.

11. There is a detailed description of how men and women dressed in Peking at the start of the twentieth century in *K'uo-fu chi* 闊斧記.

12. *TFL* 1.305–6.

13. This unverifiable statement is made by editor Yao Ling-hsi in *TFL* 1.220, who goes on to say that footbound males were also mentioned in *Liao-chai chih-i*.

14. The first Ming account is in *Shu-yüan tsa-chi* 菽園雜記, ch. 7, f. 10a, the second in *TFL* 3.72.

15. This article appeared in the May 15, 1931, issue of the *Shanghai Times* 上海時報. For information about it and the earlier stories about male footbinding, see *TFL* 1.216–20. Matignon, *La Chine Hermétique*, 263–81, describes young pederasts who, while made up as girls, were apparently natural-footed. (Cf. Ibid., Plate 28)

16. *TFL* 1.307.

17. For the translations which follow, see Li Ju-chen 李汝珍: *Ching-hua yüan* 鏡花緣, ch. 33–34, 13. His biography is in Hummel, *Eminent Chinese*, I, 472–73. For other biographical details and a discussion of this novel, see Ch'en Shou-yi, *Chinese Literature*, 590–93.

18. *Chan-yüan ching-yü* 湛淵靜語 1.1b–2a.

19. This passage was quoted by Hu Shih in *Hu Shih wen-ts'un* 胡適文存, vol. 2, 414–15. Hu Shih regarded *Ching-hua yüan* as a permanent contribution to the world's history of the emancipation of women. (Hummel, loc. cit.)

20. Yüan Mei 袁枚, *Tu-wai yü-yen* 牘外餘言. Yüan served capably in a series of official posts, but retired early in his career and became a renowned and well-paid writer. "He insisted that women should be given equal opportunity to develop their native intelligence." (Hummel, op. cit., II, 956)

21. Yü Cheng-hsieh's 兪正燮 writings against footbinding are discussed in *Chung-kuo fu-nü sheng-huo shih*, 247, 250 (Cf. *Kuei-ssu lei-kao* 癸巳類稿, *Ts'un-kao* 存稿). His biography is in Hummel, op. cit., II, 936–37.

NOTES TO CHAPTER NINE *Painful History of the Lotus Hooks*

1. Cited by Chia Shen, op. cit., 15b.

2. *San-k'o-hsi kuan ts'ung-t'an* 三可惜館叢談, cited in *TFL* 2.22–23. The information in this chapter on revolutionary attempts to eliminate footbinding has largely been taken from the essay by Li Jung-mei 李榮楣 entitled, *Chung-kuo fu-nü ch'an-tsu shih-t'an* 中國婦女纏足史譚 (in *TFL* 2.1–38).

3. *TFL* 2.27.

4. May 16, 1927, issue of the Shanghai paper *Shen-pao* 申報 (cited in *TFL* 2.28).

5. October 15, 1927, issue of *Shen-pao* (*TFL* 2.29).

6. June 24, 1928, issue of *I-shih pao* 益世報 (*TFL* 2.30).

7. June 17, 1928, issue of *New Tientsin Press* 新天津報 (*TFL* 2.31).

8. September 7, 1928, issue of *New Tientsin Press* (*TFL* 2.34).

9. August 14, 1928, issue of *I-shih pao* (*TFL* 2.32–33).

10. *TFL* 4.165.

11. *TFL* 2.273–74.

12. Viewpoint expressed in a Kiangsi news editorial, cited in *TFL* 2.279.

13. *TFL* 1.255–58. Many of the critical accounts of footbinding which follow may have been composed at the specific request of foot investigation authorities, as the price exacted for approving the writer's petition not to have to let out the feet because of extenuating circumstances.

14. *TFL* 2.50–51.

15. 萬字埠.

16. *TFL* 2.51–54.

17. *TFL* 2.55–57.

18. *TFL* 2.63–65.

19. *TFL* 2.67–69.

20. 東方遊記 (*TFL* 2.60).

21. "When the feet are completely remodelled, there is a notch in the middle of the sole deep enough to conceal a penny-piece put in edge-wise across the foot." (Fielde, *Pagoda Shadows*, 29)

22. *TFL* 2.59–63.

23. *TFL* 1.362–63; 2.338–41; 4.122–24; the *Pen-ts'ao kang-mu* 本草綱目, as cited by Toriyama, *Shina. Shinajin*, 142. These footbinding prescriptions are sometimes hard to decipher because of the local village ingredients which were used. A few other remedies are listed below.

A Hsi Shih 西施 (Chinese beauty) Bone Softening Broth consisted of a half ounce each of apricot seeds and frankincense, and two ounces each of 朴硝 and mulberry tree bark. It was boiled in a jar, after which the feet were steamed over it and inserted when it cooled. Used three times, it made the feet "soft as cotton." Burnt alabaster, soapstone, and burned alum were compounded for the alleviation of itching and peeling between the toes. This was also effective for stopping perspiration of the woman's private parts. Lime powder, glutinous rice, plums, ground camphor, and yellow lead produced an effective mixture for the peeling of carbuncles and the promotion of healing. Other foot-softening ingredients included nepeta japonica, red hibiscus, Sapan-wood iris root, myrrh, acrous gramineus, and licorice root. (See sources as cited for further information.)

24. *TFL* 2.57–59.

25. This is a summary of the account in *TFL* 3.13–19.

26. *TFL* 2.65–67.

27. *TFL* 2.183–84. Matignon, *La Chine Hermétique,* 229, mentions a northern massage by the mother in which she seized the heel-bone with one hand, the front part of the foot with the other, and bent both parts forcibly together. It was said that these efforts sometimes resulted in a fracture or dislocation of the tarsus bone.

28. The text is 膏本, which I have been unable to identify. If written instead as 膏沐, the term would mean "bandoline."

29. 濱江; located in Manchuria.

30. *TFL* 1.261–62.

31. 門頭村, near Thailand.

32. Summary of an account in *TFL* 1.258–61.

NOTES TO CHAPTER TEN *Ladies of the Bound-Foot Era*

1. My field study in Taiwan, conducted on a part-time basis, consisted of interviewing elderly ladies of diverse origins who either still practiced footbinding or had done so in their youth. Chinese friends helped me in formulating a questionnaire and in conducting the interviews in either Taiwanese or Mandarin. Whenever possible, tape recordings were made and transcribed later for greater accuracy. This aspect of the study especially benefited from the voluntary efforts of Tai Chu-yü 戴祝念, Gerald L. T. Lai 賴金鐓, Teng Hsin-sheng 鄧新聲, and Liu Kuang-hsia 劉光夏. In this chapter, the recorded interviews have been collated and rearranged by topic. Several ladies allowed photographs to be taken of their bare feet; this was never permitted by respectable women in the days when footbinding flourished.

2. The records are preserved in *Ts'ai-fei lu* 采菲錄 (abbreviated *TFL*), four monographs published between 1934 and 1938 by a Chinese scholar named Yao Ling-hsi 姚靈犀. These monographs are referred to as *TFL* 1, 2, 3, or 4, followed by the page or pages to which reference is made. I used these editions:

TFL 1. Edited by Yao Ling-hsi; his preface dated January, 1933. Reprinted January 1, 1936, by Shih-tai kung-ssu 時代公司 in Tientsin.

TFL 2. Same editor; his preface dated January, 1936. Published February 20, 1936, same as above.

TFL 3. Same editor, published December 30, 1936, by Tien-ching shu-chü 天津書局.

TFL 4. Same editor, published December 1, 1938, by Tien-ching shu-chü. A fifth book was planned, to be called *Ts'ai-fei hsin-lu* 采菲新錄. (*TFL* 4.265). van Gulik, *Sexual Life in Ancient China*, p. 218, refers to a fifth book published as a *hsü-pien* 續編, but this may be a reference instead to the second of the four books, called *Ts'ai-fei lu hsü-pien* 采菲錄續編.

These four monographs by Yao Ling-hsi represent a remarkable and comprehensive collection of materials relating to all aspects of footbinding, with impartial inclusion of opponents as well as enthusiasts of the practice. Yao collected contributions from many areas in China, and apparently published each volume after having accumulated about 350 pages of material, prefaced by illustrations. Contents included historical sources, anecdotes, poetry, discussions in question and answer form, official edicts, essays, and miscellany. The special merit of the work is that it was recorded when footbinding was still a living part of the historical scene.

Yao entitled each study *Ts'ai-fei lu* 采菲錄 (*The Record of Gathering Radishes*), alluding to a poem in the *Book of Odes* which advised that one should not reject the beautiful stems of a plant because its roots were rotten. Yao stated that he had coined this title because one should not disregard a woman's overall beauty even though the bound foot was a defect of her lower extremities. He admitted that footbinding was an evil custom and injurious to the nation's health, and went on to say: "I want to go into detail in order to find out the truth about this custom, and then later one can judge whether it is right or wrong. To forbid opium, you should know its origins and injurious qualities. In the same way, to eliminate footbinding, we should first know its history; this was my intent in compiling the monograph." (*TFL* 2. editor's preface, 3–4)

3. Cf. *Encyclopaedia Sinica*, article under Footbinding: "A Chinese writer has declared that one girl out of ten died from the after-effects of footbinding, suppuration and gangrene often occurring, causing the limb to fall off." (186–87). However, our quotation, which seems in direct contradiction to this allegation, was taken from Williams, *The Middle Kingdom*, vol. 2, 38. His remarks were made about forty years before the anti-footbinding movement got under way and were obviously put forth without ulterior motive. Inspection of missionary hospital records compiled in the late nineteenth century supports the observation by Williams. Mrs. Archibald Little, an influential writer against the custom who founded an anti-footbinding society in Shanghai in 1895, gave testimony from doctors in Shanghai, Nanking, and Chungking in such a way as to suggest that serious maladies were commonplace. (*Intimate China*, 140–44)

4. *TFL* 2 (Ch'en Wei-ch'en's 陳微塵 preface) 1.

5. The writer recalls an article in *Hsin-sheng pao* 新生報 Taiwan, (ca. Feb., 1961), describing a 101 year old Taiwanese from Su-ao 蘇澳 who had her feet bound in infancy. Provided, therefore, that the child got through the initial period, there would seem to have been no negative correlation between footbinding and longevity.

6. The following ladies were interviewed:

1) Madam Feng, our first informant, was 82 years old. She was from Hunan Province, where she had reared five sons and five daughters. Only one son had come with her to Taiwan; she was cared for by her daughter-in-law. Madam Feng still did some embroidery work, and in this way contributed to the meeting of household expenses. Her son was a major in the Chinese Air Force, and one grandson was in elementary school. Madam Feng, who was unusually lively for her age, tended to be talkative and to digress.

2) Madam Hsiung, born in 1889 in Kiangsi Province, was widowed and in relatively poor circumstances. Three children were still on the mainland, and a fourth had died in Taiwan. She had to perform such daily household tasks as cooking and washing. Her feet had been let out and were over five inches long, but she still swayed as she walked. She may have suffered from lapses in memory, for she was unable to answer two of our questions.

3) Mrs. Kuo Wu Ch'ueh, also a widow, was born in 1886 in Fukien Province. Two sons and a daughter were in Taiwan with her. She was

the first of the women interviewed who still bound her feet to the present day, and hers were the smallest. She was reticent about being photographed in her bare feet and retained a part of what appeared to be a cotton wadding. This meant that we could photograph only the big toe clearly. She was able to walk unaided, slowly but without difficulty. She had aristocratic demeanor and answered questions briefly and with reserve. When she stood, her feet protruded slightly beneath her trousers like two tiny specks.

4) Madam T'ung was born in 1895 in Hupei Province. She was one of two women whose husband had not predeceased her; we were also able to question Mr. T'ung about footbinding. Madam T'ung, whose feet had been let out and were about six inches long, seemed in excellent health. She rose every morning at five o'clock and worked around the house until eight in the evening.

5) Mrs. Ch'ĕn Shih-ch'ou, whose ancestors were Fukienese, was born in 1892 in Lung-ching, Taiwan. I was able to get this interview by stopping to chat with her in the street, complimenting her in Taiwanese on her tiny "golden lotuses." Like Mrs. Kuo (3), she still bound her feet. While I was unable to measure them, they probably did not exceed four inches. She was a very lively person and answered our questions at length.

6) Mrs. Wu Han was questioned in April, 1961, by a Taiwanese assistant, and my absence may have resulted in more candid replies being elicited. Mrs. Wu was born in Taiwan in 1878 and resides in Taichung. Her husband died when she was 28 years old, and she has been a widow for more than 50 years. She gave birth to a son, already deceased, who reared eight children. They in turn had 28 children, so Mrs. Wu has 8 grandchildren and 28 great-grandchildren. Her foot, which is still bound, is about 3½ inches long, smaller than Mrs. Ch'en's (5) and about the same size as Mrs. Kuo's (3).

7) Mrs. Yang Mien, interviewed one month later, was born in 1881 in Ch'ing-shui, Taiwan. She married when seventeen, and her husband died about twenty years ago. She has twenty-six grandchildren. She let her feet out, and they are over five inches long. The Taiwanese interviewer later stated: "When I photographed her, she took off the bindings and said that the wind made her feet feel very painful. That is why at first she did not want to remove the bandages. The old lady said that she felt very embarrassed to let men see her bare feet. This 81 year old lady was very courteous. When she walked, she swayed from side to

side as if she were a young lady. Her eyes were still good, and she was able to sew and do some work for the family. She was in remarkable condition for her age."

8) Mrs. Ch'en Cheng Chien, who now lives in Taichung, was born in Taiwan in 1890. She was interviewed in May, 1961. She married at the age of nineteen, and her husband died at the age of forty-six. She bore him two sons and now has sixteen grandchildren. Her feet were reputedly once four inches long, but she let them out.

9) Madam Liang, whose maiden name was Ch'en, was the oldest woman interviewed, eighty-nine years of age. She lived in Lung-hsi Village, Central Taiwan. The village name indicated a north Chinese origin. Through inquiries we discovered that most of the original inhabitants who had settled there more than two hundred years before were native to Shansi. From Shansi, they had gone south to Fukien and then Taiwan. There were about a thousand inhabitants in Lung-hsi.

Our venerable informant, the mother of three sons and two daughters, could still see and hear clearly. However, she was somewhat indisposed on the day we questioned her (April 15, 1961). Madam Liang was rather heavy set, with feet over five inches long. Because of her physical discomfort, we limited our questions and allowed ample time between responses. We later asked for a pair of tiny shoes as a memento of the visit, but she demurred, saying that the pair we wanted were bedroom shoes, to be worn on the day of her death. She later had another pair made for us by hand.

I was transferred to Tokyo in late May, 1961, but made arrangements to present congratulatory gifts on her ninetieth birthday. This took place in late July, 1961, but was not especially observed because she was financially unable to invite large numbers of the villagers to attend. She apologized to my interpreter for not being able to reciprocate for the gifts and said that she would pray for my "long life."

10) Mrs. Ting was 76 years old in the spring of 1961, native to the former port of Lukang in Central Taiwan. Her husband died thirteen years ago. She was questioned on April 5, 1961, and went into considerable detail in her replies, of particular value with regard to the binding process.

11) Mrs. Shih, also from Lukang, was born in 1894. She married a man four years her senior in 1912, and they were still in good health at the time of the interview. Mrs. Shih, like Mrs. Ting, answered at length. Since these two ladies were from the same place in Taiwan, their replies were often similar.

The women described above responded to a general questionnaire. In addition, there was an informal discussion with a 35 year old Taiwanese woman from Nan-t'un. The Nan-t'un informant's (12) mother, whose feet had been bound, had died 15 years ago at the age of sixty-three. Mrs. Liu Wang Tzu-chih (13), born in Fukien in 1903 and teaching in a Taichung Girls' Middle School, spoke with me in the spring of 1961 about her impressions of footbinding. She started the process while in Fukien in 1915, but gave it up three years later when she started attending middle school.

T'ung Hui-ch'uan, the husband of Madam T'ung (4), was the first man to be interviewed. He was born in Hupeh Province in 1894 and was from the same city as his wife. He revealed traditional views of a man born and reared during the bound-foot era. A Taiwanese assistant, Gerald L. T. Lai, was unable to get information from the women he queried about the origin of bound feet. However, his father, Lai Jan, born in 1901 and living in Taichung, furnished a detailed account; this was corroborated in part by the testimony of mainland ladies.

7. *TFL* 2.7.

8. *TFL* 2.8.

9. *TFL* 2.11–12; cf. Li, "The Life of a Girl in China," 63–64.

10. Cf. Trusler, *The Habitable World Described*, 16; Winterbotham, *An Historical, Geographical, and Philosophical View of the Chinese Empire*, 380. ("Scarcely is a girl born, but the nurse binds up her feet so tight, that they cannot grow; and this torture must be endured, until the foot has naturally done growing." Trusler, loc. cit.)

11. *TFL* 1.124; 127–32.

12. *TFL* 1.195–97. Editor Yao Ling-hsi states that Korean women from 1862 onward bound their feet in the New Moon, Pointed Lotus, or Wei styles, but that this was gradually prohibited by the Japanese occupation authorities.

13. The interview was granted by Mrs. Ts'ui Lee Ch'ing-yen, a member of the *yangban* class whose family has lived in Seoul for generations.

Her remarks were interpreted by Mrs. Pak Lee Sun-ai, Director of the Korean Language Institute at Yonsei University. The *yangban* bride brought along enough *poson* to her husband's home to last for three years, and additional pairs as gifts for all of his feminine relations.

14. *TFL* 1.193–94. Manchu footbinding diminished after the Revolution and had vanished by the early thirties.

15. *TFL* 2.198–99. Ta-t'ung women often used silk instead of cloth for both binding and shoes.

16. Matignon, *La Chine Hermétique*, 231.

17. *TFL* 4.121. The Hunanese writer criticized this as being extremely unsanitary.

18. *Pen-ts'ao kang-mu* 本草綱目: ch. 52, f. 4a–5a. (*Ssu-pu ts'ung-k'an* 四部叢刊 ed.) In regard to the medicinal uses of urine, it may be of interest to note that an article in *The Japan Times*, dated August 20, 1965, discussed a new drug said to be effective in dissolving blood clots blocking blood vessels and went on to state that a method had been worked out by which "...one liter of fresh, germ-free urine yields 0.3 milligrams of the compound. Fifty liters of urine are needed for one shot which contains 15 milligrams of the compound."

19. *TFL* 2.9–11.

20. *TFL* 1.199, 279; 2.172, 185–89. One writer mentions an experience with a woman who had amorous pictures embroidered on a red satin brassiere as well as in her sleeping shoes. (*TFL* 4.261)

21. *TFL* 1.168.

22. Fielde, *Pagoda Shadows*, 27–28.

23. *TFL* 3.300–301.

24. *TFL* 2.174; cf. 1.190; 2.163, 258, 264; 3.250.

25. *TFL* 3.80; 1.133.

26. *TFL* 1.46–48; 280.

27. Fielde, op. cit., 27–32.

28. Davis, *The Chinese: A General Description of the Empire of China and its Inhabitants,* 268-69. "For them footbinding was of vital importance. It was the patent of gentility. What mother would condemn her child to go through life marked as a 'big-footed' woman of the coolie class when by binding the feet a door to advancement in the social scale might be opened?... At the cost, therefore, of long-drawn agony the feet were bound and slowly crushed." (Ayscough, *Chinese Women Yesterday and Today,* 27–28)

29. Veblen, *The Theory of the Leisure Class,* 82–83, 148–50, 185–86.

30. Mrs. Feng's statement is indirectly corroborated by E. H. Parker, who stated 'hat in the early twentieth century the Empress Dowager (1835–1908) explicitly condemned footbinding (*China,* 299).

31. *TFL* 2.39.

32. *TFL* 2.37.

33. The well-known story that the fox spirit Ta-chi set a palace fashion by binding its feet is recorded in *Chien-hu chi* 堅瓠集 (*TFL* 2.13–14). Western writers in the nineteenth century heard what must have been another popular account, namely that a clubfooted Shang empress persuaded the emperor to decree footbinding in order to conceal her deformity. (See, for instance, Doolittle, *Social Life of the Chinese,* vol. 2, 197; Williams, *The Middle Kingdom,* vol. 2, 38.)

34. Terror spread among the people after the execution of the woman revolutionary Ch'iu Chin on July 15, 1907. And, as in the later period, "young girls, who had given up footbinding, feared that they might be considered revolutionary and reverted to the practice." (Ayscough, op. cit., 174)

Bibliography

I. Chinese and Japanese Works (arranged by title):

An-kuo fu-jen 安國夫人. By Nan-kung Po 南宮搏. 2 vols. Hong Kong: Huan-ch'iu t'u-shu tsa-chih ch'u-pan-she 環球圖書雜誌出版社, 1955?

Chan-yüan ching-yü 湛淵静語. By Po T'ing 白珽 (fl. late 13th c.). In *Chih-pu-tsu chai ts'ung-shu* 知不足齋叢書.

"Ch'an-tsu" 纏足. By Wu Ying-t'ao 吳瀛濤. In *Taiwan Hsin-sheng pao* 台灣新生報 (Mar. 21, 1961), 7.

Ch'an-tsu lun 纏足論. By Yüan Mei 袁枚 (1716–98). In *Hsiang-yen ts'ung-shu* 香艷叢書.

Ch'eng-chai tsa-chi 誠齋雜記. By Lin K'un 林坤 (fl. Yüan). In *Chin-tai mi-shu* 津逮秘書.

Chi-hsieh hsing-chiu 妓鞋行酒. By Shen Tè-fu 沈徳符 (1578–1642). In *Hsiang-yen ts'ung-shu.*

Chiao-ch'i chi 脚氣集. By Ch'e Jo-shui 車若水 (fl. ca. 1280). Shanghai: Commercial Press collated edition, 1919.

Ch'ih-pei ou-t'an 池北偶談. By Wang Shih-chen 王士禎 (1634–1711). In *Wang Yü-yang i-shu* 王漁洋遺書.

Chin P'ing Mei 金瓶梅. For Japanese translation of: see *Kin Hei Bai.*

Chin-shu 晉書. By Fang Hsüan-ling 房玄齡 (578–648), and others. Taipei: photolithograph of Ch'ing 清 *Wu-ying-tien* 武英殿 edition by I-wen yin-shu-kuan 藝文印書館, 2 vols., 1957. (All other standard history citations refer to this edition.)

Chin-yüan tsa-tsuan 金園雜纂. By Fang Hsün 方絢 (c. 18th c.) In *Hsiang-yen ts'ung-shu.*

Ching-hua yüan 鏡花緣. By Li Ju-chen 李汝珍. (c. 1763–c. 1830). Taipei: *Shih-chieh shu-chü* 世界書局, 1957.

"Ch'ing chin fu-nü ch'an-tsu che" 請禁婦女纏足摺. By K'ang Yu-wei 康有為 (1858–1927). In appendix to *Chung-hua fu-nü ch'an-tsu k'ao,* q.v.

Chiu T'ang-shu 舊唐書. Traditionally by Liu Hsü 劉昫 (887–946) and others; most likely by Chao Ying 趙瑩 (fl. 945) and others. 3 vols.

Cho-keng lu 輟耕錄. By T'ao Tsung-i 陶宗儀 (fl. 1368). In *Chin-tai mi-shu* 津逮秘書.

Chung-hua fu-nü ch'an-tsu k'ao 中華婦女纏足考. By Chia Shen 賈申. Peking, 1925.

Chung-kuo chin-tai shih 中國近代史. By Huang Ta-shou 黃大受. Taipei: Ta Chung-kuo t'u-shu yu-hsien kung-ssu 大中國圖書有限公司 (3 vols.), 1953–55.

"Chung-kuo fu-nü ch'an-tsu shih-t'an" 中國婦女纏足史譚. By Li Jung-mei 李榮楣. In *Ts'ai-fei lu hsü-pien.*

Chung-kuo fu-nü sheng-huo-shih 中國婦女生活史. By Ch'en Tung-yüan 陳東原. Shanghai: Commercial Press, 1937.

Feng-ch'uang hsiao-tu 楓窗小牘. By Yüan Chiung 袁褧 (fl. Ming). In *Pao-yen-t'ang mi-chi kuang-han* 寶顏堂秘笈廣函.

Fu-jen chi 婦人集. By Ch'en Wei-sung 陳維崧 (1626–82). In *Hsiang-yen ts'ung-shu.*

Fu-jen hsieh-wa k'ao 婦人鞋襪考. By Yü Huai 余懷 (1616–96). In *T'an-chi ts'ung-shu* 檀几叢書.

Fu-jen kung-tsu 婦人弓足. By Shen Te-fu 沈德符 (1578–1642). In *Hsiang-yen ts'ung-shu.*

Handwritten notes on footbinding. By Nagao Ryūzo. Compiled from 1943–45; in the writer's possession.

Hsiang-lien p'in-tsao 香蓮品藻. By Fang Hsün 方絢 (c. 18th c.) In *Hsiang-yen ts'ung-shu.*

Hsiao-chiao wen 小脚文. By K'uang-wang-sheng 曠望生 (a pseudonym). In *Hsiang-yen ts'ung-shu.*

Hsin T'ang-shu 新唐書. By Ou-yang Hsiu 歐陽修 (1007–72), Sung Ch'i 宋祁 (993–1061), and others. 3 vols.

Hsin Yüan-shih 新元史. By K'o Shao-min 柯劭忞 (1850–1933). 3 vols.

Hu Shih wen-ts'un 胡適文存. By Hu Shih 胡適 (1891–1962). Taipei: Yüan-tung t'u-shu kung-ssu 遠東圖書公司, 4 vols., 1953.

I-lin fa-shan 藝林伐山. By Yang Shen 楊慎 (1488–1559). In *Han-hai ts'ung-shu* 函海叢書.

Kai-yü ts'ung-k'ao 陔餘叢考. By Chao I 趙翼 (1727–1814). In *Ou-pei ch'üan-chi* 甌北全集.

Kin Hei Bai 金瓶梅. Ed. and Trans. by Ono Shinobu 小野忍 and Chida Kuichi 千田九一. 3 vols., illustrated. Tokyo: Heibonsha, 1962.

Ku-chin shih-wu k'ao 古今事物考. By Wang San-p'in 王三聘 (fl. Ming). In *Hsü Chih-pu-tsu chai ts'ung-shu* 續知不足齋叢書.

Kuan-yüeh ch'a 貫月査. By Fang Hsün (c. 18th c.). In *Hsiang-yen ts'ung-shu.*

Kuei-ssu lei-kao 癸巳類稿. By Yü Cheng-hsieh 俞正燮 (1775–1840). In *An-hui ts'ung-shu* 安徽叢書.

Kuei-ssu ts'un-kao 癸巳存稿. By Yü Cheng-hsieh. In *Lien-yün-i ts'ung-shu* 連筠簃叢書.

Lang-huan chi 瑯環記. By I Shih-chen 伊世珍 (fl. Yüan). In *Chin-tai mi-shu.*

Lao hsüeh-an pi-chi 老學庵筆記. By Lu Fang-weng 陸放翁 (1125–1210). In *Pei-hai ts'ung-shu* 稗海叢書.

Li-tai jen-wu nien-li-pei-chuan tsung-piao 歷代人物年里碑傳綜表. Edited by Chiang Liang-fu 羌亮夫 and collated by T'ao Ch'iu-ying 陶秋英. Shanghai, 1959.

"Lien-ch'ü mi-chi" 蓮趣秘記. By Chih-lien 知蓮 (a pseudonym). In *Ts'ai-fei lu ti-ssu-pien.*

"Lien-miao" 蓮妙. By Ai-t'u-sheng 愛特生 (a pseudonym). In *Ts'ai-fei lu ti-ssu-pien.*

Ling-nan tsa-chi 嶺南雜記. By Wu Chen-fang 吳震方 (fl. 1679). In *Hsiao-fang-hu-chai yü-ti ts'ung-ch'ao* 小方壺齋輿地叢鈔.

"Lun Tung-fu ch'ing shih ch'an-tsu chin-ling shih" 論東撫請設纏足禁令事. Anonymous. In *Tung-fang tsa-chih* 東方雜誌. 1:11 (Dec., 1904), 144–46.

Ming-shih 明史. By Chang T'ing-yü 張廷玉 (1672–1755) and others.

Nan-shih 南史. By Li Yen-shou 李延壽 (fl. 1st half 7th c.) and others.

Nan-ts'un cho-keng lu 南村輟耕録. See *Cho-keng lu.*

Nan-yüeh pi-chi 南越筆記. By Li T'iao-yüan 李調元 (1734–1803). In *Han-hai* 函海.

Pen-ts'ao kang-mu 本草綱目. By Li Shih-chen 李時珍 (1518–93) and others. In *Ssu-pu ts'ung-k'an* 四部叢刊.

Pi-tsou-chai yü-t'an chieh-lu 敝帚齋餘談節録. By Shen Te-fu 沈德符 (1578–1642). In *Hsiang-yen ts'ung-shu.*

Sha-jen pi-chi 傻人筆記. By Ku Huai 谷懷. Taipei: Kuo-min ch'u-pan-she 國民出版社, 1956.

Sheng-shih wei-yen 盛世危言. By Cheng Kuan-ying 鄭觀應, also called T'ao-chai 陶齋 and Kuan-ying 官應 (fl. end 19th c.). Block-print ed., author's preface dated 1892.

Shih-hua tsung-kuei 詩話總龜. By Jüan Yüeh 阮閱 (fl. 1123). In *Ssu-pu ts'ung-k'an.*

"Shina fujin tensoku no kigen" 支那婦人纏足の起原. By Naka Michiyo 那珂通世. IX. 6, *Shigaku zasshi* (June 10, 1898), 496–520.

Shina fūzoku 支那風俗. By Inoue Kobai 井上紅梅. 3 vols. Shanghai, 1919–20.

"Shina kanzoku no joshi ni okonawaruru tensoku no fū" 支那漢族の女子に行はるる纏足の風. By Inō Yoshinori 伊能嘉矩. In *Tōkyō jinruigakkai zasshi* 東京人類學會雜誌 No. 229, April 20, 1905, 301–11.

Shina minzokushi 支那民俗誌. By Nagao Ryūzo 永尾龍造. Vols. 1, 2, 6. Tokyo, 1940, 1941, and 1942, respectively.

Shina no otoko to onna 支那の男と女. By Gotō Asatarō 後藤朝太郎. Tokyo: Daitō shuppansha 大東出版社, 1939.

Shina. Shinajin 支那. 支那人. By Toriyama Kiichi 鳥山喜一. Tokyo: Iwanami shoten 岩波書店, 1942.

"Shinsen ni kawaigarareta onna" 神仙にかわいがられた女. By Okuno Shintarō 奥野信太郎. In *(Bungei shunjū) Manga Tokuhon* (October, 1962), 68–73.

Shu-yüan chui-t'an 菽園贅談. By Ch'iu Shu-yüan 邱菽園 (fl. late 17th c.?). Cited in *Shina minzokushi*.

Shu-yüan tsa-chi 菽園雜記. By Lu Yung 陸容 (fl. 1465). In *Shou-shan-ko ts'ung-shu* 守山閣叢書.

Shun-hsi ching-hua 瞬息京華. By Lin Yutang 林語堂. Taipei: Tung-ya ch'u-pan-she 東亜出版社, 1957.

Ssu-k'u ch'üan-shu tsung-mu 四庫全書總目. By Chi Yün 紀昀 (1724–1815) and others. Taipei: I-wen yin-shu kuan, 1957.

Sung-shih 宋史. By T'o-t'o 托托 (1313–55) and others.

Sung-shu 宋書. By Shen Yüeh 沈約 (441–513) and others.

Ta T'ang hsin-yü 大唐新語. By Liu Su 劉肅 (1188–1263). In *T'ang-jen shuo-hui pen* 唐人說會本.

"Taiwan fujin no kotsuban ni tsuite narabi ni seitai keisoku" 台灣婦人の體盤ニ就テ並ニ生體計測. By Tsunoda Hideo 角田秀雄. In *Taiwan Igakkai zasshi* 台灣醫學會雜誌 No. 29, January, 1905, 179–210.

T'an-ch'ien hsin-lu 丹鉛新錄. By Hu Ying-lin 胡應麟 (1551–1602). In *Shao-shih shan-fang pi-ts'ung hsü-chi* 少室山房筆叢續集.

T'an-ch'ien tsung-lu 丹鉛總録. By Yang Shen 楊慎 (1488–1559). In *Yang-shih Chiao-chung-t'ang k'e-pen* 楊氏教忠堂刻本.

T'an-yüan t'i-hu 譚苑醍湖. By Yang Shen 楊慎. In *Han-hai* 函海.

T'ang-yin kuei-ch'ien 唐音癸籤. By Hu Chen-heng 湖震亨 (fl. Ming). In *Shuang-yü-t'ang ts'ung-shu* 双與堂叢書.

T'ang yü-lin 唐語林. By Wang Tang 王讜 (fl. early 12th c.). Shanghai: Ku-tien wen-hsüeh ch'u-pan she, 1957; also in *Shou-shan-ko ts'ung-shu.*

"Tensoku" てんそく. By a Mr. Takenouchi 竹之内. Tokyo: *Dai hyakka jiten* 大百科事典 (vol. 18, 1932), 264–65.

"Tensoku" てんそく. By Kanazeki Takao 金关丈夫. Tokyo: *Sekai dai hyakka jiten* 世界大百科字典 (ca. 1955?), 349–50.

"T'ien Kuei-fei" 田貴妃. By Tu Fu-weng 杜負翁. In *Chung-yang jih-pao* 中央日報 (April 22, 1961), 7.

T'ien-lu shih-yü 天禄識餘. By Kao Shih-ch'i 高士奇 (1645–1703). In *Shuo-ling ch'ien-chi* 説鈴前集.

"T'ien-tsu shih-hua" 天足史話. By Chieh-jen 介人(a pseudonym). Taipei: *Tzu-yu pao* 自由報, July 23, 1960.

Ting-an wen-chi 定盦文集. By Kung Tzu-chen 龔自珍 (1792–1841). In *Ssu-pu ts'ung-k'an.*

Tsa-shih mi-hsin 雜事秘辛. Author unknown, early Han attribution considered spurious; probably Six Dynasties period. In *Kuang Han Wei ts'ung-shu pieh-shih* 廣漢魏叢書別史.

Ts'ai-fei hsin-lu 采菲新録: name of a fifth book planned after 1938 by Yao Ling-hsi but perhaps not published. (See *TFL* 4.365).

Ts'ai-fei lu 采菲録. Edited by Yao Ling-hsi 姚靈犀. Tientsin: Shih-tai kung-ssu 時代公司, reprinted January 1, 1936.

Ts'ai-fei lu hsü-pien 采菲録續編. Edited by Yao Ling-hsi. Tientsin: Shih-tai kung-ssu. February 20, 1936.

Ts'ai-fei lu ti-san-pien 采菲録第三編. Edited by Yao Ling-hsi. Tientsin: T'ien-ching shu-chü 天津書局. December 30, 1936.

Ts'ai-fei lu ti-ssu-pien 采菲録第四編. Edited by Yao Ling-hsi. Tientsin: T'ien-ching shu-chü. December 1, 1938.

Ts'ai-lien ch'uan 采蓮船. By Fang Hsün (c. 18th c.). In *Hsiang-yen ts'ung-shu.*

"Tsui-lien ssu-nüeh chi" 醉蓮肆虐記. By Wu-ssu lao-jen 五四老人 (a pseudonym). In *Ts'ai-fei lu ti-ssu-pien.*

Tu-wai yü-yen 牘外餘言. By Yüan Mei 袁枚 (1716–98). In *Sui-yüan san-shih-chung* 隋園三十種.

T'u-shu wen-chien lu 圖書聞見録. By Kuo Jo-hsü 郭若虛 (fl. 1070). In *Ssu-pu ts'ung-k'an hsü-pien.*

T'ung-su pien 通俗編. By Che Hao 翟灝 (died 1788). In *Han-hai* 函海.

Wakan yakuyō shokubutsu 和漢薬用植物. By Karomai Tatsuo 刈米達夫 and Kimura Yushirō 木村雄四郎. Tokyo: Hirokawa shoten 廣川書店, 1949.

Wen-chien chin-lu 聞見近録. By Wang Kung 王鞏 (fl. latter half 11th c.). In *Hsüeh-hai lei-pien* 學海類編.

Yeh-huo pien 野獲編. By Shen Te-fu 沈徳符 (1578–1642). In *Ch'ien-t'ang Yao-shih Fu-li shan-fang* 錢塘姚氏扶荔山房.

Yin-an so-yü 蚓菴瑣語. By Li Wang-fu 李王逋 (fl. late 17th c.?). In *Shuo-ling hou-chi* 説鈴後集.

II. Works in English and French (arranged by author):

Anonymous. "Anti-footbinding," *Encyclopaedia Sinica*, (1917), 29–30.

Anonymous. "Footbinding," *Encyclopaedia Sinica*, (1917), 186–87.

Anonymous. "Letter About Footbinding," *The Spectator*, (March 19, 1898), 406–7.

Anonymous. "Small feet of the Chinese females; remarks on the origin of the custom of compressing the feet; the extent and effects of the practice; with an anatomical description of a small foot," *The Chinese Repository*, III. 12 (Canton, April, 1835), 537–42.

Arlington, L. C. "Footbinding," *The New China Review*, I, no. 1 (March, 1919), 92–94.

———. "Further Notes on Footbinding," *The New China Review*, II (1920), 211–14.

Ayscough, Florence. *Chinese Women Yesterday and Today*. London, 1938.

Bashford, James W. *China, An Interpretation*. New York, 1919.

Beal, Samuel, ed. and trans. *Buddhist Records of the Western World*. 2 vols., London,, 1906.

Beasley, W. G., and Pulleyblank, E. G., editors. *Historians of China and Japan*. London, 1962.

Belgion, Montgomery. *Love in the Western World*. New York, 1957. (ed. and trans. Denis de Rougemont, *L'Amour et l'Occident*, France, 1939.)

Blake, Henry A. *China*. London, 1909.

Chavannes, Edouard. review of Virchow, *Das Skelett eines verkruppelten Chinesinnen Fuszes*, *T'oung pao*, IV (1903), 419.

Ch'en Shou-yi. *Chinese Literature*. New York, 1961.

Chung Cheng. "Feet," *New Chinese Stories*. Taipei, 1961, 3–12.

Davis, John F. *A General Description of the Empire of China*. 2 vols. London, 1836.

Doolittle, Justus. *Social Life of the Chinese*. 2 vols. New York, 1865.

Eberhard, Wolfram. *Chinese Festivals*. New York, 1952.

Egerton, Clement, ed. and trans. *The Golden Lotus*. 4 vols. London, 1955.

Fielde, Adele M. *Pagoda Shadows*. London, 1887.

Fielding, William J. *Strange Customs of Courtship and Marriage*. New York, 1956.

Gamble, Sidney D. "The Disappearance of Footbinding in Tinghsien," *American Journal of Sociology*, (September, 1943), 181–83.

Gichner, Lawrence E. *Erotic Aspects of Chinese Culture*. Privately published, 1957.

Giles, Herbert A. *Adversaria Sinica*. Shanghai, 1914.

Goodrich, L. Carrington. *A Short History of the Chinese People*. New York, 1950.

Gray, Archdeacon J. H. *China; A History of the Laws, Manners, and Customs of the People*. 2 vols. London, 1878.

Hsu, Francis L. K. *Americans and Chinese, Two Ways of Life*. New York, 1953.

Hummel, Arthur W., ed. *Eminent Chinese of the Ch'ing Period*. 2 vols. Washington, 1943.

Ku Hung-ming. *Spirit of the Chinese People*. Taipei, 1956.

Levy, Howard S. *Harem Favorites of an Illustrious Celestial*. Taichung, 1958.
———. *Lament Everlasting (The Death of Yang Kuei-fei)*. Tokyo, 1962.
———. "T'ang Courtesans, Ladies and Concubines," *Orient/West*, VII, 3 (March 1962), 49–64.
———. "Ladies, Consorts and Concubines in Chinese Literature," Tokyo: unpublished manuscript.

Li, Yieni Tsao. "The Life of a Girl in China," *Annals of the American Academy of Political and Social Science*, (January, 1912), 63–64.

Lin Yutang. *My Country and My People*. New York, 1937.

Little, Mrs. Archibald. *Intimate China*. London, 1899.

Mahler, Jane Gaston. *The Westerners Among the Figurines of the T'ang Dynasty of China.* Rome, 1959.

Matignon, Dr. J. J. *La Chine Hermétique.* Paris, 1936.

Morache, Medical Inspector. *Note sur la deformation du Pied chez les Femmes Chinoises.* (Cited by Matignon, *La Chine Hermétique,* but unavailable to me.)

Parker, E. H. *China.* London, 1917.

Parshley, H. M. *A History of Sex.* London, 1961. (Ed. and trans. Simone de Beauvoir, *Le Deuxieme Sexe,* 2 vols., France, 1949.)

Suh-ho. "In Praise of Footbinding," *The New Republic,* (Dec. 18, 1915), 170–72.

Tanizaki Junichiro. *The Key.* New York, 1962.

Trusler, Dr. John. *The Habitable World Described.* Vol. 6; London, 1790.

van Gulik, R. H. *Sexual Life in Ancient China.* Leiden, 1961.

Veblen, Thorstein. *The Theory of the Leisure Class.* New York, 1945.

Vincent, Dr. Eugene. *La Médecine en Chine au XXe Siecle.* Paris, 1915.

Wang Ts'ang-pao. *La Femme dans la Société Chinoise.* Paris, 1933.

Werner, E. T. C., and Tedder, Henry R., editors. *Descriptive Sociology of the Chinese.* (Compiled and abstracted upon the plan organized by Herbert Spencer.) London, 1910.

Williams, S. Wells. *The Middle Kingdom.* 2 vols. New York, 1857.

Winterbotham, W. *An Historical, Geographical, and Philosophical View of the Chinese Empire.* London, 1795.

Index